Mastering Unit Testing Using Mockito and JUnit

An advanced guide to mastering unit testing using Mockito and JUnit

Sujoy Acharya

PUBLISHING

BIRMINGHAM - MUMBAI

Mastering Unit Testing Using Mockito and JUnit

First published: July 2014

Production reference: 1080714

Published by Packt Publishing Ltd.
Livery Place
35 Livery Street
Birmingham B3 2PB, UK.

ISBN 978-1-78398-250-9

www.packtpub.com

Credits

Author
Sujoy Acharya

Reviewers
Jose Muanis Castro

Alexey Grigorev

Daniel Pacak

Commissioning Editor
Amarabha Banerjee

Acquisition Editor
Meeta Rajani

Content Development Editor
Balaji Naidu

Technical Editors
Neha Mankare

Edwin Moses

Copy Editor
Mradula Hegde

Project Coordinator
Leena Purkait

Proofreaders
Simran Bhogal

Maria Gould

Ameesha Green

Indexer
Rekha Nair

Graphics
Abhinash Sahu

Production Coordinator
Melwyn D'sa

Cover Work
Melwyn D'sa

Cover Image
Disha Haria

About the Author

Sujoy Acharya works as a software architect with Siemens Technology and Services Pvt Ltd. (STS). He grew up in a joint family and pursued his graduation in Computer Science and Engineering. His hobbies are watching movies and sitcoms, playing outdoor sports, and reading books.

He likes to research upcoming technologies. His major contributions are in the fields of Java, J2EE, SOA, Ajax, GWT, and the Spring framework.

He has authored *Test-Driven Development with Mockito, Packt Publishing*. He designs and develops healthcare software products. He has over 10 years of industrial experience and has architected and implemented large-scale enterprise solutions.

I would like to thank my wife, Sunanda, for her patience and endless support in spending many hours reviewing my draft and providing valuable inputs.

I would also like to thank my mother and late father for their support, blessings, and encouragement.

To my one-year-old kid, Abhigyan, I am sorry I couldn't be around with you as much as we all wanted, and often, I had to get you away from the laptop. I love you very much.

About the Reviewers

Jose Muanis Castro holds an Information Systems degree. Originally from Rio de Janeiro, he now lives in Brooklyn with his wife and kids. He is a software engineer at The New York Times, where he works with recommendation systems on the personalization team. Previously, he worked on the CMS and publishing platforms at Globo.com, the biggest media portal of Brazil.

He is a seasoned engineer with a history of hands-on experience in several languages. He's passionate about continuous improvement in Agile and Lean processes. With years of experience in automation, right from testing to deploying, he constantly switches hats between development and operations. When he's not coding, he enjoys riding his bike around. His Twitter handle is @muanis.

> I'm thankful to my wife Márcia and my kids, Vitoria and Rafael, for understanding that I couldn't be there at times with them while I was helping to review this book.

Alexey Grigorev is an experienced software developer with several years of professional Java programming. From the beginning, he successfully adopted the best practices in Extreme Programming (XP), one of which is testing, and drove his teammates to use it. In many cases, he witnessed testing save projects when under constantly developing requirements his team managed to quickly deliver the changes.

Right now, he is a freelancer who specializes in machine learning and data mining, and he also successfully adopts TDD and testing in these fields to ensure the reliability of his applications.

For any questions, you can contact him via alexey.s.grigoriev@gmail.com.

Daniel Pacak is a self-made software engineer who fell in love with coding during his studies of Nuclear Physics at Warsaw University of Technology. This was back in 2006 when no one cared about unit testing at all. He acquired his professional experience by working on several business-critical projects, mainly web applications, for clients in financial services, telecommunications, e-commerce, and the travel industry.

When he's not coding, he enjoys lifting weights in the gym close to his office.

www.PacktPub.com

Support files, eBooks, discount offers, and more

You might want to visit www.PacktPub.com for support files and downloads related to your book.

Did you know that Packt offers eBook versions of every book published, with PDF and ePub files available? You can upgrade to the eBook version at www.PacktPub.com and as a print book customer, you are entitled to a discount on the eBook copy. Get in touch with us at service@packtpub.com for more details.

At www.PacktPub.com, you can also read a collection of free technical articles, sign up for a range of free newsletters and receive exclusive discounts and offers on Packt books and eBooks.

http://PacktLib.PacktPub.com

Do you need instant solutions to your IT questions? PacktLib is Packt's online digital book library. Here, you can access, read and search across Packt's entire library of books.

Why subscribe?

- Fully searchable across every book published by Packt
- Copy and paste, print and bookmark content
- On demand and accessible via web browser

Free access for Packt account holders

If you have an account with Packt at www.PacktPub.com, you can use this to access PacktLib today and view nine entirely free books. Simply use your login credentials for immediate access.

Table of Contents

Preface

If you've been a software developer for a long time, you have certainly participated in software conferences or developer forums and experienced many interesting conversations. They start out well with one of the developers describing a cool development process that he/she follows, and then another developer strikes with a cutting-edge technology or tool or a mind-boggling enterprise integration pattern that he/she works with. Each speaker attempts to outdo the last speaker. Old timers speak about ancient machines that had to be programmed with punch cards or switches, where they had only few bytes of RAM, or they start describing COBOL as a dynamic language that follows the Model View Presenter pattern. Ask them three questions: "How do you unit test your program?", "Can you alleviate high blood pressure by monitoring your pressure more often?", and "Have you ever maintained your own code?"

I asked the first question to more than 200 developers. Believe me, 80 percent of developers replied, "We pay our testers or we have skilled testers." Five percent said, "Our customers test the software." Now the remaining 15 percent do unit testing and use print statements or write JUnit tests.

It is insane to keep doing things the same way and expect them to improve. Any program is only as good as it is useful; so, before applying complex tools, patterns, or APIs, we should verify whether our software functions or not. We should configure our development environment to provide us quick feedback of what is being developed. Automated JUnit tests help us verify our assumptions continuously. Side effects are detected quickly and this saves time.

As Martin Fowler states *Any fool can write code that a computer can understand. Good programmers write code that humans can understand.*

We can write obfuscated code to impress our peers, but writing readable code is an art. Readability is a code quality.

Can you treat high blood pressure by monitoring your blood pressure more often? No, you need medication. Similarly, we should analyze our code to improve our code quality. Static code analysis tools suggest corrective actions, which means we should continuously monitor our code quality.

Always code as though the guy who ends up maintaining your code will be a violent psychopath who knows where you live. We work in brand new greenfield projects and also in existing brownfield projects. Greenfield projects always follow test-driven development to deliver maintainable and testable code.

Test-driven development is an evolutionary development approach. It offers test-first development where the production code is written only to satisfy a test. The simple idea of writing a test first reduces the extra effort of writing unit tests after coding. In test-driven development, test doubles and mock objects are extensively used to mock out external dependencies. Mockito is an open source mock unit testing framework for Java. It allows mock object creation, verification, and stubbing.

As Winston Churchill states *We make a living by what we get, but we make a life by what we give.*

We inherit the legacy code from someone else—it may come from a very old existing project, from other teams who cannot maintain the code, or may be acquired from another company. However, it is our duty to improve the quality.

This book is an advanced-level guide that will help software developers to get complete expertise in unit testing in the JUnit framework using Mockito as the mocking framework. The focus of the book is to provide readers with comprehensive details on how effectively JUnit tests can be written. Build scripts can be customized to automate unit tests, code quality can be monitored using static code analysis tools and code quality dashboards, and tests can be written for the Web and database components. Legacy code can be refactored. Test-driven development and Mockito can be used for software development; JUnit best practices can be followed.

Armed with the knowledge of advanced JUnit concepts, test automation, build scripting tools, the mocking framework, code coverage tools, static code analysis tools, web tier unit testing, database tier unit testing, test-driven development, and refactoring legacy code, you will be pleasantly surprised as how quickly and easily you can write high-quality clean, readable, testable, maintainable, and extensible code. With these kinds of skills in your next software conference, you can impress the participants.

What this book covers

Chapter 1, JUnit 4 – a Total Recall, covers the unit testing concept, the JUnit 4 framework, the Eclipse setup, and advance features of JUnit 4. It covers the JUnit 4 framework briefly to get you up and running. We will discuss the concept surrounding JUnit essentials, annotations, assertion, the @RunWith annotation, and exception handling so that you have an adequate background on how JUnit 4 works. Advanced readers can skip to the next section. JUnit 4++ explores the advanced topics of JUnit 4 and deep dives into the following topics: parameterized test, matchers and assertThat, assumption, theory, timeout, categories, rules, test suites, and test order.

Chapter 2, Automating JUnit Tests, focuses on getting the reader quickly started with the Extreme Programming (XP) concept, Continuous Integration (CI), benefits of CI, and JUnit test automation using various tools such as Gradle, Maven, Ant, and Jenkins. By the end of this chapter, the reader will be able to write build scripts using Gradle, Maven, and Ant and configure Jenkins to execute the build scripts.

Chapter 3, Test Doubles, illustrates the concept of test doubles and explains various test double types, such as mock, fake, dummy, stub, and spy.

Chapter 4, Progressive Mockito, distills the Mockito framework to its main core and provides technical examples. No previous knowledge of mocking is necessary. By the end of this chapter, the reader will be able to use advanced features of the Mockito framework; start behavior-driven development using Mockito; and write readable, maintainable, and clean JUnit tests using Mockito.

Chapter 5, Exploring Code Coverage, unfolds the code coverage concept, code coverage tools, and provides step-by-step guidance to generate coverage reports using various build scripts. The following topics are covered: code coverage; branch and line coverage; coverage tools—Clover, Cobertura, EclEmma, and JaCoCo; measuring coverage using Eclipse plugins; and using Ant, Maven, and Gradle to generate reports. By the end of this chapter, the reader will be able to configure Eclipse plugins and build scripts to measure code coverage.

Chapter 6, Revealing Code Quality, explores the static code analysis and code quality improvement. By the end of this chapter, the reader will be able to configure the SONAR dashboard, set up Eclipse plugins, configure Sonar runner, and build scripts to analyze code quality using PMD, FindBugs, and Checkstyle.

Chapter 7, Unit Testing the Web Tier, deals with unit testing the web tier or presentation layer. It covers unit testing servlets, playing with Spring MVC, and working with the Model View Presenter pattern. By the end of this chapter, the reader will be able to unit test the web tier components and isolate the view components from the presentation logic.

Chapter 8, Playing with Data, covers the unit testing of the database layer. Topics such as separating concerns, unit testing the persistence logic, simplifying persistence with Spring, verifying the system integrity, and writing integration tests with Spring are explained. By the end of this chapter, the reader will be able to unit test the data access layer components in isolation from the database, write neat JDBC code using Spring, and write integration tests using the Spring API.

Chapter 9, Solving Test Puzzles, explains the importance of unit testing in greenfield and brownfield projects. Topics such as working with testing impediments, identifying constructor issues, realizing initialization issues, working with private methods, working with final methods, exploring static method issues, working with final classes, learning new concerns, exploring static variables and blocks, and test-driven development are covered. By the end of this chapter, the reader will be able to write unit tests for the legacy code; refactor the legacy code to improve the design of existing code; start writing simple, clean, and maintainable code following test-first and test-driven developments; and refactor code to improve code quality.

Chapter 10, Best Practices, focuses on JUnit guidelines and best practices for writing clean, readable, and maintainable JUnit test cases. It covers working with assertions, handling exceptions, and working with test smells. By the end of this chapter, the reader will be able to write clean and maintainable test cases.

What you need for this book

You will need the following software to be installed before you run the examples:

- Java 6 or higher: JDK 1.6 or higher can be downloaded from the following Oracle website:

  http://www.oracle.com/technetwork/java/javase/downloads/index.html

- Eclipse editor: The latest version of Eclipse is Kepler (4.3). Kepler can be downloaded from the following website:

  http://www.eclipse.org/downloads/

- Mockito is required for creation, verification of mock objects, and stubbing. It can be downloaded from the following website:

  https://code.google.com/p/mockito/downloads/list

Who this book is for

This book is for advanced to novice level software testers or developers who use Mockito in the JUnit framework. Reasonable knowledge and understanding of unit testing elements and applications is required.

This book is ideal for developers who have some experience in Java application development as well as some basic knowledge of JUnit testing, but it covers the basic fundamentals of JUnit testing, test automation, static code analysis, legacy code refactoring, and test-driven development to get you acquainted with these concepts before using them.

Conventions

In this book, you will find a number of styles of text that distinguish between different kinds of information. Here are some examples of these styles, and an explanation of their meaning.

Code words in text, database table names, folder names, filenames, file extensions, pathnames, dummy URLs, user input, and Twitter handles are shown as follows: "The `afterClass` and `beforeClass` methods are executed only once."

A block of code is set as follows:

```
@Test
public void currencyRoundsOff() throws Exception {
  assertNotNull(CurrencyFormatter.format(100.999));
  assertTrue(CurrencyFormatter.format(100.999).
    contains("$"));
  assertEquals("$101.00",
    CurrencyFormatter.format(100.999));
}
```

When we wish to draw your attention to a particular part of a code block, the relevant lines or items are set in bold:

```
public class LocaleTest {
  private Locale defaultLocale;
  @Before
  public void setUp() {
    defaultLocale = Locale.getDefault();
    Locale.setDefault(Locale.GERMANY);
  }
  @After
  public void restore() {
    Locale.setDefault(defaultLocale);
```

```
    }
    @Test
    public void currencyRoundsOff() throws Exception {
      assertEquals("$101.00",
        CurrencyFormatter.format(100.999));
    }
  }
```

Any command-line input or output is written as follows:

```
green(com.packtpub.junit.recap.rule.TestWatcherTest) success!
```

New terms and **important words** are shown in bold. Words that you see on the screen, in menus or dialog boxes for example, appear in the text like this: "Click on **Java build path** on the left-hand side and open the **Libraries** tab."

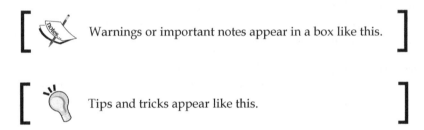

Warnings or important notes appear in a box like this.

Tips and tricks appear like this.

Reader feedback

Feedback from our readers is always welcome. Let us know what you think about this book—what you liked or may have disliked. Reader feedback is important for us to develop titles that you really get the most out of.

To send us general feedback, simply send an e-mail to feedback@packtpub.com, and mention the book title via the subject of your message.

If there is a topic that you have expertise in and you are interested in either writing or contributing to a book, see our author guide on www.packtpub.com/authors.

Customer support

Now that you are the proud owner of a Packt book, we have a number of things to help you to get the most from your purchase.

Downloading the example code

You can download the example code files for all Packt books you have purchased from your account at http://www.packtpub.com. If you purchased this book elsewhere, you can visit http://www.packtpub.com/support and register to have the files e-mailed directly to you.

Errata

Although we have taken every care to ensure the accuracy of our content, mistakes do happen. If you find a mistake in one of our books—maybe a mistake in the text or the code—we would be grateful if you would report this to us. By doing so, you can save other readers from frustration and help us improve subsequent versions of this book. If you find any errata, please report them by visiting http://www.packtpub.com/submit-errata, selecting your book, clicking on the **errata submission form** link, and entering the details of your errata. Once your errata are verified, your submission will be accepted and the errata will be uploaded on our website, or added to any list of existing errata, under the Errata section of that title. Any existing errata can be viewed by selecting your title from http://www.packtpub.com/support.

Piracy

Piracy of copyright material on the Internet is an ongoing problem across all media. At Packt, we take the protection of our copyright and licenses very seriously. If you come across any illegal copies of our works, in any form, on the Internet, please provide us with the location address or website name immediately so that we can pursue a remedy.

Please contact us at copyright@packtpub.com with a link to the suspected pirated material.

We appreciate your help in protecting our authors, and our ability to bring you valuable content.

Questions

You can contact us at questions@packtpub.com if you are having a problem with any aspect of the book, and we will do our best to address it.

1
JUnit 4 – a Total Recall

This chapter covers the unit testing concept, the JUnit 4 framework, the Eclipse setup, and the advanced features of JUnit 4. In JUnit 4, you will be introduced to the JUnit framework briefly to get you up and running. We will discuss the concept surrounding JUnit essentials, annotations, assertion, the `@RunWith` annotation, and exception handling so that you have an adequate background on how JUnit 4 works. Advanced readers can skip to the next section.

In JUnit 4++, we will explore the advanced topics of JUnit 4 and deep dive into parameterized tests, Hamcrest matchers and `assertThat`, the assumption, theory, timeout, categories, rules, test suites, and tests order.

Defining unit testing

A test is an assessment of our knowledge, a proof of concept, or an examination of data. A class test is an examination of our knowledge to ascertain whether we can go to the next level. For software, it is the validation of functional and nonfunctional requirements before it is shipped to a customer.

Unit testing code means validation or performing the sanity check of code. Sanity check is a basic test to quickly evaluate whether the result of a calculation can possibly be true. It is a simple check to see whether the produced material is coherent.

It's a common practice to unit test the code using print statements in the main method or by executing the application. Neither of them is the correct approach. Mixing up production code with tests is not a good practice. Testing logic in the production code is a code smell, though it doesn't break the code under the test. However, this increases the complexity of the code and can create severe maintenance problem or cause system failure if anything gets misconfigured. Print statements or logging statements are executed in the production system and print unnecessary information. They increase execution time and reduce code readability. Also, junk logging information can hide a real problem, for instance, you may overlook a critical deadlock or a hung thread warning because of excessive logging of junk.

Unit testing is a common practice in **test-driven development** (TDD). TDD is an evolutionary development approach. It offers test-first development where the production code is written only to satisfy a test, and the code is refactored to improve its quality. In TDD, unit tests drive the design. You write code to satisfy a failing test, so it limits the code you write to only what is needed. The tests provide a fast, automated regression for refactoring and new enhancements.

Kent Beck is the originator of Extreme Programming and TDD. He has authored many books and papers.

Generally, all tests are included in the same project but under a different directory/folder. Thus, a `org.packt.Bar.java` class will have a `org.packt.BarTest.java` test. These will be in the same package (`org.packt`) but will be organized in the: `src/org/foo/Bar.java` and `test/org/foo/BarTest.java` directories, respectively.

Our customers do not execute the unit tests, so we don't deliver the test source folder to them. Having the code and test in the same package allows the test to access protected and default methods/properties. This is particularly useful while working with the legacy code.

Java code can be unit tested using a code-driven unit testing framework. The following are a few of the available code-driven unit testing frameworks for Java:

- SpryTest
- Jtest
- JUnit
- TestNG

JUnit is the most popular and widely used unit testing framework for Java. We will explore JUnit 4 in the next section.

Working with JUnit 4

JUnit is a unit testing framework for Java. It allows developers to unit test the code elegantly. Apparently, TestNG is cleaner than JUnit, but JUnit is far more popular than TestNG. JUnit has a better mocking framework support such as Mockito, which offers a custom JUnit 4 runner.

The latest version of JUnit (4.11) can be downloaded from `https://github.com/junit-team/junit/wiki/Download-and-Install`.

JUnit 4 is an annotation-based, flexible framework. Its predecessor has many downsides. The following are the advantages of JUnit 4 over its predecessor:

- Instead of inheriting from `junit.framework.Testcase`, any class can be a test class

- The `setUp` and `tearDown` methods are replaced by the `@before` and `@after` annotations

- Any public method annotated as `@test` can be a test method

In this chapter, we will use **Eclipse** to execute the JUnit tests; in the following chapters, we will be using **Ant**, **Maven**, and **Gradle** to execute tools. Eclipse is an integrated development environment, and can be used to develop applications in Java. It can be downloaded from `http://www.eclipse.org/downloads/`. As of today, the latest IDE version is KEPLER (4.3).

> Since 2006, Eclipse releases a project annually. It started with the name **Callisto** (starts with a C). Lexicographically, Eclipse project names go like C, E, G, H, I, J, K, and L.
>
> In 2014, they will release the **Luna** (which starts with L) version. Between 2006 and now, they released **Europa** (E), **Ganymede** (G), **Galileo** (G), **Helios** (H), **Indigo** (I), **Juno** (J), and **Kepler** (K).

In the following section, we will set up Eclipse and execute our first JUnit test.

Setting up Eclipse

You can skip this section if you know how to install Eclipse and add JUnit JAR to the `classpath` project. The following are the steps to set up Eclipse:

1. Visit `http://www.eclipse.org/downloads/`. From the dropdown, select the operating system—**Windows**, **Mac**, or **Linux**—and then click on the hardware architecture hyperlink, that is, **32 Bit** or **64 Bit**, and download the binary, as shown in the following screenshot:

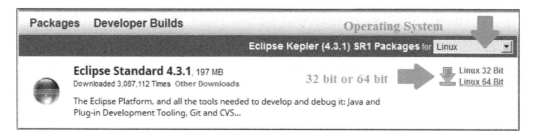

2. Extract the binary and launch Eclipse, for example, click on `Eclipse.exe` in Windows to launch Eclipse.

3. Create a new workspace (for example, in Windows, enter `C:\dev\junit` or in Linux or Mac enter `/user/local/junit`; Eclipse will create the directories). Once the workspace is open, press *Ctrl + N* or navigate to **File | New**; it will open a wizard. Select **Java Project** and click on **Next**. Enter `JUnitTests` as the project name and click on **Finish**. This will create a Java project named `JUnitTests`.

4. Download the `junit.jar` and `hamcrest-core.jar` packages from `https://github.com/junit-team/junit/wiki/Download-and-Install` and copy the jars to the `JUnitTests` project folder.

5. You can add the JAR to the `classpath` project in two ways; either right-click on both JAR, select **Build Path**, and then click on **Add to build path**. Or, right-click on the project and select the **Properties** menu item. Click on **Java build path** on the left-hand side and open the **Libraries** tab. Then, click on the **Add JARs...** button, and it will open a pop-up window. Expand the **JUnitTests** project from the pop up, select the two JAR (`junit.jar` and `hamcrest-core.jar`), and add them to **Libraries**. We are now ready with the Eclipse setup.

Running the first unit test

JUnit 4 is an annotation-based framework. It doesn't force you to extend the `TestCase` class. Any Java class can act as a test. In this section, we will uncover the JUnit 4 annotations, assertions, and exceptions.

We will examine the annotations before writing our first test.

Exploring annotations

The `@Test` annotation represents a test. Any `public` method can be annotated with the`@Test` annotation with `@Test` to make it a test method. There's no need to start the method name with test.

We need data to verify a piece of code. For example, if a method takes a list of students and sorts them based on the marks obtained, then we have to build a list of students to test the method. This is called data setup. To perform the data setup, JUnit 3 defines a `setUp()` method in the `TestCase` class. A test class can override the `setUp()` method. The method signature is as follows:

```
protected void setUp() throws Exception
```

JUnit 4 provides a @Before annotation. If we annotate any public void method of any name with @Before, then that method gets executed before every test execution.

Similarly, any method annotated with @After gets executed after each test method execution. JUnit 3 has a tearDown() method for this purpose.

JUnit 4 provides two more annotations: @BeforeClass and @AfterClass. They are executed only once per test class. The @BeforeClass and @AfterClass annotations can be used with any public static void methods. The @BeforeClass annotation is executed before the first test and the @AfterClass annotation is executed after the last test. The following example explains the annotation usage and the execution sequence of the annotated methods.

Let's write our first test by performing the following steps:

1. We will create a test class under a test source package. Create a **Source folder** named test and create a SanityTest.java Java class under package com.packtpub.junit.recap.

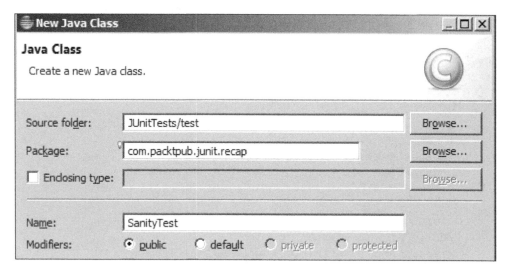

It is a good practice to create test classes with a Test suffix. So, a MyClass class will have a MyClassTest test class. Some code coverage tools ignore tests if they don't end with a Test suffix.

2. Add the following code to the `SanityTest` class:

```java
import org.junit.After;
import org.junit.AfterClass;
import org.junit.Before;
import org.junit.BeforeClass;
import org.junit.Test;

public class SanityTest {

  @BeforeClass
  public static void beforeClass() {
    System.out.println("***Before Class is invoked");
  }

  @Before
  public void before() {
    System.out.println("_____");
    System.out.println("\t Before is invoked");
  }
  @After
  public void after() {
    System.out.println("\t After is invoked");
    System.out.println("=================");
  }

  @Test
  public void someTest() {
    System.out.println("\t\t someTest is invoked");
  }

  @Test
  public void someTest2() {
    System.out.println("\t\t someTest2 is invoked");
  }

  @AfterClass
  public static void afterClass() {
    System.out.println("***After Class is invoked");
  }
}
```

In the preceding class, we created six methods. Two test methods are annotated with @Test. Note that two methods (beforeClass and afterClass) are static and the other four are nonstatic. A static method annotated with @BeforeClass is invoked only once, that is, before the test class is instantiated, and @AfterClass is invoked after the class is done with all the execution.

3. Run the test. Press *Alt + Shift + X* and *T* or navigate to **Run | Run As | JUnit Test**. You will see the following console (System.out.println) output:

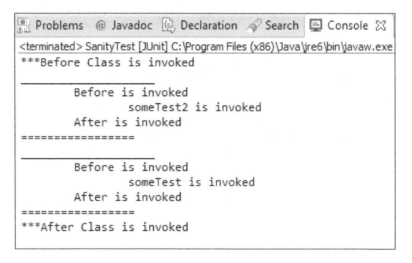

```
Problems   @ Javadoc   Declaration   Search   Console
<terminated> SanityTest [JUnit] C:\Program Files (x86)\Java\jre6\bin\javaw.exe
***Before Class is invoked

_____
        Before is invoked
                someTest2 is invoked
        After is invoked
==================

_____
        Before is invoked
                someTest is invoked
        After is invoked
==================
***After Class is invoked
```

Check whether the before and after methods are executed before and after every test run. However, the order of the test method execution may vary. In some runs, someTest may be executed before someTest2 or vice versa. The afterClass and beforeClass methods are executed only once.

Congratulations! We successfully ran our first JUnit 4 test.

 @Before and @After can be applied to any `public void` methods. @AfterClass and @BeforeClass can be applied to only `public static void` methods.

Verifying test conditions with Assertion

Assertion is a tool (a predicate) used to verify a programming assumption (expectation) with an actual outcome of a program implementation; for example, a programmer can expect that the addition of two positive numbers will result in a positive number. So, he or she can write a program to add two numbers and assert the expected result with the actual result.

The `org.junit.Assert` package provides static overloaded methods to assert expected and actual values for all primitive types, objects, and arrays.

The following are the useful assert methods:

- `assertTrue(condition)` or `assertTrue(failure message, condition)`: If the condition becomes false, the assertion fails and `AssertionError` is thrown. When a failure message is passed, the failure message is thrown.

- `assertFalse(condition)` or `assertFalse(failure message, condition)`: If the condition becomes true, the assertion fails and `AssertionError` is thrown.

- `assertNull`: This checks whether the object is null, otherwise throws `AssertionError` if the argument is not null.

- `assertNotNull`: This checks whether the argument is not null; otherwise, it throws `AssertionError`.

- `assertEquals(string message, object expected, object actual)`, or `assertEquals(object expected, object actual)`, or `assertEquals(primitive expected, primitive actual)`: This method exhibits an interesting behavior if primitive values are passed and then the values are compared. If objects are passed, then the `equals()` method is invoked. Moreover, if the actual value doesn't match the expected value, `AssertionError` is thrown.

- `assertSame(object expected, object actual)`: This supports only objects and checks the object reference using the == operator. If two different objects are passed, then `AssertionError` is thrown.

- `assertNotSame`: This is just the opposite of `assertSame`. It fails when the two argument references are the same.

Sometimes double can lead to surprising results due to the representation that Java uses to store doubles. Any operation on a double value can lead to an unexpected result. Assert doesn't rely on double comparison; so, assertEquals(double expected, double actual) is deprecated.

Declare a double variable sum = .999+ .98. The sum variable should add the values and store 1.98, but when you print the value in your machine, you will get 1.9889999999999999 as the output. So, if you assert sum with a double value 1.98, the test will fail.

The assert method provides an overloaded method for the double value assertion, that is, assertEquals(double expected, double actual, double delta). During comparison, if the difference between the expected and the actual value is less than the delta value, the result is considered passed.

For monetary calculations, it is recommended to use BigDecimal instead of doubles.

We will use the assert methods in the test as follows:

1. Create a AssertTest test class under com.packtpub.junit.recap. Add the following lines to the class:

```
package com.packtpub.junit.recap;

import org.junit.Assert;
import org.junit.Test;

public class AssertTest {

  @Test
  public void assertTrueAndFalseTest() throws Exception {
    Assert.assertTrue(true);
    Assert.assertFalse(false);
  }

  @Test
  public void assertNullAndNotNullTest() throws Exception {
    Object myObject = null;
    Assert.assertNull(myObject);

    myObject = new String("Some value");
    Assert.assertNotNull(myObject);
  }
}
```

In the preceding code, `assertTrueAndFalseTest` sends `true` to `assertTrue` and `false` to `assertFalse`. So, the test should not fail.

In `assertNullAndNotNullTest`, we are passing `null` to `assertNull` and a non-null `String` to `assertNotNull`; so, this test should not fail.

Run the tests. They should be green.

2. We will examine `assertEquals` and add the following test and static import the `assertEquals` method:

```
import static org.junit.Assert.assertEquals;


@Test
public void assertEqualsTest() throws Exception {
    Integer i = new Integer("5");
    Integer j = new Integer("5");;
    assertEquals(i,j);
}
```

In the preceding code, we defined two `Integer` objects, i and j, and they are initialized with 5. Now, when we pass them to `assertEquals`, the test passes, as the `assertEquals` method calls `i.equals(j)` and not `i == j`. Hence, only the values are compared, not the references.

The `assertEquals` method works on all primitive types and objects. To verify a double value, either use the overloaded `assertEquals(actual, expected, delta)` method or just use `BigDecimal` instead of using `Double`.

3. Add a test to verify the `assertNotSame` behavior and static import the `assertNotSame` method:

```
import static org.junit.Assert.assertNotSame;
@Test
public void assertNotSameTest() throws Exception {
    Integer i = new Integer("5");
    Integer j = new Integer("5");;
    assertNotSame(i , j);
}
```

The `assertNotSame` method fails only when the expected object and the actual object refers to the same memory location. Here, i and j hold the same value but the memory references are different.

4. Add a test to verify the `assertSame` behavior and static import the `assertSame` method:

```
import static org.junit.Assert.assertSame;
@Test
public void assertSameTest() throws Exception {
  Integer i = new Integer("5");
  Integer j = i;
  assertSame(i,j);
}
```

The `assertSame` method passes only when the expected object and the actual object refer to the same memory location. Here, `i` and `j` hold the same value and refer to the same location.

Working with exception handling

To test an error condition, exception handling feature is important. For example, an API needs three objects; if any argument is null, then the API should throw an exception. This can be easily tested. If the API doesn't throw an exception, the test will fail.

The `@Test` annotation takes the `expected=<<Exception class name>>.class` argument.

If the expected exception class doesn't match the exception thrown from the code, the test fails. Consider the following code:

```
@Test(expected=RuntimeException.class)
public void exception() {
  throw new RuntimeException();
}
```

This is only one solution. There are several other methods that are generally considered to be better solutions. Utilizing `@Rule` in JUnit 4.8+ and assigning `ExpectedException` is a stronger solution because you can inspect the message as well as the type. We have covered `@Rule` in the *Working with JUnit 4++ section* of this chapter.

Exploring the @RunWith annotation

Test runners execute the JUnit tests. Eclipse has a built-in native graphical runner. JUnit 4 provides tools to define the suite to be run and to display its results.

When a class is annotated with `@RunWith` or the class extends a class annotated with `@RunWith`, JUnit will invoke the class that it references to run the tests on that class, instead of using the built-in runner. The `@RunWith` annotation is used to change the nature of the test class. It can be used to run a test as a parameterized test or even a Spring test, or it can be a Mockito runner to initialize the mock objects annotated with a `@Mock` annotation.

The `@RunWith` annotation takes an argument. The argument must be a class extended from `org.junit.runner.Runner`.

`JUnit4.class` is an example of a runner. This class aliases the current default JUnit 4 class runner.

`Suite` is a standard runner that allows us to build a suite that contains tests from many packages. The following is an example of `@RunWith`:

```
@RunWith(Suite.class)
public class Assumption {


}
```

Working with JUnit 4++

This section explores the advanced features of the JUnit 4 framework and includes the following topics: parameterized test, Hamcrest matchers and assertThat, assumption, theory, timeout, categories, rules, test suites, and tests order.

Ignoring a test

Suppose a failing test blocks you to check-in a mission critical code, and you come to know that the owner of the code is on a vacation. What do you do? You try to fix the test or just comment out or delete the test to proceed with your check-in (committing files to a source control such as SVN), or you wait until the test is fixed.

Sometimes we comment out tests because the feature is not developed. JUnit came up with a solution for this. Instead of commenting a test, we can just ignore it by annotating the test method with `@Ignore`. Commenting out a test or code is bad as it does nothing but increases the code size and reduces its readability. Also, when you comment out a test, then the test report doesn't tell you anything about the commented-out test; however, if you ignore a test, then the test report will tell you that something needs to be fixed as some tests are ignored. So, you can keep track of the ignored test.

Use `@Ignore("Reason: why do you want to ignore?")`. Giving a proper description explains the intention behind ignoring the test. The following is an example of, where a test method is ignored because the holiday calculation is not working:

```
@Test
@Ignore("John's holiday stuff failing")
public void when_today_is_holiday_then_stop_alarm() {
}
```

The following is a screenshot from Eclipse:

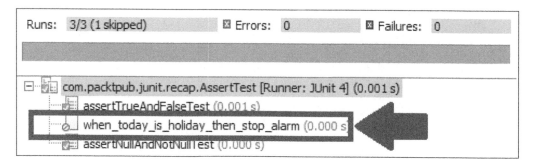

You can place the `@Ignore` annotation on a test class, effectively ignoring all the contained tests.

Executing tests in order

JUnit was designed to allow execution in a random order, but typically they are executed in a linear fashion and the order is not guaranteed. The JUnit runner depends on reflection to execute the tests. Usually, the test execution order doesn't vary from run to run; actually, the randomness is environment-specific and varies from JVM to JVM. So, it's better that you never assume they'll be executed in the same order and depend on other tests, but sometimes we need to depend on the order.

For example, when you want to write slow tests to insert a row into a database, then first update the row and finally delete the row. Here, unless the insert function is executed, delete or update functions cannot run.

JUnit 4.11 provides us with an `@FixMethodOrder` annotation to specify the execution order. It takes `enum MethodSorters`.

To change the execution order, annotate your test class using `@FixMethodOrder` and specify one of the following available `enum MethodSorters` constant:

- `MethodSorters.JVM`: This leaves the test methods in the order returned by the JVM. This order may vary from run to run.

- `MethodSorters.NAME_ASCENDING`: This sorts the test methods by the method name in the lexicographic order.

- `MethodSorters.DEFAULT`: This is the default value that doesn't guarantee the execution order.

We will write a few tests to verify this behavior.

Add a `TestExecutionOrder` test and create tests, as shown in the following code snippet:

```
public class TestExecutionOrder {
  @Test    public void edit() throws Exception {
    System.out.println("edit executed");
  }
  @Test    public void create() throws Exception {
    System.out.println("create executed");
  }
  @Test    public void remove() throws Exception {
    System.out.println("remove executed");
  }
}
```

Run the tests. The execution order may vary, but if we annotate the class with `@FixMethodOrder(MethodSorters.NAME_ASCENDING)`, the tests will be executed in the ascending order as follows:

```
@FixMethodOrder(MethodSorters.NAME_ASCENDING)
public class TestExecutionOrder { ... }
```

The following Eclipse screenshot displays the test execution in the ascending order:

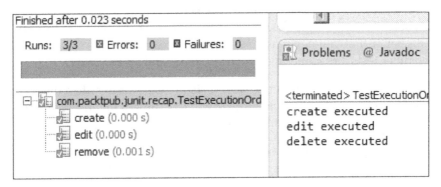

Learning assumptions

In multisite projects, sporadically, a date or time zone tests fail in a local CI server but run fine in other servers in a different time zone. We can choose to not run those automatic tests in our local server.

Sometimes our tests fail due to a bug in a third-party code or external software, but we know that after some specific build or version, the bug will be fixed. Should we comment out the code and wait until the build is available?

In many projects, **Jenkins** (for test automation) and **SONAR** (for code-quality metrics) run in a server. It has been observed that due to low resources, the automatic tests run forever when SONAR is processing and the tests run simultaneously.

JUnit has the answer to all these issues. It recommends using an `org.junit.Assume` class.

Like `Assert`, `Assume` offers many static methods, such as `assumeTrue(condition)`, `assumeFalse(condition)`, `assumeNotNull(condition)`, and `assumeThat(condition)`. Before executing a test, we can check our assumption using the `assumeXXX` methods. If our assumption fails, then the `assumeXXX` methods throw `AssumptionViolatedException`, and the JUnit runner ignores the tests with failing assumptions.

So, basically, if our assumption is not true, the tests are just ignored. We can assume that the tests are run in the EST time zone; if the tests are run somewhere else, they will be ignored automatically. Similarly, we can assume that the third-party code version is higher than the build/version 123; if the build version is lower, the tests will be ignored.

Let's write the code to validate our assumption about `Assume`.

Here, we will try to solve the SONAR server issue. We will assume that SONAR is not running. If SONAR runs during the test execution, the assumption will fail and the tests will be ignored.

Create an `Assumption` test class. The following is the body of the class:

```
public class Assumption {

  boolean isSonarRunning = false;
  @Test
  public void very_critical_test() throws Exception {
    isSonarRunning = true;
    Assume.assumeFalse(isSonarRunning);
```

```
        assertTrue(true);
    }


}
```

Here, for simplicity, we added a `isSonarRunning` variable to replicate a SONAR server facade. In the actual code, we can call an API to get the value. We will set the variable to `false`. Then, in the test, we will reset the value to `true`. This means SONAR is running. So, our assumption that SONAR is not running is false; hence, the test will be ignored.

The following screenshot shows that the test is ignored. We didn't annotate the test using `@Ignore`:

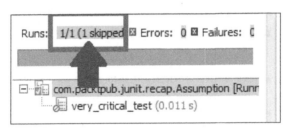

When we change the value of the `isSonarRunning` variable to `false`, as given in the following code snippet, the test will be executed:

```
public void very_critical_test() throws Exception {
    isSonarRunning = false;
    Assume.assumeFalse(isSonarRunning);
    assertTrue(true);
}
```

Continuous integration tools such as Jenkins can run multiple tools such as Sonar to acquire code-quality metrics. It's always a good practice to have a build pipeline where the code quality is only checked after the tests pass. This prevents the CPU-intensive tasks from occurring at the same time.

Assumption is also used in the `@Before` methods, but be careful not to overuse it. Assumption is good for use with TDD where one writes pretests ahead of time.

Exploring the test suite

To run multiple test cases, JUnit 4 provides `Suite.class` and the `@Suite.SuiteClasses` annotation. This annotation takes an array (comma separated) of test classes.

Create a `TestSuite` class and annotate the class with `@RunWith(Suite.class)`. This annotation will force Eclipse to use the suite runner.

Next, annotate the class with `@Suite.SuiteClasses({ AssertTest.class, TestExecutionOrder.class, Assumption.class })` and pass comma-separated test class names.

The following is the code snippet:

```
import org.junit.runner.RunWith;
import org.junit.runners.Suite;

@RunWith(Suite.class)
@Suite.SuiteClasses({ AssertTest.class, TestExecutionOrder.class,
  Assumption.class })
public class TestSuite {

}
```

During execution, the suite will execute all the tests. The following is a screenshot of the suite run. Check whether it runs seven tests out of the three test fixtures: `AssertTest`, `TestExecutionOrder`, and `Assumption`.

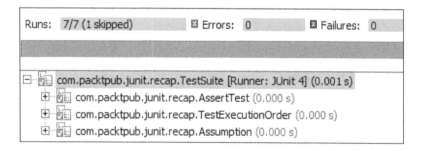

A test suite is created for group-related tests such as a group of data access, API usage tests, or a group of input validation logic tests.

Asserting with assertThat

Joe Walnes created the `assertThat(Object actual, Matcher matcher)` method. General consensus is that `assertThat` is readable and more useful than `assertEquals`. The syntax of the `assertThat` method is as follows:

```
public static void assertThat(Object actual, Matcher matcher
```

Here, `Object` is the actual value received and `Matcher` is an implementation of the `org.hamcrest.Matcher` interface. This interface comes from a separate library called `hamcrest.jar`.

A matcher enables a partial or an exact match for an expectation, whereas `assertEquals` uses an exact match. `Matcher` provides utility methods such as `is`, `either`, `or`, `not` , and `hasItem`. The `Matcher` methods use the **builder pattern** so that we can combine one or more matchers to build a composite matcher chain. Just like `StringBuilder`, it builds a string in multiple steps.

The following are a few examples of matchers and `assertThat`:

- `assertThat(calculatedTax, is(not(thirtyPercent)) );`
- `assertThat(phdStudentList, hasItem(DrJohn) );`
- `assertThat(manchesterUnitedClub, both( is(EPL_Champion)).` `and(is(UEFA_Champions_League_Champion)) );`

The preceding examples are more English than a JUnit test code. So, anyone can understand the intent of the code and test, and a matcher improves readability.

Hamcrest provides a utility matcher class called `org.hamcrest.CoreMatchers`.

A few utility methods of `CoreMatchers` are `allOf`, `anyOf`, `both`, `either`, `describedAs`, `everyItem`, `is`, `isA`, `anything`, `hasItem`, `hasItems`, `equalTo`, `any`, `instanceOf`, `not`, `nullValue`, `notNullValue`, `sameInstance`, `theInstance` `,startsWith`, `endsWith`, and `containsString`. All these methods return a matcher.

We worked with `assertEquals`; so, let's start with `equalTo`. The `equalTo` method is equivalent to `assertEquals`.

Comparing matchers – equalTo, is, and not

Create a `AssertThatTest.java` JUnit test and static import `org.hamcrest.CoreMatchers.*;` as follows:

```
import static org.hamcrest.CoreMatchers.not;
import static org.hamcrest.CoreMatchers.is;
import static org.junit.Assert.assertThat;

import org.junit.Test;

public class AssertThatTest {

  @Test
  public void verify_Matcher() throws Exception {
```

```
        int age = 30;
        assertThat(age, equalTo(30));
        assertThat(age, is(30));

        assertThat(age, not(equalTo(33)));
        assertThat(age, is(not(33)));
    }
}
```

Set the `age` variable to `30` and then likewise for `assertEquals` and call `equalTo`, which here is `Matcher`. The `equalTo` method takes a value. If the `Matcher` value doesn't match the actual value, then `assertThat` throws an `AssertionError` exception.

Set the `age` variable value to `29` and rerun the test. The following error will occur:

```
java.lang.AssertionError:
    Expected: <30>
        but: was <29>
    at org.hamcrest.MatcherAssert.assertThat(MatcherAssert.java:20)
```

The `is(a)` attribute takes a value and returns a Boolean and behaves similar to `equalTo(a)`. The `is(a)` attribute is the same as `is(equalTo(a))`.

The `not` attribute takes a value or a matcher. In the preceding code, we used `assertThat(age, is(not(33)));`. This expression is nothing but `age is not 33` and is more readable than the `assert` methods.

Working with compound value matchers – either, both, anyOf, allOf, and not

In this section, we will use `either`, `both`, `anyOf`, `allOf`, and `not`. Add the following test to the `AssertThatTest.java` file:

```
@Test
    public void verify_multiple_values() throws Exception {

        double marks = 100.00;
        assertThat(marks, either(is(100.00)).or(is(90.9)));

        assertThat(marks, both(not(99.99)).and(not(60.00)));

        assertThat(marks, anyOf(is(100.00),is(1.00),is(55.00),
            is(88.00),is(67.8)));
```

```
        assertThat(marks, not(anyOf(is(0.00),is(200.00))));

        assertThat(marks, not(allOf(is(1.00),is(100.00), is(30.00)))));
    }
```

In the preceding example, a `marks` double variable is initialized with a value of `100.00`. This variable value is asserted with an `either` matcher.

Basically, using `either`, we can compare two values against an actual or calculated value. If any of them match, then the assertion is passed. If none of them match, then `AssertionError` is thrown.

The `either(Matcher)` method takes a matcher and returns a `CombinableEitherMatcher` class. The `CombinableEitherMatcher` class has a `or(Matcher other)` method so that `either` and `or` can be combined.

The `or(Matcher other)` method is translated to `return (new CombinableMatcher(first)).or(other);` and finally to `new CombinableMatcher(new AnyOf(templatedListWith(other)));`.

Using `both`, we can compare two values against an actual or calculated value. If any of them don't match, then the `AssertionError` exception is thrown. If both of them match, then the assertion is passed.

A numeric value such as a math score cannot be equal to both 60 and 80. However, we can negate the expression. If the math score is 80, then using the `both` matcher we can write the expression as `assertThat (mathScore , both (not(60)). and(not (90)))`.

The `anyOf` matcher is more like `either` with multiple values. Using `anyOf`, we can compare multiple values against an actual or calculated value. If any of them match, then the assertion is passed. If none of them match, then the `AssertionError` exception is thrown.

The `allOf` matcher is more like `both` with multiple values. Using `allOf`, we can compare multiple values against an actual or calculated value. If any of them don't match, then the `AssertionError` exception is thrown. Similar to `both`, we can use `allOf` along with `not` to check whether a value does or doesn't belong to a set.

In the preceding example, using `allOf` and `not`, we checked whether the `marks` attribute is not `1`, `100`, or `30`.

Working with collection matchers – hasItem and hasItems

In the previous section, we asserted a value against multiple values. In this section, we will assert a collection of values against a value or numerous values.

Consider the following example. A salary list is populated with three values: 50.00, 200.00, and 500.00. Use hasItem to check whether a value exists in a collection, and use hasItems to check whether multiple values exist in a collection, as shown in the following code:

```
@Test
public void verify_collection_values() throws Exception {

    List<Double> salary =Arrays.asList(50.0, 200.0, 500.0);

    assertThat(salary, hasItem(50.00));
    assertThat(salary, hasItems(50.00, 200.00));
        assertThat(salary, not(hasItem(1.00)));
}
```

The hasItem matcher has two versions: one takes a value and the other takes a matcher. So, we can check a value in a collection using hasItem, or check whether a value doesn't exist in a collection using not and hasItem. The hasItems matcher operates on a set of values.

Exploring string matchers – startsWith, endsWith, and containsString

In this section, we will explore the string matchers. CoreMatchers has three built-in string matcher methods. In the following example, a String variable name is assigned a value and then we assert that the name starts with a specific value, contains a value, and ends with a value:

```
@Test
  public void verify_Strings() throws Exception {
    String name = "John Jr Dale";
    assertThat(name, startsWith("John"));
    assertThat(name, endsWith("Dale"));
    assertThat(name, containsString("Jr"));
  }
```

The `startsWith` matcher operates on string only. It checks whether the string starts with the given string. The `endsWith` matcher checks whether the string ends with the given string. The `containsString` matcher checks whether the string contains another string.

Sometimes, a method calls to return a JSON response. Using `containsString`, a specific value can be asserted.

> Note that `startsWith`, `endsWith`, and `containsStrings` are not the only string matchers. Other built-in matchers such as `both`, `either`, `anyOf`, and so on, can be applied to a `String` object.

Exploring built-in matchers

`JUnitMatchers` has built-in matcher methods, but all of these methods are deprecated. Use Hamcrest matchers instead of using `JUnitMatchers`.

Building a custom matcher

We can build our own matchers to use in `assertThat`. How about building a `matcher` that will compare two values and return `true` only if the actual object is less than or equal to the expected value?

Call it a `lessThanOrEqual` matcher. It should be allowed to use with any object that can be compared so that we can use an `Integer` or `Double` or `String` type or any custom class that implements the `Comparable` interface.

For example, `assertThat(100, lessThanOrEqual(200))` should pass, but `assertThat(100, lessThanOrEqual(50))` should fail and `assertThat("john123", lessThanOrEqual("john123"))` should pass, but `assertThat("john123", lessThanOrEqual("john12"))` should fail.

Follow the ensuing steps to build the `lessThanOrEqual` matcher:

1. Create a `LessThanOrEqual` class under the `com.packtpub.junit.recap` package.

2. To build a custom matcher, a class should implement the `Matcher` interface. However, Hamcrest recommends extending `org.hamcrest.BaseMatcher` rather than implementing the `Matcher` interface. So, we will extend `BaseMatcher`. The `BaseMatcher` class is an abstract class, and it doesn't implement `describeTo(Description description)` and `matches(Object t)`.

The `public boolean matches(Object obj)` method is invoked by `assertThat`. If this method returns `false`, then an `AssertionError` exception is thrown.

The `public void describeTo(Description description)` method is invoked when `matches(Object obj)` returns `false`. This method builds the description of an expectation.

The following code snippet explains how `assertThat` works:

```
if(!matcher.matches(actual)){
        Description description =
          new StringDescription();
        description.appendText(reason).
          appendText("\nExpected: ).
          appendDescriptionOf(matcher).
          appendText("\n    but: ");

        matcher.describeMismatch(actual, description);
        throw new AssertionError(description.toString());
}
```

Note that when `matcher.matches()` returns `false`, the description is built from the actual value and the matcher. The `appendDescriptionOf()` method calls the `describeTo()` method of the matcher to build the error message.

Finally, `matcher.describeMismatch(actual, description)` appends the string `but: was <<actual>>`.

3. The `lessThanOrEqual` class needs to compare two objects, so the `Matcher` class should be operated on the `Comparable` objects. Create a generic class that operates with any type that implements the `Comparable` interface, as follows:

```
public class LessThanOrEqual<T extends Comparable<T>> extends
BaseMatcher<Comparable<T>> {

}
```

4. Now we need to implement the `describeTo` and `matches` methods. The `assertThat` method will pass the actual value to the matcher's `matches(Object o)` method, and `lessThanOrEqual` will accept a value to compare with the actual. So, in the `matches` method, we need two comparable objects: one passed as a parameter and the other passed to a matcher object. The expected value is passed during the `matcher` object instantiation as follows:

```
assertThat (actual, matcher(expectedValue)).
```

We will store the `expectedValue` during the `Matcher` object creation and use it in the `matches()` method to compare the `expectedValue` with the `actual` as follows:

```
public class LessThanOrEqual<T extends Comparable<T>>
  extends BaseMatcher<Comparable<T>> {
  private final Comparable<T> expectedValue;

  public LessThanOrEqual(T expectedValue) {
   this.expectedValue = expectedValue;
  }


  @Override
  public void describeTo(Description description) {
    description.appendText(" less than or equal(<=)
      "+expectedValue);
  }


  @Override
  public boolean matches(Object t) {
    int compareTo = expectedValue.compareTo((T)t);
    return compareTo > -1;
  }
}
```

The preceding `LessThanOrEqual` class should return `true` only if `expectedValue.compareTo(actual) >= 0` and then the `describeTo()` method appends the string `"less than or equals (<=) "+ expectedValue` text to the `description`, so that if the assertion fails, then the `"less than or equals (<=) "+ expectedValue` message will be shown.

5. The `assertThat` method takes a matcher but `new`
    `LessThanOrEqual(expectedValue)` doesn't look good. We will create a
    `static` method in the `LessThanOrEqual` class to create a new object of
    `LessThanOrEqual`. Call this method from the `assertThat` method as follows:

```
@Factory
public static<T extends Comparable<T>>  Matcher<T>
  lessThanOrEqual(T t) {
  return new LessThanOrEqual(t);
  }
```

    The `@Factory` annotation isn't necessary but needed for a Hamcrest tool.
    When we create many custom matchers, then it becomes annoying to import
    them all individually. Hamcrest ships with a `org.hamcrest.generator.`
    `config.XmlConfigurator` command-line tool that picks up predicates
    annotated with the `@Factory` annotation and collects them in a `Matcher` class
    for easy importing.

6. Static import the `LessThanOrEqual` class and add a test to `AssertThatTest.`
    `java` to validate the custom matcher, as shown in the following code:

```
@Test
public void lessthanOrEquals_custom_matcher() throws
  Exception
{
  int actualGoalScored = 2;
  assertThat(actualGoalScored, lessThanOrEqual(4));
  assertThat(actualGoalScored, lessThanOrEqual(2));

  double originalPI = 3.14;
  assertThat(originalPI, lessThanOrEqual(9.00));

  String authorName = "Sujoy";
  assertThat(authorName, lessThanOrEqual("Zachary"));
}
```

    This test should pass.

7. How about testing the code with a greater value? In Java, `Integer.MAX_`
    `VALUE` holds the maximum integer value and `Integer.MIN_VALUE` holds the
    minimum integer value. If we expect that the maximum value will be greater
    than or equal to the minimum value, then the assertion should fail. Consider
    the following code snippet:

```
int maxInt = Integer.MAX_VALUE;
assertThat(maxInt, lessThanOrEqual(Integer.MIN_VALUE));
```

This will throw the following error:

```
java.lang.AssertionError:
   Expected:  less than or equals(<=) -2147483648
      but: was <2147483647>
   at org.hamcrest.MatcherAssert.assertThat(MatcherAssert.java:20)
   at org.junit.Assert.assertThat(Assert.java:865)
```

Creating parameterized tests

Parameterized tests are used for multiple iterations over a single input to stress the object in test. The primary reason is to reduce the amount of test code.

In TDD, the code is written to satisfy a failing test. The production code logic is built from a set of test cases and different input values. For example, if we need to build a class that will return the factorial of a number, then we will pass different sets of data and verify that our implementation passes the validation.

We know that the factorial of 0 is 1, the factorial of 1 is 1, the factorial of 2 is 2, the factorial of 3 is 6, the factorial of 4 is 24, and so on.

So, if we write tests such as `factorial_of_1_is_1` and `factorial_of_4_is_24`, then the test class will be polluted very easily. How many methods will we write?

We can create two arrays: one with the expected values and the other with the original numbers. Then, we can loop through the arrays and assert the result. We don't have to do this because the JUnit 4 framework provides us with a similar solution. It gives us a `Parameterized` runner.

We read about the `@RunWith` annotation in the preceding section. `Parameterized` is a special type of runner and can be used with the `@RunWith` annotation.

Parameterized comes with two flavors: constructor and method.

Working with parameterized constructors

Perform the following steps to build a parameterized test with a constructor:

1. Create a source folder `src` and add a `Factorial.java` class under `src/com.packtpub.junit.recap`.

2. Implement the factorial algorithm. Add the following code to the
    `Factorial.java` class:

    ```
    package com.packtpub.junit.recap;

    public class Factorial {

      public long factorial(long number) {
        if(number == 0) {
          return 1;
        }

        return number*factorial(number-1);
      }
    }
    ```

3. Add a `ParameterizedFactorialTest.java` test under `test/`
    `com.packtpub.junit.recap` and annotate the class with `@`
    `RunWith(Parameterized.class)` as follows:

    ```
    import org.junit.runner.RunWith;
    import org.junit.runners.Parameterized;

    @RunWith(Parameterized.class)
    public class ParameterizedFactorialTest {

    }
    ```

4. Add a method to create a dataset for factorial algorithm. The method should
    return `Collection` of the `Object []` method. We need a collection of two
    dimensional arrays to hold the numbers and factorial values. To define the
    data parameters, annotate the method with `@Parameters`.

    The following code snippet defines a `@parameters` method
    `factorialData()`:

    ```
    @Parameters
    public static Collection<Object[]> factorialData() {
      return Arrays.asList(new Object[][] {

        { 0, 1 }, { 1, 1 }, { 2, 2 }, { 3, 6 },
          { 4, 24 }, { 5, 120 },{ 6, 720 }
      });
    }
    ```

    Check whether the arrays hold the number and the expected factorial result
    (0's factorial is 1, 5's factorial is 120, and so on).

5. The `Parameterized` runner needs a constructor to pass the collection of data. For each row in the collection, the 0th array element will be passed as the 1st constructor argument, the next index will be passed as 2nd argument, and so on, as follows:

```
private int number;
private int expectedResult;

public ParameterizedFactorialTest(int input,
   int expected) {
      number= input;
      expectedResult= expected;
}
```

In the test class, we added two members to hold the number and the expected factorial value. In the constructor, set these values. The `Parameterized` runner will loop through the data collection (annotated with a `@Parameters` annotation) and pass the values to the constructor.

For example, it will pass 0 as input and 1 as expected, then 1 as input and 1 as expected, and so on.

6. Now, we need to add a test method to assert the number and the factorial as follows:

```
@Test
public void factorial() throws Exception {
  Factorial fact = new Factorial();
  assertEquals(fact.factorial(number),expectedResult);
}
```

We created a `Factorial` object and passed the number to get the actual result and then asserted the actual value with `expectedResult`. Here, the runner will create seven instances of the test class and execute the test method.

The following screenshot shows the result of the test run taken from Eclipse:

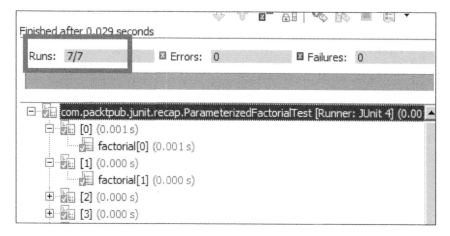

Note that the seven tests run and the tests names are [0] factorial[0], [1] factorial[1], and so on till [6].

If the dataset returns an empty collection, the test doesn't fail; actually, nothing happens.

If the number of parameters in the object array and the constructor argument don't match, then a `java.lang. IllegalArgumentException: wrong number of arguments` exception is thrown. For example, { 0, 1, 3 } will throw an exception as 3 arguments are passed, but constructor can accept only 2.

If the constructor is not defined but the data set contains a value, then the `java.lang.IllegalArgumentException: wrong number of arguments` exception is thrown.

Working with parameterized methods

We learned about the parameterized constructor; now we will run the parameterized test excluding the constructor. Follow the ensuing steps to run the test using the `@Parameter` annotation:

1. Add a `ParameterizeParamFactorialTest.java` test class.

2. Copy the content from the constructor test and delete the constructor. Change the class members to public, as follows:

```
@RunWith(Parameterized.class)
public class ParameterizeParamFactorialTest {

  @Parameters
  public static Collection<Object[]> factorialData() {
    return Arrays.asList(new Object[][] {

      { 0, 1 }, { 1, 1 }, { 2, 2 }, { 3, 6 },
        { 4, 24 }, { 5, 120 },{ 6, 720 }
    });
  }


  public int number;
  public int expectedResult;



  @Test
  public void factorial() throws Exception {
    Factorial fact = new Factorial();
    assertEquals(fact.factorial(number),expectedResult);
  }
}
```

3. If we run the test, it will fail as the reflection process won't find the matching constructor. JUnit provides an annotation to loop through the dataset and set the values to the class members. `@Parameter(value=index)` takes a value. The value is the array index of the data collection object array. Make sure that the `number` and `expectedResult` variables are `public`; otherwise, the security exception will be thrown. Annotate them with the following parameters:

```
@Parameter(value=0)
public int number;
@Parameter(value=1)
public int expectedResult;
```

Here, for each row in the data collection, the `number` variable will hold the 0th index of the array and the `expectedResult` variable will hold the 1st index.

4. Run the test; seven tests will be executed.

Giving a name

In the constructor example, we found that the test names are assigned with indexes such as [0], [1], and so on. So, if a test fails, then it is not easy to identify the data. To identify an individual test case in a parameterized test, a name is required. The `@Parameters` annotation allows placeholders that are replaced at runtime, and we can use them. The following are the placeholders:

- `{index}`: This represents the current parameter index
- `{0}`, `{1}`,...: This represents the first, second, and so on, parameter values

The following code snippet annotates the dataset with the name placeholders:

```
@Parameters(name = "{index}: factorial({0})={1}")
  public static Collection<Object[]> factorialData() {
     return Arrays.asList(new Object[][] {

         { 0, 1 }, { 1, 1 }, { 2, 2 }, { 3, 6 },
            { 4, 24 }, { 5, 120 },{ 6, 720 }
     });
  }
```

Eclipse has a bug that chops off the name.

Working with timeouts

JUnit tests are automated to get quick feedback after a change in the code. If a test runs for a long time, it violates the quick feedback principle. JUnit provides a timeout value (in milliseconds) in the `@Test` annotation to make sure that if a test runs longer than the specified value, the test fails.

The following is an example of a timeout:

```
@Test(timeout=10)
public void forEver() throws Exception {
  Thread.sleep(100000);
}
```

Here, the test will fail automatically after 10 milliseconds. The following is an Eclipse screenshot that shows the error:

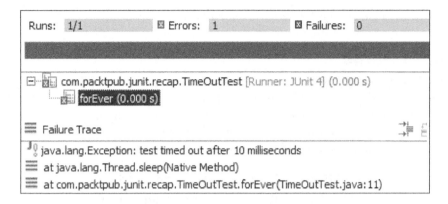

Exploring JUnit theories

A theory is a kind of a JUnit test but different from the typical example-based JUnit tests, where we assert a specific data set and expect a specific outcome. JUnit theories are an alternative to JUnit's parameterized tests. A JUnit theory encapsulates the tester's understanding of an object's universal behavior. This means whatever a theory asserts is expected to be true for all data sets. Theories are useful for finding bugs in boundary-value cases.

Parameterized tests allow us to write flexible data-driven tests and separate data from the test methods. Theories are similar to parameterized tests—both allow us to specify the test data outside of the test case.

Parameterized tests are good but they have the following drawbacks:

- Parameters are declared as member variables. They pollute the test class and unnecessarily make the system complex.

- Parameters need to be passed to the single constructor or variables need to be annotated, simply making the class incomprehensible.

- Test data cannot be externalized.

Theory comes up with many annotations and a runner class. Let's examine the important annotations and classes in theory, as follows:

- `@Theory`: Like `@Test`, this annotation identifies a theory test to run. The `@Test` annotation doesn't work with a theory runner.

- `@DataPoint`: This annotation identifies a single set of test data (similar to `@Parameters`), that is, either a static variable or a method.

- @DataPoints: This annotation identifies multiple sets of test data, generally an array.

- @ParametersSuppliedBy: This annotation provides the parameters to the test cases.

- Theories: This annotation is a JUnit runner for the theory-based test cases and extends org.junit.runners.BlockJUnit4ClassRunner.

- ParameterSupplier: This is an abstract class that gives us the handle on the parameters that we can supply to the test case.

We will start with a simple theory and then explore more. Perform the following steps:

1. Create a MyTheoryTest.java class and annotate the class with @RunWith(Theories.class). To run a theory, this special runner is required. Consider the following code:

   ```
   @RunWith(Theories.class)
   public class MyTheoryTest {

   }
   ```

2. Now run the test. It will fail with the java.lang.Exception: No runnable methods error because no theory is defined yet. Like the @Test annotation, we will define a method and annotate it with @Theory as follows:

   ```
   @RunWith(Theories.class)
   public class MyTheoryTest {

     @Theory
     public void sanity() {
       System.out.println("Sanity check");
     }
   }
   ```

   Run the theory, and it will be executed with no error. So, our theory setup is ready.

3. Define a public static String with a name variable and annotate this variable with @DataPoint. Now execute the test, nothing special happens. If a theory method (annotated with @Theory) takes an argument and a variable annotated with @DataPoint matches the type, then the variable is passed to the theory during execution. So, change the sanity method and add a String argument to pass @DataPoint to the sanity() method, as follows:

   ```
   @RunWith(Theories.class)
   public class MyTheoryTest {
     @DataPoint public static String name ="Jack";
   ```

```
    @Theory
    public void sanity(String aName) {
        System.out.println("Sanity check "+aName);
    }
}
```

Now run the theory. It will pass the @DataPoint name to the sanity(String aName) method during execution and the name will be printed to the console.

4. Now, add another static @DataPoint, call it mike, and rename the name variable to jack, as follows:

```
@RunWith(Theories.class)
public class MyTheoryTest {
    @DataPoint public static String jack ="Jack";
    @DataPoint public static String mike ="Mike";

    @Theory
    public void sanity(String aName) {
        System.out.println("Sanity check "+aName);
    }
}
```

During theory execution, both the @DataPoint variables will be passed to the sanity(String aName) method. The output will be as follows:

```
<terminated> MyTheoryTest [JUnit]
Sanity check Jack
Sanity check Mike
```

5. Now, slightly modify the sanity() method—rename the aName argument to firstName and add a second String argument, lastName. So now the sanity method takes the String arguments, fistName and lastName. Print these variables using the following code:

```
@RunWith(Theories.class)
public class MyTheoryTest {
    @DataPoint public static String jack ="Jack";
    @DataPoint public static String mike ="Mike";

    @Theory
    public void sanity(String firstName, String lastName) {
        System.out.println("Sanity check "+firstName+",
          "+lastName);
    }
}
```

When executed, the output will be as follows:

```
<terminated> MyTheoryTest [JUnit]
Sanity check Jack, Jack
Sanity check Jack, Mike
Sanity check Mike, Jack
Sanity check Mike, Mike
```

So, 2 x 2 = 4 combinations are used. When the multiple @DataPoint annotations are defined in a test, the theories apply to all possible well-typed combinations of data points for the test arguments.

6. So far we have only examined single-dimension variables. The @DataPoints annotation is used to provide a set of data. Add a static char array to hold the character variables and add a Theory method to accept two characters. It will execute the theory with 9 (3 ^ 2) possible combinations as follows:

```
@DataPoints  public static char[] chars =
        new char[] {'A', 'B', 'C'};
@Theory
public void build(char c, char d) {
   System.out.println(c+" "+d);
}
```

The following is the output:

```
<terminated> MyTheoryTest [JUnit]
A A
A B
A C
B A
B B
B C
C A
C B
C C
```

Externalizing data using @ParametersSuppliedBy and ParameterSupplier

So far, we have covered how to set up test data using `@DataPoint` and `@DataPoints`. Now, we will use external classes to supply data in our tests using `@ParametersSuppliedBy` and `ParameterSupplier`. To do this, perform the following steps:

1. Create an `Adder.java` class. This class will have two overloaded `add()` methods to add numbers and strings. We will unit test the methods using theory.

   The following is the `Adder` class:

   ```java
   public class Adder {

     public Object add(Number a, Number b) {
       return a.doubleValue()+b.doubleValue();
     }

     public Object add(String a, String b) {
       return a+b;
     }
   }
   ```

2. Create an `ExternalTheoryTest.java` theory as follows:

   ```java
   @RunWith(Theories.class)
   public class ExternalTheoryTest {

   }
   ```

3. We will not use `@DataPoints` to create data. Instead, we will create a separate class to supply numbers to validate the `add` operation. JUnit provides a `ParameterSupplier` class for this purpose. `ParameterSupplier` is an abstract class, and it forces you to define a method as follows:

   ```java
   public abstract List<PotentialAssignment>
     getValueSources(ParameterSignature parametersignature);
   ```

   `PotentialAssignment` is an abstract class that JUnit theories use to provide test data to test methods in a consistent manner. It has a static `forValue` method that you can use to get an instance of `PotentialAssignment`.

   Create a `NumberSupplier` class to supply different types of numbers: `float`, `int`, `double`, `long`, and so on. Extend the `ParameterSupplier` class as follows:

   ```java
   import
     org.junit.experimental.theories.ParameterSignature;
   ```

```
import org.junit.experimental.theories.ParameterSupplier;
import
  org.junit.experimental.theories.PotentialAssignment;

public  class NumberSupplier extends ParameterSupplier {
  @Override
    public List<PotentialAssignment>
    getValueSources(ParameterSignature sig) {
      List<PotentialAssignment> list = new
        ArrayList<PotentialAssignment>();
      list.add(PotentialAssignment.forValue("long",
        2L));
      list.add(PotentialAssignment.forValue("float",
        5.00f));
      list.add(PotentialAssignment.forValue("double",
          89d));
      return list;
  }

};
```

Check whether the overridden method creates a list of
PotentialAssignment values of different numbers.

4. Now, modify the theory to add two numbers. Add a theory method
    as follows:

```
import org.junit.experimental.theories.ParametersSuppliedBy;
import org.junit.experimental.theories.Theories;
import org.junit.experimental.theories.Theory;
import org.junit.runner.RunWith;

@RunWith(Theories.class)
public class ExternalTheoryTest {

  @Theory
  public void adds_numbers(
  @ParametersSuppliedBy(NumberSupplier.class) Number num1,
  @ParametersSuppliedBy(NumberSupplier.class) Number num2)
  {
    System.out.println(num1 + " and " + num2);
  }

}
```

Check the `adds_numbers` method; two `Number` arguments `num1` and `num2` are annotated with `@ParametersSuppliedBy(NumberSupplier.class)`.

When this theory is executed, the `NumberSupplier` class will pass a list.

5. Execute the theory; it will print the following result:

```
<terminated> ExternalTh
2 and 2
2 and 5.0
2 and 89.0
5.0 and 2
5.0 and 5.0
5.0 and 89.0
89.0 and 2
89.0 and 5.0
89.0 and 89.0
```

6. Now, we can check our `Adder` functionality. Modify the theory to assert the result.

Create an instance of the `Adder` class and call the `add` method by passing `num1` and `num2`. Add the two numbers and `assert` the value with the results of `Adder`.

The `assertEquals(double, double)` method is deprecated as the double value calculation results in an unpredictable result. So, the `assert` class adds another version of `assertEquals` for `doubles`; it takes three arguments: actual, expected, and a delta. If the difference between the `actual` and the `expected` value is greater than or equal to delta, then the assertion passes as follows:

```
@RunWith(Theories.class)
public class ExternalTheoryTest {

  @Theory
  public void adds_numbers(
  @ParametersSuppliedBy(NumberSupplier.class) Number num1,
  @ParametersSuppliedBy(NumberSupplier.class) Number num2) {
    Adder anAdder = new Adder();
    double expectedSum =
      num1.doubleValue()+num2.doubleValue();
    double actualResult = (Double)anAdder.add(num1, num2);
    assertEquals(actualResult, expectedSum, 0.01);
  }

}
```

The `Adder` class has an `add` method for `String`. Create a `StringSupplier` class to supply `String` values to our theory and modify the theory class to verify the `add (String, String)` method behavior. You can assert the `Strings` as follows:

- ○ `String expected = str1+str2;`
- ○ `assertEquals(expected, actual);`

Here, `str1` and `str2` are the two method arguments of the theory.

Dealing with JUnit rules

Rules allow very flexible addition or redefinition of the behavior of each test method in a test class. Rules are like **Aspect Oriented Programming (AOP)**; we can do useful things before and/or after the actual test execution. You can find more information about AOP at `http://en.wikipedia.org/wiki/Aspect-oriented_programming`.

We can use the inbuilt rules or define our custom rule.

In this section, we will look at the inbuilt rules and create our custom Verifier and WatchMan rule.

Playing with the timeout rule

The timeout rule applies the same timeout to all the test methods in a class. Earlier, we used the timeout in the `@Test` annotation as follows:

```
@Test(timeout=10)
```

The following is the syntax of the timeout rule:

```
import org.junit.Rule;
import org.junit.Test;
import org.junit.rules.Timeout;

public class TimeoutTest {

    @Rule
    public Timeout globalTimeout =  new Timeout(20);

    @Test
    public void testInfiniteLoop1() throws InterruptedException{
      Thread.sleep(30);
    }
```

```
@Test
public void testInfiniteLoop2() throws InterruptedException{
   Thread.sleep(30);
}

}
```

When we run this test, it times out after 20 milliseconds. Note that the timeout is applied globally to all methods.

Working with the ExpectedException rule

The ExpectedException rule is an important rule for handling exceptions. It allows you to assert the expected exception type and the exception message, for example, your code may throw a generic exception (such as IllegalStateException) for all failure conditions, but you can assert the generic exception message to verify the exact cause.

Earlier, we used @Test(expected=Exception class) to test the error conditions.

The ExpectedException rule allows in-test specification of expected exception types and messages.

The following code snippet explains how an exception rule can be used to verify the exception class and the exception message:

```
public class ExpectedExceptionRuleTest {

   @Rule
   public ExpectedException thrown= ExpectedException.none();

   @Test
   public void throwsNothing() {

   }

   @Test
   public void throwsNullPointerException() {
      thrown.expect(NullPointerException.class);
      throw new NullPointerException();
   }

   @Test
   public void throwsIllegalStateExceptionWithMessage() {
      thrown.expect(IllegalStateException.class);
```

```
        thrown.expectMessage("Is this a legal state?");

        throw new IllegalStateException("Is this a legal state?");
    }
}
```

The `expect` object sets the expected exception class and `expectMessage` sets the expected message in the exception. If the message or exception class doesn't match the rule's expectation, the test fails. The `ExpectedException` object thrown is reset on each test.

Unfolding the TemporaryFolder rule

The `TemporaryFolder` rule allows the creation of files and folders that are guaranteed to be deleted when the test method finishes (whether it passes or fails). Consider the following code:

```
@Rule
public TemporaryFolder folder = new TemporaryFolder();

@Test
public void testUsingTempFolder() throws IOException {
    File createdFile = folder.newFile("myfile.txt");
    File createdFolder = folder.newFolder("mysubfolder");

}
```

Exploring the ErrorCollector rule

The `ErrorCollector` rule allows the execution of a test to continue after the first problem is found (for example, to collect all the incorrect rows in a table and report them all at once) as follows:

```
import org.junit.rules.ErrorCollector;
import static org.hamcrest.CoreMatchers.equalTo;

public class ErrorCollectorTest {

    @Rule
    public ErrorCollector collector = new ErrorCollector();

    @Test
    public void fails_after_execution() {
    collector.checkThat("a", equalTo("b"));
    collector.checkThat(1, equalTo(2));
```

```
        collector.checkThat ("ae", equalTo ("g"));
    }
}
```

In this example, none of the verification passes but the test still finishes its execution, and at the end, notifies all errors.

The following is the log—the arrows indicate the errors—and also note that only one test method is being executed but Eclipse indicates three failures:

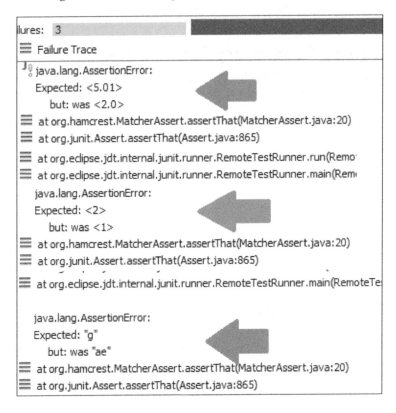

Working with the Verifier rule

Verifier is a base class of `ErrorCollector`, which can otherwise turn passing tests into failing tests if a verification check fails. The following example demonstrates the `Verifier` rule:

```
public class VerifierRuleTest {
    private String errorMsg = null;

    @Rule
```

```
public TestRule rule = new Verifier() {
  protected void verify() {
    assertNull("ErrorMsg should be null after each test
      execution",errorMsg);
  }
};


@Test
public void testName() throws Exception {
  errorMsg = "Giving a value";
}
}
```

Verifier's `verify` method is executed after each test execution. If the `verify` method defines any assertions, and that assertion fails, then the test is marked as failed.

In the preceding example, the test should not fail as the test method doesn't perform any comparison; however, it still fails. It fails because the Verifier rule checks that after every test execution, the `errorMsg` string should be set as null, but the test method sets the value to `Giving a value`; hence, the verification fails.

Learning the TestWatcher rule

`TestWatcher` (and the deprecated `TestWatchman`) are base classes for rules that take note of the testing action, without modifying it. Consider the following code:

```
@FixMethodOrder(MethodSorters.NAME_ASCENDING)
public class TestWatcherTest {

  private static String dog = "";

  @Rule
  public TestWatcher watchman = new TestWatcher() {
    @Override
    public Statement apply(Statement base,
      Description description) {
      return super.apply(base, description);
    }

    @Override
    protected void succeeded(Description description) {
      dog += description.getDisplayName() + " " + "success!\n";
    }
```

```
        @Override
        protected void failed(Throwable e, Description description) {
           dog += description.getDisplayName() + " " +
             e.getClass().getSimpleName() + "\n";
        }

        @Override
        protected void starting(Description description) {
           super.starting(description);
        }

        @Override
        protected void finished(Description description) {
           super.finished(description);
        }
    };

    @Test
    public void red_test() {
       fail();
    }

    @Test
    public void green() {
    }

    @AfterClass
    public static void afterClass() {
       System.out.println(dog);
    }
}
```

We created a `TestWatcher` class to listen to every test execution, collected the failure, and success instances, and at the end, printed the result in the `afterClass()` method.

The following is the error shown on the console:

```
green(com.packtpub.junit.recap.rule.TestWatcherTest) success!

red_test(com.packtpub.junit.recap.rule.TestWatcherTest) AssertionError
```

Working with the TestName rule

The `TestName` rule makes the current test name available inside test methods. The `TestName` rule can be used in conjunction with the `TestWatcher` rule to make a unit testing framework compile a unit testing report.

The following test snippet shows that the test name is asserted inside the test:

```
public class TestNameRuleTest {

  @Rule
    public TestName name = new TestName();

    @Test
    public void testA() {
      assertEquals("testA", name.getMethodName());
    }

    @Test
    public void testB() {
      assertEquals("testB", name.getMethodName());
    }
}
```

The following section uses the `TestName` rule to get the method name before test execution.

Handling external resources

Sometimes JUnit tests need to communicate with external resources such as files or databases or server sockets. Dealing with external resources is always messy because you need to set up state and tear it down later. The `ExternalResource` rule provides a mechanism that makes resource handling a bit more convenient.

Previously, when you had to create files in a test case or work with server sockets, you had to set up a temporary directory, or open a socket in a `@Before` method and later delete the file or close the server in an `@After` method. But now, JUnit provides a simple AOP-like mechanism called the `ExternalResource` rule that makes this setup and cleanup work the responsibility of the resource.

The following example demonstrates the `ExternalResource` capabilities. The `Resource` class represents an external resource and prints the output in the console:

```java
class Resource{
  public void open() {
    System.out.println("Opened");
  }

  public void close() {
    System.out.println("Closed");
  }

  public double get() {
    return Math.random();
  }
}
```

The following test class creates `ExternalResource` and handles the resource lifecycle:

```java
public class ExternalResourceTest {
  Resource resource;
  public @Rule TestName name = new TestName();

  public @Rule ExternalResource rule = new ExternalResource() {
    @Override protected void before() throws Throwable {
      resource = new Resource();
      resource.open();
      System.out.println(name.getMethodName());
    }

    @Override protected void after()   {
      resource.close();
      System.out.println("\n");
    }
  };

  @Test
  public void someTest() throws Exception {
    System.out.println(resource.get());
  }

  @Test
  public void someTest2() throws Exception {
    System.out.println(resource.get());
  }
}
```

The anonymous `ExternalResource` class overrides the `before` and `after` methods of the `ExternalResource` class. In the `before` method, it starts the resource and prints the test method name using the `TestName` rule. In the `after` method, it just closes the resource.

The following is the test run output:

```
Opened
someTest2
0.5872875884671511
Closed

Opened
someTest
0.395586457988541
Closed
```

Note that the resource is opened before test execution and closed after the test. The test name is printed using the `TestName` rule.

Exploring JUnit categories

The `Categories` runner runs only the classes and methods that are annotated with either the category given with the `@IncludeCategory` annotation or a subtype of that category. Either classes or interfaces can be used as categories. Subtyping works, so if you use `@IncludeCategory(SuperClass.class)`, a test marked `@Category({SubClass.class})` will be run.

We can exclude categories by using the `@ExcludeCategory` annotation.

We can define two interfaces using the following code:

```
public interface SmartTests { /* category marker */ }
public interface CrazyTests { /* category marker */ }

public class SomeTest {
  @Test
  public void a() {
    fail();
  }

  @Category(CrazyTests.class)
  @Test
  public void b() {
  }
```

```
}

@Category({CrazyTests.class, SmartTests.class})
public class OtherTest {
  @Test
  public void c() {

  }
}

@RunWith(Categories.class)
@IncludeCategory(CrazyTests.class)
@SuiteClasses( { SomeTest.class, OtherTest.class }) // Note that
Categories is a kind of Suite
public class CrazyTestSuite {
  // Will run SomeTest.b and OtherTest.c, but not SomeTest.a
}

@RunWith(Categories.class)
@IncludeCategory(CrazyTests.class)
@ExcludeCategory(SmartTests.class)
@SuiteClasses( { SomeTest.class, OtherTest.class })
public class CrazyTestSuite {
  // Will run SomeTest.b, but not SomeTest.a or OtherTest.c
}
```

Summary

This JUnit refresher chapter covers both the basic and advanced usage of JUnit.

The basic section covers the annotation based on JUnit 4 testing, assertion, the @RunWith annotation, exception handling, and the Eclipse setup for running the JUnit tests.

The advanced section covers parameterized tests, matchers and assertThat, a custom lessThanOrEqual() matcher, assumption, theory, a custom NumberSupplier class, timeout, categories, TestName, ExpectedException, TemporaryFolder, ErrorCollector, Verifier and TestWatcher rules, test suites, and executing tests in order.

By now, you will be able to write and execute JUnit 4 tests and be familiar with the advanced concepts of JUnit 4.

Chapter 2, Automating JUnit Tests, focuses on getting you quickly started with project-building tools and test automation. It provides an overview of continuous integration, explores the incremental Gradle build and Maven build lifecycle, Ant scripting, and Jenkins automation using Gradle, Maven, and Ant scripts.

2
Automating JUnit Tests

In this chapter, you will be introduced to the concept of **Extreme Programming (XP)**, **Continuous Integration (CI)**, the benefits of CI, and JUnit test automation using various tools.

The following topics will be covered in this chapter:

- CI
- Gradle automation
- Maven project management
- Ant
- Jenkins

Continuous Integration

In college, I was working on a critical steganography (image watermarking) project and simultaneously developing a module on my home computer, where I integrated my changes with other changes on the college server. Most of my time was wasted in integration. After manual integration, I would find everything broken; so, integration was terrifying.

When CI is not available, development teams or developers make changes to code and then all the code changes are brought together and merged. Sometimes, this merge is not very simple; it involves the integration of lots of conflicting changes. Often, after integration, weird bugs crop up and a working module may start to fail, as it involves a complete rework of numerous modules. Nothing goes as planned and the delivery is delayed. As a result, the predictability, cost, and customer service are affected.

CI is an XP concept. It was introduced to prevent integration issues. In CI, developers commit the code periodically, and every commit is built. Automated tests verify the system integrity. It helps in the incremental development and periodic delivery of the working software.

Benefits of CI

CI is meant to make sure that we're not breaking something unconsciously in our hurry. We want to run the tests continuously, and we need to be warned if they fail.

In a good software development team, we'd find **test-driven development** (TDD) as well as CI.

CI requires a listener tool to keep an eye on the version control system for changes. Whenever a change is committed, this tool automatically compiles and tests the application (sometimes it creates a WAR file, deploys the WAR/EAR file, and so on).

If compilation fails, or a test fails, or deployment fails, or something goes wrong, the CI tool immediately notifies the concerned team so that they can fix the issue.

CI is a concept; to adhere to CI, tools such as Sonar and FindBugs can be added to the build process to track the code quality, and they automatically monitor the code quality and code coverage metrics. Good quality code gives us confidence that a team is following the right path. Technical debts can be identified very quickly, and the team can start reducing the debts. Often, CI tools have the ability to present dashboards pertaining to quality metrics.

In a nutshell, CI tools enforce code quality, predictability, and provide quick feedback, which reduces the potential risk. CI helps to increase the confidence in the build. A team can still write very poor quality code, even test poor quality code, and the CI will not care.

Numerous CI tools are available on the market, such as Go, Bamboo, TeamCity, CruiseControl, and Jenkins. However, CruiseControl and Jenkins are the widely used ones.

Jenkins supports various build scripting tools. It integrates almost all sorts of projects and is easy to configure. In this chapter, we will work with Jenkins.

CI is just a generic conduit to run the commands; often, build tools are used to execute the commands, and then the CI tool collects the metrics produced by the commands or build tools. Jenkins needs build scripts to execute tests, compile the source code, or even deploy deliverables. Jenkins supports different build tools to execute the commands—Gradle, Maven, and Ant are the widely used ones. We will explore the build tools and then work with Jenkins.

You can download the code for this chapter. Extract the ZIP file. It contains a folder named `Packt`. This folder has two subfolders: `gradle` and `chapter02`. The `gradle` folder contains the basic Gradle examples and the `chapter02` folder contains the Java projects and Ant, Gradle, and Maven build scripts.

Gradle automation

Gradle is a build automation tool. Gradle has many benefits such as loose structure, ability to write scripts to build, simple two-pass project resolution, dependency management, remote plugins, and so on.

The best feature of Gradle is the ability to create a **domain-specific language** (DSL) for the build. An example would be generate-web-service-stubs or run-all-tests-in-parallel.

 A DSL is a programming language specialized for a domain and focuses on a particular aspect of a system. HTML is an example of DSL. We cannot build an entire system with a DSL, but DSLs are used to solve problems in a particular domain. The following are the examples of DSLs:

- A DSL for building Java projects
- A DSL for drawing graph

It's one of the **unique selling point** (USP) is an incremental build. It can be configured to build a project only if any resource has changed in the project. As a result, the overall build execution time decreases.

Gradle comes up with numerous preloaded plugins for different projects types. We can either use them or override.

Unlike Maven or Ant, Gradle is not XML based; it is based on a dynamic language called **Groovy**. Groovy is a developer-friendly **Java Virtual Machine** (JVM) language. Its syntax makes it easier to express the code intent and provides ways to effectively use expressions, collections, closures, and so on. Groovy programs run on JVM; so, if we write Java code in a Groovy file, it will run. Groovy supports DSL to make your code readable and maintainable.

Groovy's home page is `http://groovy.codehaus.org/`.

 We can use Ant or Maven in a Gradle script. Gradle supports the Groovy syntax. Gradle provides support for Java, Web, Hibernate, GWT, Groovy, Scala, OSGi, and many other projects.

Big companies such as LinkedIn and Siemens use Gradle. Many open source projects, such as Spring, Hibernate, and Grails use Gradle.

Getting started

Java (jdk 1.5 +) needs to be installed before executing a Gradle script. The steps to do this are as follows:

1. Go to the command prompt and run `java -version`; if Java is not installed or the version is older than 1.5, install the latest version from the Oracle site.

2. Gradle is available at `http://www.gradle.org/downloads`. Once the download is complete, extract the media. You will find that it includes a `bin` directory. Open the command prompt and go to the `bin` directory. You can extract the media to any directory you want. For example, if you extract the Gradle media under `D:\Software\gradle-1.10`, then open the command prompt and go to `D:\Software\gradle-1.10\bin`.

3. Now, check the Gradle version using the `gradle -v` command. It will show you the version and other configuration. To run the Gradle from anywhere in your computer, create a `GRADLE_HOME` environment variable and set the value to the location where you extracted the Gradle media.

4. Add `%GRADLE_HOME%\bin` (in Windows) to the `PATH` variable (export `GRADLE_ HOME` and `PATH` to `bash_login` in Linux and `bashrc` in Mac).

5. Open a new command prompt, go to any folder, and run the same command `gradle -v` again to check whether the `PATH` variable is set correctly.

The other option is to use the Gradle wrapper (`gradlew`) and allow the batch file (or shell script) to download the version of Gradle specific to each project. This is an industry standard for working with Gradle, which ensures that there's consistency among Gradle versions. The Gradle wrapper is also checked into the source code control along with the build artifacts.

Gradling

In the programming world, "Hello World" is the starting point. In this section, we will write our first "Hello World" Gradle script. A Gradle script can build one or more projects. Each project can have one or more tasks. A task can be anything like compiling Java files or building a WAR file.

 To execute a task, we will create a `build.gradle` file and execute the `gradle` command to run a build. Gradle will look for a file named `build.gradle` in the current directory. To execute a build file other than `build.gradle`, use the `-b <file name>` option.

We will create a task to print "Hello World" on the console. Perform the following steps:

1. Open a text editor and enter the following:

```
task firstTask << {
   println 'Hello world.'
}
```

   Save the file as `build.gradle`.

2. Open the command prompt and browse to the folder where you saved the `build.gradle` file. Run the `gradle firstTask` command, or if you saved the file under `D:\Packt\gradle`, simply open the command prompt and run `gradle -b D:\Packt\gradle\build.gradle firstTask`.

   The following information will be printed on the command prompt:

   ```
   :firstTask
   Hello world.
   BUILD SUCCESSFUL
   ```

Here, `task` defines a Gradle task and `<<` defines a task called `firstTask` with a single closure to execute. The `println` command is Groovy's equivalent to Java's `System.out.println`.

When we executed the task using its name, the output shows the task name and then printed the **Hello world** message.

> Using the `-q` option, we can turn off the Gradle messages. If we run `gradle -q -b build.gradle firstTask`, then it will print only **Hello world**.

Ordering subtasks using doFirst and doLast

A task can contain many subtasks. Subtasks can be defined and ordered using the `doFirst` and `doLast` keywords. The following code snippet describes the Java method style task definition and subtask ordering:

```
task aTask(){
  doLast{
   println 'Executing last.'
  }

  doFirst {
        println 'Running 1st'
  }
}
```

Here, we defined a task named aTask using the Java method style. The task aTask contains two closure keywords: doLast and doFirst.

The doFirst closure is executed once the task is invoked, and the doLast closure is executed at the end.

When we run gradle aTask, it prints the following messages:

```
:aTask
Running 1st
Executing last.

BUILD SUCCESSFUL
```

Default tasks

In Ant, we can define a default target; similarly, Gradle provides options for default tasks using the keyword defaultTasks 'taskName1', ...'taskNameN'.

The defaultTasks 'aTask' keyword defines aTask as a default task. So now if we only execute gradle with no task name, then it will invoke the default task.

The task dependency

In Ant, a target depends on another target, for example, a Java code compile task may depend on cleaning of the output folder; similarly, in Gradle, a task may depend on another task. The dependency is defined using the dependsOn keyword. The following syntax is used to define a task dependency:

```
secondTask.dependsOn 'firstTask'
```

Here, secondTask depends on firstTask.

Another way of defining task dependency is passing the dependency in a method-like style. The following code snippet shows the method argument style:

```
task secondTask (dependsOn: 'firstTask') {

  doLast {
      println 'Running last'
    }

  doFirst {
      println 'Running first'
    }

}
```

Execute `gradle secondTask`; it will first execute the dependent task `firstTask` and then execute the task `secondTask` as follows:

```
:firstTask
Hello world.
:secondTask
Running first
Running last
```

Another way of defining intertask dependency is using `secondTask.dependsOn = ['firstTask']` or `secondTask.dependsOn 'firstTask'`.

 We can abbreviate each word of a task name in a camel case to execute a task. For example, the task name `secondTask` can be abbreviated to `sT`.

Daemon

Each time the `gradle` command is invoked, a new process is started, the Gradle classes and libraries are loaded, and the build is executed. Loading classes and libraries take time. Execution time can be reduced if a JVM, Gradle classes, and libraries, are not loaded each time. The `--daemon` command-line option starts a new Java process and preloads the Gradle classes and libraries; so, the first execution takes time. The next execution with the `--daemon` option takes almost no time because only the build gets executed—the JVM, with the required Gradle classes and libraries is already loaded. The configuration for daemon is often put into a `GRADLE_OPTS` environment variable; so, the flag is not needed on all calls. The following screenshot shows the execution of daemon:

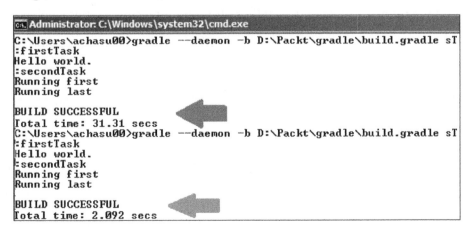

Note that the first build took 31 seconds, whereas the second build tool took only 2 seconds.

To stop a daemon process, use `gradle -stop` the command-line option.

Gradle plugins

Build scripts are monotonous, for example, in a Java build script, we define the source file location, third-party JAR location, clean output folder, compile Java files, run tests, create JAR file, and so on. Almost all Java project build scripts look similar.

This is something similar to duplicate codes. We resolve the duplicates by refactoring and moving duplicates to a common place and share the common code. Gradle plugins solve this repetitive build task problem by moving the duplicate tasks to a common place so that all projects share and inherit the common tasks instead of redefining them.

A plugin is a Gradle configuration extension. It comes with some preconfigured tasks that, together, do something useful. Gradle ships with a number of plugins and helps us write neat and clean scripts.

In this chapter, we will explore the Java and Eclipse plugins.

The Eclipse plugin

The Eclipse plugin generates the project files necessary to import a project in Eclipse.

Any Eclipse project has two important files: a `.project` file and a `.classpath` file. The `.project` file contains the project information such as the project name and project nature. The `.classpath` file contains the classpath entries for the project.

Let's create a simple Gradle build with the Eclipse plugin using the following steps:

1. Create a folder named `eclipse`, then a file named `build.gradle`, and add the following script:

   ```
   apply plugin: 'eclipse'
   ```

   To inherit a plugin nature, Gradle uses the `apply plugin: '<plug-in name>'` syntax.

2. Open the command prompt and check all the available tasks using the `gradle tasks --all` command. This will list the available Eclipse plugin tasks for you.

3. Now run the `gradle eclipse` command. It will generate only the `.project` file, as the command doesn't know what type of project needs to be built. You will see the following output on the command prompt:

```
:eclipseProject

:eclipse

BUILD SUCCESSFUL
```

4. To create a Java project, add `apply plugin: 'java'` to the `build.gradle` file and rerun the command. This time it will execute four tasks as follows:

```
:eclipseClasspath

:eclipseJdt

:eclipseProject

:eclipse
```

5. Open the `Eclipse` folder (the location where you put the `build.gradle` file). You will find the `.project` and `.classpath` files and a `.settings` folder. For a Java project, a **Java Development Tools (JDT)** configuration file is required. The `.settings` folder contains the `org.eclipse.jdt.core.prefs` file.

Now, we can launch Eclipse and import the project. We can edit the `.project` file and change the project name.

Normally, a Java project depends on third-party JARs, such as the JUnit JAR and Apache utility JARs. In the next section, we will learn how a classpath can be generated with JAR dependencies.

The Java plugin

The Java plugin provides some default tasks for your project that will compile and unit test your Java source code and bundle it into a JAR file.

The Java plugin defines the default values for many aspects of the project, such as the source files' location and Maven repository. We can follow the conventions or customize them if necessary; generally, if we follow the conventional defaults, then we don't need to do much in our build script.

Let's create a simple Gradle build script with the Java plugin and observe what the plugin offers. Perform the following steps:

1. Create a `java.gradle` build file and add the `apply plugin: 'java'` line.

2. Open the command prompt and type in `gradle -b java.gradle tasks --all`. This will list the Java plugin tasks for you.

3. To build a project, we can use the build task; the build depends on many tasks. Execute the `gradle -b java.gradle build` command. The following screenshot shows the output:

```
D:\Packt\gradle\eclipse>gradle -b java.gradle build
:compileJava UP-TO-DATE
:processResources UP-TO-DATE
:classes UP-TO-DATE
:jar
:assemble UP-TO-DATE
:compileTestJava UP-TO-DATE
:processTestResources UP-TO-DATE
:testClasses UP-TO-DATE
:test UP-TO-DATE
:check UP-TO-DATE
:build

BUILD SUCCESSFUL
```

Since no source code was available, the build script didn't build anything. However, we can see the list of available tasks—build tasks are dependent on compile, JAR creation, test execution, and so on.

Java plugins come with a convention that the build source files will be under `src/main/java`, relative to the project directory. Non-Java resource files such as the XML and properties files will be under `src/main/resources`. Tests will be under `src/test/java`, and the test resources under the `src/test/resources`.

To change the default Gradle project source file directory settings, use the `sourceSets` keyword. The `sourceSets` keyword allows us to change the default source file's location.

A Gradle script must know the location of the `lib` directory to compile files. The Gradle convention for library locations is repositories. Gradle supports the local `lib` folder, external dependencies, and remote repositories.

Gradle also supports the following repositories:

- **Maven repository**: Maven can be configured on our local machine, on a network machine, or even the preconfigured central repository.
  - ○ **Maven central repository**: Maven's central repository is located at `http://repo1.maven.org/maven2`. The `mavenCentral()` groovy method can be used to load dependencies from the centralized Maven repository. The following is an example of accessing the central repository:

    ```
    repositories {
        mavenCentral()
    }
    ```

○ **Maven local repository**: If we have a local Maven repository, we can use the `mavenLocal()` method to resolve dependencies as follows:

```
repositories {
    mavenLocal()
}
```

The `maven()` method can be used to access repositories configured on the intranet. The following is an example of accessing an intranet URL:

```
repositories {
    maven {
        name = 'Our Maven repository name'
        url = '<intranet URL>'
    }
}
```

The `mavenRepo()` method can be used with the following code:

```
repositories {
    mavenRepo(name: '<name of the repository>',
        url: '<URL>')
}
```

A secured Maven repository needs user credentials. Gradle provides the `credentials` keyword to pass user credentials. The following is an example of accessing a secured Maven repository:

```
repositories {
    maven(name: repository name') {
        credentials {
            username = 'username'
            password = 'password'
        }
        url = '<URL>'
    }
}
```

- **Ivy repository**: This is a remote or local ivy repository. Gradle supports the same Maven methods for ivy. The following is an example of accessing an ivy repository and a secured ivy repository:

```
repositories {
    ivy(url: '<URL>', name: '<Name>')
    ivy {
    credentials
     {
        username = 'user name'
            password = 'password'
     }
        url = '<URL>'
    }
}
```

- **Flat directory repository**: This is a local or network directory. The following is an example of accessing a local directory:

```
repositories {
    flatDir(dir: '../thirdPartyFolder',
      name: '3rd party library')
    flatDir {
        dirs '../springLib', '../lib/apacheLib',
          '../lib/junit'
        name = ' Configured libraries for spring,
          apache and JUnit'
    }
}
```

Gradle uses `flatDir()` to locate a local or network-shared library folder. Here, `dir` is used to locate a single directory and `dirs` with directory locations separated by commas are used to locate distributed folders.

In this section, we will create a Java project, write a test, execute the test, compile source or test files, and finally build a JAR file. Perform the following steps:

1. Create a `build.gradle` build script file under `packt\chapter02\java`.

2. Add Eclipse and Java plugin support using the following lines of code:

```
apply plugin: 'eclipse'
apply plugin: 'java'
```

3. We will write a JUnit test, so our project will be dependent on JUnit JARs. Create a `lib` directory under `packt\chapter02` and copy the `hamcrest-core-1.3.jar` and `junit-4.11.jar` JARs (we downloaded these JARs in *Chapter 1, JUnit 4 – a Total Recall*).

4. In this example, we will use the flat directory repository. We created a `lib` directory for JUnit JARs. Add the following lines to the `build.gradle` file to configure our repository:

```
repositories {
    flatDir(dir: '../lib', name: 'JUnit Library')
}
```

We have a single `lib` folder; so, we will use `flatDir` and `dir` conventions.

A repository can have numerous library files, but we may need only some of them. For example, source file compilation doesn't require the JUnit JARs but test files and test execution need them.

Gradle comes with dependency management. The dependencies keyword is used to define dependencies.

The closure dependencies support the following default types:

- **Compile**: These are the dependencies required to compile the source of the project.

- **Runtime**: These dependencies are required by the production classes at runtime. By default, these also include the compile time dependencies.

- **testCompile**: These dependencies are required to compile the test source of the project. By default, they also include the compiled production classes and the compile-time dependencies.

- **testRuntime**: These dependencies are required to run the tests. By default, they also include the compile, runtime, and testCompile dependencies.

Each dependency type needs a coordinate: a group, name, and version of a dependent JAR.

Some websites, such as `mvnrepository.com`, can help us to come up with a ready-to-copy-paste dependency string, such as `http://mvnrepository.com/artifact/org.springframework/spring-aop/3.1.1.RELEASE`.

Suppose we need to include the `org.springframework.aop-3.1.1.RELEASE.jar` file in our classpath (here `org.springframework` is the group, `aop` is the name, and `3.1.1.RELEASE` is the version). We can simply write `org.springframework:aop:3.1.1.RELEASE` to identify `aop.jar`.

5. Tests need JUnit JAR support. Add the following lines to our `build.gradle` file to add the JUnit dependency:

```
dependencies {
    testCompile group: 'junit', name: 'junit',
      version: '4.11'
    testCompile group: '', name: 'hamcrest-core',
      version: '1.3'
}
```

Or simply add the following lines to the file:

```
dependencies {
    testCompile 'junit:junit:4.11', ':hamcrest-core:1.3'
}
```

6. Generate an Eclipse project using the Eclipse plugin and issue the `gradle eclipse` command. The `eclipse` command will execute three tasks: `eclipseClasspath`, `eclipseJdt`, and `eclipseProject`.

Go to the `\chapter02\java` folder, and you will find a `.classpath` and a `.project` file. Open the `.classpath` file and check whether `junit-4.11` and `hamcrest-core-1.3.jar` have been added as `classpathentry`.

The following screenshot shows the `gradle eclipse` command output:

The following screenshot shows the content of the generated `.classpath` file:

7. Launch Eclipse and import the project by navigating to **File | Import | Existing Projects into Workspace**. Now browse to the `D:\Packt\ chapter02\java` folder and import the project. Eclipse will open the `java` project—the Java community's best practice is to keep the test and source code files under the same package but in a different source folder. Java code files are stored under `src/main/java`, and test files are stored under `src/ test/java`. Source resources are stored under `src/main/resources`.

    We need to create the `src/main/java`, `src/main/resources`, and `src/ test/java` folders directly under the Java project.

    The following screenshot displays the folder structure:

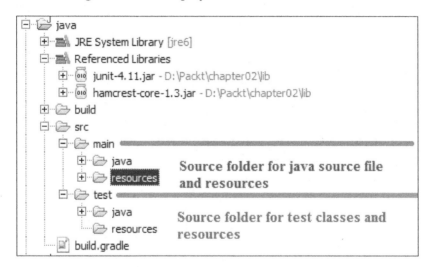

8. Right-click on the leaf folders (the `java` and `resources` folders under `src/ main` and `src/test`, respectively); a pop-up menu will open. Now, go to **Build Path | Use as Source Folder**.

    The following screenshot shows the action:

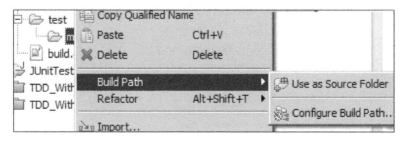

9. We will create a Java class and unit test the behavior; the Java class will read from a properties file and return an `enum` type depending on the value provided in the properties file. Reading a file from the test is not recommended as I/O operations are unpredictable and slow; your test may fail to read the file and take time to slow down the test execution. We can use mock objects to stub the file read, but for simplicity, we will add two methods in the service class—one will take a `String` argument and return an `enum` type, and the other one will read from a properties file and call the first method with the value. From the test, we will call the first method with a string. The following are the steps to configure the project:

    1. Add an `environment.properties` properties file under `/java/src/main/resources` and add `env = DEV` in that file.

    2. Create an `enum` file in the `com.packt.gradle` package under the `/java/src/main/java` source package:

        ```
        public enum EnvironmentType {
           DEV, PROD, TEST
        }
        ```

    3. Create a Java class to read the properties file as follows:

        ```
        package com.packt.gradle;

        import java.util.ResourceBundle;

        public class Environment {
          public String getName() {
            ResourceBundle resourceBundle =
              ResourceBundle.getBundle("environment");
            return resourceBundle.getString("env");
          }
        }
        ```

    4. Create a `EnvironmentService` class to return an `enum` type depending on the environment setup as follows:

        ```
        package com.packt.gradle;
        public class EnvironmentService {

          public EnvironmentType getEnvironmentType() {
            return getEnvironmentType(new
              Environment().getName());
          }
          public EnvironmentType getEnvironmentType(String name) {
            if("dev".equals(name)) {
              return EnvironmentType.DEV;
        ```

```
      }else if("prod".equals(name)) {
        return EnvironmentType.PROD;
      }
      return null;
    }
  }
```

The get EnvironmentType() method calls the Environment class to read the properties file value and then calls the getEnvironmentType(String name) method with the read value to return an enum type.

5. Add a test class under /src/test/java in the com.packt.gradle package. The following is the code:

```
package com.packt.gradle;
import static org.junit.Assert.*;
import static org.hamcrest.CoreMatchers.*;
import org.junit.Test;

public class EnvironmentServiceTest {
EnvironmentService service = new EnvironmentService();
@Test
public void returns_NULL_when_environment_not_configured()
{
    assertNull(service.getEnvironmentType("xyz"));  }

@Test
public void production_environment_configured(){
    EnvironmentType environmentType =
      service.getEnvironmentType("prod");
    assertThat(environmentType,
      is(EnvironmentType.PROD));
  }
}
```

Here, the returns_NULL_when_environment_not_configured() test passes xyz to the getEnvironmentType method and expects that the service will return null, assuming that there won't be any xyz environment. In another test, it passes the prod value to the getEnvironmentType method and expects that a type will be returned.

10. Now open the command prompt and run `gradle build`; it will compile the source and test files, execute the test, and finally create a JAR file.

   To execute only the tests, run `gradle test`.

   Open the `\chapter02\java\build` folder, and you will find three important folders:

   ○ `libs`: This folder contains the build output JARs — `Java.jar`

   ○ `reports`: This folder contains the HTML test results

   ○ `test-results`: This folder contains the XML format test execution result and the time taken to execute each test

   The following screenshot shows the test execution result in the HTML format:

Gradle is an intelligent build tool, and it supports incremental build. Rerun the `gradle build` command. It will just skip the tasks and say UP-TO-DATE. The following is a screenshot of the incremental build:

```
D:\Packt\chapter02\java>gradle build
:compileJava UP-TO-DATE
:processResources UP-TO-DATE
:classes UP-TO-DATE
:jar UP-TO-DATE
:assemble UP-TO-DATE
:compileTestJava UP-TO-DATE
:processTestResources UP-TO-DATE
:testClasses UP-TO-DATE
:test UP-TO-DATE
:check UP-TO-DATE
:build UP-TO-DATE
```

If we make a change to the test class, only test tasks will be executed. The following are the test tasks: `compileTestJava`, `testClasses`, `test`, `check`, and `build`.

In next chapters, we will explore more on Gradle. Do you want to dive deep now? If so, you can visit `http://www.gradle.org/docs/current/userguide/userguide.html`.

Maven project management

Maven is a project build tool. Using Maven, we can build a visible, reusable, and maintainable project infrastructure.

Maven provides plugins for visibility: the code quality/best practices is visible through the PMD/checkstyle plugin, the XDOC plugin generates project content information, the JUnit report plugin makes the failure/success story visible to the team, the project activity tracking plugins make the daily activity visible, the change log plugin generates the list of changes, and so on.

As a result, a developer knows what APIs or modules are available for use; so, he or she doesn't invent the wheel (rather, he or she reuses the existing APIs or modules). This reduces the duplication and allows a maintainable system to be created.

In this section, we will explore the Maven architecture and rebuild our Gradle project using Maven.

Installation

A prerequisite for Maven is the **Java Development Kit (JDK)**. Make sure you have JDK installed on your computer.

The following are the steps to set up Maven:

1. Download the Maven media. Go to `http://maven.apache.org/download.html` to get the latest version of Maven.

2. After downloading Maven, extract the archive to a folder; for example, I extracted it to `D:\Software\apache-maven-3.1.1`.

3. For Windows OS, create an environment variable named `M2_HOME` and point it to the Maven installation folder. Modify the `PATH` variable and append `%M2_HOME%\bin`.

4. For Linux, we need to export the `PATH` and `M2_HOME` environment variables to the `.bashrc` file. Open the `.bashrc` file and edit it with the following text:

    ```
    export M2_HOME=/home/<location of Maven installation>
    export PATH=${PATH}:${M2_HOME}/bin
    ```

5. For Mac, the `.bash_login` file needs to be modified with following text:

```
export M2_HOME=/usr/local/<maven folder>
export PATH=${PATH}:${M2_HOME}/bin
```

6. Check the installation and execute the `mvn -version` command. This should print the Maven version. The following is a screenshot of the output:

```
D:\>mvn -version
Apache Maven 3.1.1 (0728685237757ffbf44136acec
Maven home: D:\SoftWare\apache-maven-3.1.1
Java version: 1.7.0_25, vendor: Oracle Corporation
Java home: C:\Program Files\Java\jdk1.7.0_25\jre
Default locale: en_US, platform encoding: Cp1252
OS name: "windows 7", version: "6.1", arch: "amd64"
```

Maven is installed so we can start exploring Maven. Eclipse users with the `m2eclipse` plugin installed already have Maven, which they can directly use from Eclipse and they don't have to install Maven.

The Archetype plugin

In Maven, Archetype is a project-template generation plugin.

Maven allows us to create a project infrastructure from scratch from a list of predefined project types. The Maven command `mvn archetype:generate` generates a new project skeleton.

The `archetype:generate` command loads a catalog of available project types. It tries to connect to the central Maven repository at `http://repo1.maven.org/maven2`, and downloads the archetype catalog.

 To get the latest catalog, you should be connected to the Internet.

Follow the ensuing steps to generate a Java project skeleton:

1. Create a folder hierarchy `/Packt/chapter02/maven`, open the command prompt, and browse to the `/Packt/chapter02/maven` folder.

2. Issue a `mvn archetype:generate` command; you will see a large list of archetypes being downloaded, each with a number, a name, and a short description.

   It will prompt you to enter an archetype number. Type in the default `maven-archetype-quickstart` archetype. In my case, the number is 343.

The following screenshot shows you that the number 343 is default:

```
910: remote -> sk.seges.sesam:sesam-annotation
911: remote -> tk.skuro:clojure-maven-archetype
912: remote -> uk.ac.rdg.resc:edal-ncwms-based-webapp
Choose a number or apply filter (format:
[groupId:]artifactId, case sensitive contains): 343:
```

 To get the entire catalog on Windows OS, enter the mvn archetype:generate > archetype.txt command. This will populate the text file with the project type list.

3. Enter 343 or just hit *Enter* to select the default. Next, it will prompt you to select a version. Hit *Enter* to select the default.

4. Now it will ask you to provide a groupId. A groupId is the root package for multiple projects, and org.springframework is the groupId for all Spring projects. Enter org.packt as groupId.

5. Next, it will ask for artifactId. This is the project name and aop is the artifactId for org.springframework.aop-3.1.1.RELEASE. Enter Demo for the artifactId.

6. Maven will ask for the version and the default is 1.0-SNAPSHOT. The version is your project's version, and here 3.1.1.RELEASE is the version for the org.springframework.aop-3.1.1.RELEASE project. We will accept the default. Hit *Enter* to accept the default.

7. Now you will be prompted to enter the package name. Enter com.packt.edu as package's name.

8. Finally, it will show you what you entered. Review it and accept it as shown in the following screenshot:

```
Confirm properties configuration:
groupId: org.packt
artifactId: Demo
version: 1.0-SNAPSHOT
package: com.packt.edu
 Y:  :
```

Open the `/Packt/chapter02/maven` folder; you will see the `Demo` project folder is created with the following file structure:

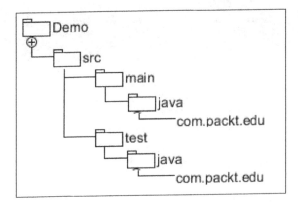

The Maven convention for the source Java file is `src/main/java` and the test source file is `src/test/java`.

Maven will automatically create a Java file `App.java` under `src/main/java/com/packt/edu` and a test file `AppTest` under `src/test/java/com/packt/edu`.

Also, it will create an XML file `pom.xml` directly under `Demo`. This file will be used for building the project. In the next section, we will read about the POM file.

The Project Object Model (POM) file

Every Maven project contains a `pom.xml` file, which is a project metadata file.

A POM file can contain the following sections:

- Project coordinates such as `<groupId/>`, `<artifactId/>`, `<version/>`, `<dependency>`, and inheritance through `<modules/>` and `<parent/>`

  Open the `pom.xml` file in the `Demo` folder; it contains the following coordinate details:

  ```
  <groupId>org.packt</groupId>
  <artifactId>Demo</artifactId>
  <version>1.0-SNAPSHOT</version>
  <packaging>jar</packaging>
  ```

- The build details in `<build>` and `<reporting>`

- Project visibility details such as `<name>`, `<organization>`, `<developers>`, `<url>`, and `<contributors>`

  Our generated `pom.xml` contains the following details:

  ```
  <name>Demo</name>
  <url>http://maven.apache.org</url>
  ```

- Project environment details such as `<scm>`, `<repository>`, and `<mailingList>`

Project dependency

In a multimodule project, a project can depend on many other projects. For example, say we depend on JUnit. Maven automatically discovers the required artifact dependencies. This is very useful as we depend on many open source projects. It's always useful, be it an open source or a close source project.

Do you remember the Gradle dependency closure? It has four default types for Compile, Runtime, testCompile, and testRuntime.

Similarly, Maven has the following dependency scopes:

- **Compile**: Code compile time classpath dependency; this is the default scope. If not, it is explicitly defined and then the compile time scope is set.
- **Runtime**: This is required at runtime.
- **Test**: This dependency is required for test code compilation and test execution.
- **Provided**: The JDK or environment dependency at runtime.

A parent project defines dependencies using the following code snippet:

```
<dependencies>
    <dependency>
        <groupId>junit</groupId>
        <artifactId>junit</artifactId>
        <version>4.11</version>
        <scope>test</scope>
    </dependency>
</dependencies>
```

All child projects inherit the dependency by just adding the `<dependency>` tag as follows:

```
<dependency>
    <groupId>junit</groupId>
    <artifactId>junit</artifactId>
</dependency>
```

The build life cycle

The build life cycle clearly defines the process of building and distributing a particular project artifact.

Maven has the following three built-in build life cycles:

- **Default**: This life cycle handles the compile, test, packaging, deployment, and many more functions
- **Clean**: This life cycle generally cleans the build artifacts generated by the previous build(s)
- **Site**: This life cycle takes care of generation and deployment of the project's site documentation

Now, we will compile and test our Demo project.

In this section, we will work with compile, test, and package targets of the default life cycle.

Compiling the project

Perform the following steps to compile the project:

1. Open the command prompt and browse to \Packt\chapter02\maven\Demo. Maven needs a pom.xml file to compile a project.

2. Type in mvn compile; it will compile the project and create class files under \Demo\target\classes. The following screenshot shows the output:

```
D:\Packt\chapter02\maven\Demo>mvn compile
[INFO] Scanning for projects...
[INFO]
[INFO] ------------------------------------------------------------------------
[INFO] Building Demo 1.0-SNAPSHOT
[INFO] ------------------------------------------------------------------------
Downloading: http://repo.maven.apache.org/maven2/junit/junit/
Downloaded: http://repo.maven.apache.org/maven2/junit/junit/4.11/
Downloading: http://repo.maven.apache.org/maven2/org/hamcrest/
Downloaded: http://repo.maven.apache.org/maven2/org/hamcrest/
Downloading: http://repo.maven.apache.org/maven2/org/hamcrest/
Downloaded: http://repo.maven.apache.org/maven2/org/hamcrest/
[INFO]
[INFO] --- maven-resources-plugin:2.6:resources (default-resources) @ Demo ---
[INFO] Using 'UTF-8' encoding to copy filtered resources.
[INFO] skip non existing resourceDirectory
[INFO]
[INFO] --- maven-compiler-plugin:2.5.1:compile (default-compile) @ Demo ---
[INFO] Compiling 1 source file to D:\Packt\chapter02\maven\Demo\target\classes
[INFO]
[INFO] BUILD SUCCESS
[INFO] ------------------------------------------------------------------------
[INFO] Total time: 17.810s
[INFO] Finished at: Sun Feb 02 15:30:02 IST 2014
[INFO] Final Memory: 11M/120M
[INFO] ------------------------------------------------------------------------
```

Testing the project

To execute the tests in Demo, open the command prompt and type in `mvn test`; it will download JUnit JARs and surefire JARs for test compilation and test report generation respectively and then execute the test. The following screenshot shows the output:

```
 T E S T S

Running com.packt.edu.AppTest
Tests run: 1, Failures: 0, Errors: 0, Skipped: 0, Time elapsed: 0.125 sec

Results :

Tests run: 1, Failures: 0, Errors: 0, Skipped: 0

[INFO] ------------------------------------------------------------------------
[INFO] BUILD SUCCESS
[INFO] ------------------------------------------------------------------------
[INFO] Total time: 14.295s
[INFO] Finished at: Sun Feb 02 15:37:30 IST 2014
[INFO] Final Memory: 12M/157M
[INFO] ------------------------------------------------------------------------
```

Packaging the project

The `mvn package` command compiles source code, compiles tests, executes tests, and finally builds a JAR. It will generate `Demo-1.0-SNAPSHOT.jar` in `\Packt\chapter02\maven\Demo\target`.

The clean life cycle

The `mvn clean` command removes the `target` folder and deletes all the content. Run the command and check that the `target` folder has been deleted from `\Packt\chapter02\maven\Demo\`.

The site life cycle

The `mvn site` command generates a detailed project report in the HTML format under the target or site. It includes About, Plugin Management, Distribution Management, Dependency Information, Source Repository, Mailing Lists, Issue Tracking, Continuous Integration, Project Plugins, Project License, Project Team, Project Summary, and Dependencies.

Refer to `http://maven.apache.org/guides/index.html` to explore more on Maven.

The next section covers the Apache Ant.

Another neat tool (Ant)

Ant is a Java-based build tool from the Apache Software Foundation. Ant's build files are written in XML. You need Java to execute an Ant task.

Download Apache Ant from `http://ant.apache.org/`, extract the media, and create an `ANT_HOME` variable and set the value to the extracted location. Edit `PATH` and append `%ANT_HOME%\bin` in Windows. For Mac or Linux OS, you need to export `ANT_HOME` and `PATH` as described in the *Installation* section of *Maven project management* earlier in this chapter.

Ant needs a `build.xml` file to execute tasks. Ant supports the `-f` option to specify a build script; so the `ant -f myBuildFile.xml` command will work.

We will create a build script and execute the Maven project (`\Packt\chapter02\maven\Demo`) using Ant. Follow the ensuing steps:

1. Create an XML file `build.xml` in `\Packt\chapter02\maven\Demo`.

2. Add the following lines in the `build.xml` file:

    ```xml
    <?xml version="1.0"?>
    <project name="Demo"  basedir=".">
      <property name="src.dir" location="src/main/java" />
      <property name="build.dir" location="bin" />
      <property name="dist.dir" location="ant_output" />
    </project>
    ```

    The `<project>` tag is a defined tag in Ant. You can name your project, and `Demo` is the name of the project. Next, we will set properties; a property can have a name and value or location. Here, `src.dir` is a property name, and this property can be accessed from any task using the `${src.dir}` syntax. The `location` attribute refers to a relative location from the `build.xml` file. Since `src/main/java` contains the source file, we set the location value to `src/main/java`. The other two properties, `build.dir` and `dist.dir`, will be used by the Java compiling task to compile class files and generate the JAR file.

3. Do you remember the clean task in Maven? Ant doesn't provide default targets. We have to define a `clean` target to remove old build outputs, and we will call Ant's `<delete>` command to delete directories. Then, using the `<mkdir>` command, we will recreate the directories:

    ```xml
    <target name="clean">
      <delete dir="${build.dir}" />
      <delete dir="${dist.dir}" />
    </target>
    <target name="makedir">
    ```

```
    <mkdir dir="${build.dir}" />
    <mkdir dir="${dist.dir}" />
</target>
```

Note that we added two targets using the `<target>` tag. Each target is identified using a name. We will call the `clean` target to delete `build.dir` (generated `.class` files) and `dist.dir` (build output JARs).

4. Compile task is inbuilt in Gradle/Maven, but Ant doesn't have any inbuilt compile targets; so, we will create a target to compile Java files as follows:

```
<target name="compile" depends="clean, makedir">
  <javac srcdir="${src.dir}" destdir="${build.dir}">
  </javac>
</target>
```

Use the `<javac>` command to compile Java files. The `<javac>` command accepts `srcdir` and `destdir`. Compiler reads Java files from `srcdir` and generates class files to `destdir`.

A target may depend on another, and `depends` allows us to pass comma-separated target names. Here, compile target depends on `clean` and `makedir`.

5. The compilation is done. Now, we will create `jar` from the class files using the `<jar>` command as follows:

```
<target name="jar" depends="compile">
    <jar destfile="${dist.dir}\${ant.project.name}.jar"
      basedir="${build.dir}">
    </jar>
  </target>
```

The `jar` target needs to know the class file's location and destination. The `destfile` attribute refers to the destination JAR file name and location and `basedir` refers to the class file location. Check whether we used `${dist.dir}\${ant.project.name}.jar` to represent the destination JAR file name and folder. Here, `${dist.dir}` refers to the destination folder, and `${ant.project.name}.jar` represents the JAR name. `${ant.project.name}` is the name (`Demo`) we mentioned in the `<project>` tag.

6. The Ant script is ready to compile and create a JAR. Open the command prompt, go to `\Packt\chapter02\maven\Demo` and issue an `ant jar` command. Here, `jar` depends on `compile` and `compile` depends on `clean` and `makedir`. So, the `jar` command will create two directories, `bin` and `ant_output`, compile the Java file and generate the `.class` file in the bin folder, and finally create a `Demo.jar` JAR in the `ant_output` folder.

7. The compilation is done; now, it's time to execute the tests. Tests need JUnit JARs and generated source class files to compile and execute. We have created the `lib` directory for Gradle in `\Packt\chapter02\lib` and kept the JUnit 4 JARs in it. We will use this `lib`. Add three properties for the test source file directory, library directory, and test report as follows:

```
<property name="test.dir" location="src/test/java" />
<property name="lib.dir" location="../../lib" />
<property name="report.dir" location="${dist.dir}/report" />
```

Check whether the `lib.dir` location is relative to the `build.xml` location. The `test.dir` attribute points to `src/test/main` and test reports will be generated inside `ant_output/report`.

8. Path allows us to refer to a directory or to a file path. We will define a `jclass.path` path to refer to all JAR files under the `lib` directory and generated `.class` files as follows:

```
<path id="jclass.path">
  <fileset dir="${lib.dir}/">
    <include name="**/*" />
  </fileset>
  <pathelement location="${build.dir}" />
</path>
```

The `<fileset>` tag takes a directory location and `<include>` takes a file name or regular expression. The `**/*` value means all the directories and files are in `${lib.dir}`. The `pathelement` attribute refers to the `bin` directory where the compiled class files are put.

9. Now, we need to compile test files. Add a `testcompile` target and use the `javac` command. Pass `test.dir` as `srcdir` for compilation. Add `<classpath>` to refer the `jclass.path` value. This will compile the test files. Consider the following code snippet:

```
<target name="testcompile" depends="compile">
  <javac srcdir="${test.dir}" destdir="${build.dir}">
    <classpath refid="jclass.path" />
  </javac>
</target>
```

10. Add another target to execute the JUnit test. Ant has a `junit` command to run tests. Pass `jclass.path` to point the `lib` directory and generated files as follows:

```
<target name="test" depends="testcompile">
  <junit printsummary="on" fork="true" haltonfailure="yes">
    <classpath refid="jclass.path" />
    <formatter type="xml" />
    <batchtest todir="${report.dir}">
      <fileset dir="${test.dir}">
        <include name="**/*Test*.java" />
      </fileset>
    </batchtest>
  </junit>
</target>
```

Issue the `ant test` command. This command compiles and executes the tests.

We can set a default task in the `build.xml` file in the `<project>` tag. The syntax is `<project name="Demo" default="task name" basedir=".">`. Now, we don't have to specify a target name.

Our Ant script is ready for compiling Java files, executing tests, and generating reports. In the next section, we will set up Jenkins and use the build scripts.

To explore more on how to compile web archives and learn advanced topics, go to `http://ant.apache.org/`.

Jenkins

Jenkins is an open source CI tool written in Java. It runs on any web container compliant with Servlet Specification 2.4. The new Apache Tomcat server is an example of a web container with which Jenkins can be integrated as a Windows service.

Jenkins supports various source control platforms, such as CVS, SVN, Git, Mercurial, and ClearCase through the use of plugins.

It can execute automated builds on Ant and Maven projects. Jenkins is free (MIT license) and runs on many operating systems. Jenkins doesn't allow you to create a Gradle project, but you can create a free-style project and build Gradle projects.

To install Jenkins on your local machine, follow the instructions at `https://wiki.jenkins-ci.org/display/JENKINS/Installing+Jenkins`.

Once Jenkins is installed, we will perform the following steps to configure Jenkins:

1. Launch the Jenkins URL; from the home page go to **Manage Jenkins | Configure system**.

2. Now you need to set up the JDK. Go to the **JDK** section, click on **JDK installations** and then click on **Add JDK**. Uncheck the **Install automatically** checkbox, and enter a **Name** and **JAVA_HOME** path. You can add as many JDKs as you want. **Name** and **JAVA_HOME** location uniquely identify the version of JDK. In your project, you can refer to the JDK you want to use. The following screenshot shows the installation of JDK:

JDK		
JDK installations	JDK Name	Java6
	JAVA_HOME	C:\Program Files\Java\jdk1.6.0_35
	☐ Install automatically	
	Add JDK	

3. Now, set up Maven. Go to the **Maven** section and click on **Maven installations**. Now, click on **Add Maven**, uncheck the **Install automatically** checkbox, enter a **Name**, and set it to **MAVEN_HOME**.

In general, if the checkbox **Install automatically** is checked, then Jenkins will ask you to select a version of the tool and download the version. You can install or add multiple versions of the software and just give a unique name. For example, you can add a name, Maven3, to refer to Maven Version 3.1.1 and add Maven2 to refer to Version 2.2.1. In your build job, Jenkins will show you the list and select the appropriate version you need. The following screenshot shows the installation of Maven:

Maven		
Maven installations	Maven Name	Maven
	MAVEN_HOME	D:\SoftWare\apache-maven-3.1.1
	☐ Install automatically	
	Add Maven	

4. Go to the **Ant** section and click on **Ant installations**. Then, click on **Add Ant**, uncheck the **Install automatically** checkbox, enter a **Name**, and set it to **ANT_HOME**.

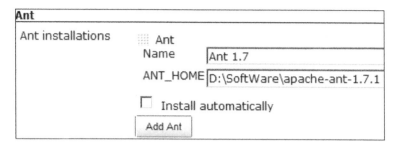

Our basic configuration is complete. Next, we will start building a Java project using Gradle.

The Gradle project

Jenkins doesn't come with Gradle. You need to install a plugin as follows:

1. Launch the Jenkins URL; from the home page, go to **Manage Jenkins | Manage Plugins**. Go to the **Available** tab; in the **Filter** textbox (located at the right top corner of the page), enter `gradle`. It will bring you **Gradle Plugin**. Check the checkbox associated with **Gradle Plugin** and click on **Install without restart**.

   This will install the **Gradle plugin**. Jenkins will show you the progress of installation. Once the installation is over, you need to configure Gradle, like we did for Ant and Maven. Refer to the following screenshot to install **Gradle plugin**:

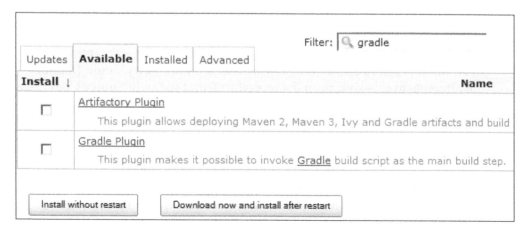

2. From the home page, go to **Manage Jenkins | Configure System**. Scroll down to the **Gradle** section and click on Gradle installation. Then, click on **Add Gradle**, uncheck the **Install automatically** checkbox, enter a **Name**, and set **GRADLE_HOME**.

Gradle		
Gradle installations	Gradle name	gradle1.10
	GRADLE_HOME	D:\SoftWare\gradle-1.10
	☐ Install automatically	
	Add Gradle	

3. Go back to the home page. The Jenkins convention for project building is **job**. A job runs continuously, invokes scripts, and gives feedback. To set up an automated build process, the user has to configure a job. Click on the **create new jobs** hyperlink to add a new project type. Jenkins supports several types of build jobs. Two most commonly used jobs are the free-style builds and the Maven 2/3 builds. The free-style projects allow you to configure any sort of build job; this job type is highly flexible and configurable. However, you can install plugins for other types.

   The following screenshot displays how to create a `gradleProject` free-style job:

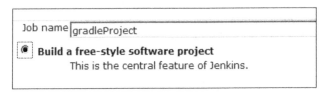

4. The free-style project has several settings. In **Advance Project Options**, you can set **Quiet period** (time to wait after a build), **Retry Count** (number of attempts to checkout from the repository), and so on. In **Source Code Management**, you can choose a version control tool type. Version control is one of the most important things in CI. It keeps track of software versions, we can revert our changes at any point in time, look at file history, and much more. By default, Jenkins comes with the source code management tool plugins, CVS and SVN, but we can install plugins to support other types, such as Git and Rational ClearCase. We didn't configure any version control tool yet; so, choose **None,** as shown in the following screenshot:

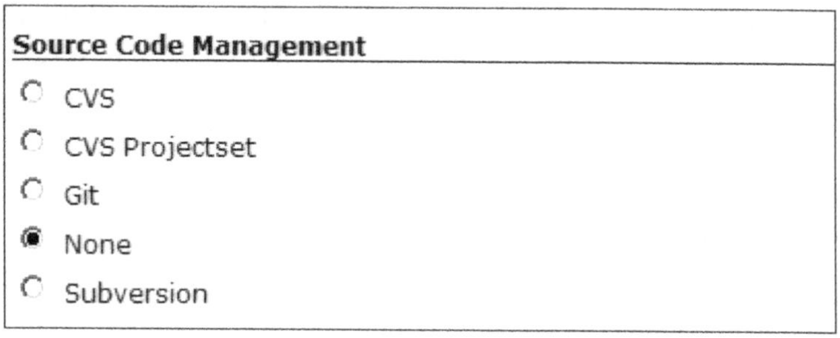

Source Code Management

- ○ CVS
- ○ CVS Projectset
- ○ Git
- ● None
- ○ Subversion

5. Next is the **Build Trigger** event, and the build trigger knows when to start a job. There are several types:

   ○ **Build after other projects are built**: This implies that the job will be invoked after another job

   ○ **Build periodically**: This signifies the periodic schedule for cron expressions, that is, every 5 minutes or every 30 minutes and so on

   ○ **Poll SCM**: This implies polling the version control location after a specific time set in the **Schedule** option

   We don't have other jobs or a version control tool, so choose **Build periodically** and set **Schedule** to **H/5****** to execute the build every 5 minutes, as shown in the following screenshot:

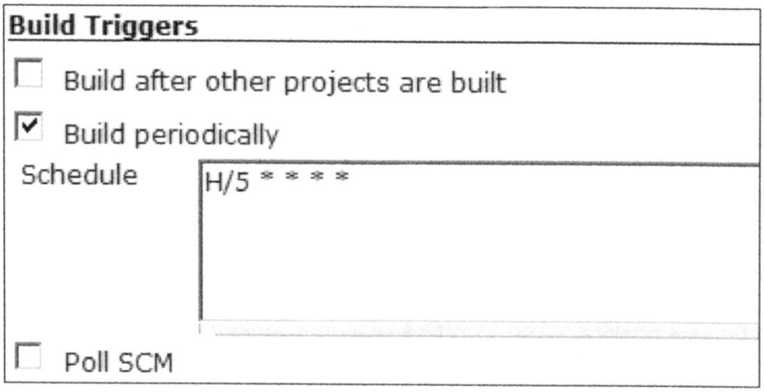

Build Triggers

- ☐ Build after other projects are built
- ☑ Build periodically

  Schedule   `H/5 * * * *`

- ☐ Poll SCM

6. The next section is **Build**. You can add several steps to a build. Click on **Add build step**. It will show you a step; choose **Invoke Gradle script** to call our Gradle project, as shown in the following screenshot:

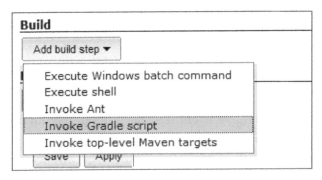

7. Now click on the **Invoke Gradle** radio button and choose the Gradle version we added. In the **Tasks** field, enter `build` to invoke the build task; you can add multiple tasks here. In the **Build File** field, enter the full path of your Gradle build file `\Packt\chapter02\java\build.gradle`, as shown in the following screenshot:

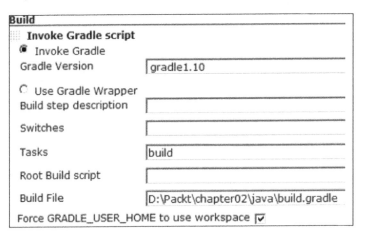

8. Now click on **Save**. Jenkins will take you to the project's home page. Click on the **Build Now** hyperlink. It will start building our first project. It will show you a build history table with a build number, such as **#1 Feb 4. 2014 09:18:45 PM**. Click on the **build#** hyperlink and then click on **Console Output**. It will show you the build log. The following screenshot shows our Gradle build log:

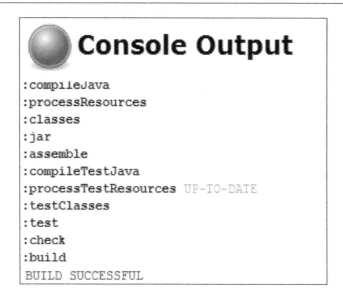

9. Now go back to the home page; it shows you the list of all builds and their status. It has a weather column—when all builds are failing, the weather shows a cloudy image, and when all builds are passing, the weather becomes sunny. You can invoke a build by clicking on the wheel symbol to the right of each build row. Refer to the following screenshot:

Our Gradle build configuration is complete. Automatically, after every five minutes, the build will be kicked off. We can configure a post build action to send an e-mail after each build. That way, if a build fails, then immediately a mail will be sent, and the concerned person can take care of the issue. So, the feedback cycle is faster.

In the next section, we will configure a Maven job.

The Maven project

In this section, we will configure Jenkins to execute a Maven build job. Please perform the following steps:

1. Click on the **New Job** hyperlink to add a new project type. Select **Build a maven2/3 project** and enter a job name, as shown in the following screenshot:

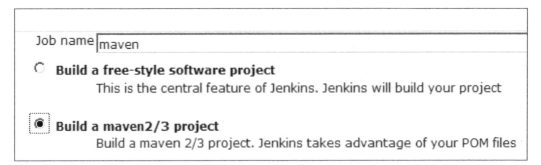

2. On the details page, choose **Source Code Management** as **None**, **Build Triggers** as **Build periodically**, and set **H/5****** to execute the build in every 5 minutes.

3. Next, go to the **Build** section and set the **Root POM** value; set the full file path location of your pom.xml file in the Demo project. You can leave the **Goals and options** section blank. Gradle will issue the default mvn install command. Refer to the following screenshot:

Build	
Root POM	D:\Packt\chapter02\maven\Demo\pom.xml
Goals and options	

4. Now click on **Save**. Jenkins will take you to the project's home page. Click on the **Build Now** hyperlink and it will start building our first project. It will show you a build history table with a build number such as **#1 Feb 4. 2014 09:18:45 PM**. Click on the **build#** hyperlink and then click on **Console Output**. It will show you the following build log:

```
Executing Maven:   -B -f D:\Packt\chapter02\maven\Demo\pom.xml
install

[INFO] Scanning for projects...


[INFO] Building Demo 1.0-SNAPSHOT
```

```
[INFO] Downloading: http://repo.maven.apache.org/maven2/org/
apache/maven/plugin

(226 KB at 33.4 KB/sec)

[INFO] BUILD SUCCESS

[INFO] Total time: 2:28.150s

[

[JENKINS] Archiving D:\Packt\chapter02\maven\Demo\pom.xml to org.
packt/Demo/1.0-SNAPSHOT/Demo-1.0-SNAPSHOT.pom

[JENKINS] Archiving D:\Packt\chapter02\maven\Demo\target\Demo-1.0-
SNAPSHOT.jar to org.packt/Demo/1.0-SNAPSHOT/Demo-1.0-SNAPSHOT.jar

channel stopped

Finished: SUCCESS
```

5. Check whether Jenkins issued the `mvn install` command, created the JAR, and installed the artifacts in the `.m2` repository.

Building the Ant project

We will set up a free-style software project to build using Ant. The following are the steps:

1. Open the Jenkins URL, click on **New Job,** and select **Build a free-style software project**. Enter the name, `ant`, and then click on **Ok**.

2. We don't have source code management, so skip this section. Go to **Build Triggers** and set the **H/5 * * * *** value to kick off build automatically in every 5 minutes.

3. Go to the **Build** section and add a **Invoke Ant** build step, as shown in the following screenshot:

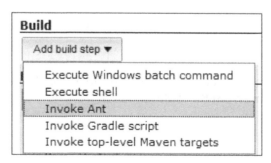

4. Select an Ant version from the dropdown, set `jar` as **Targets**; `jar` will invoke test and compile. In **Build File**, browse to our `build.xml` file location and set the value, as shown in the following screenshot:

Invoke Ant	
Ant Version	Ant 1.7
Targets	jar
Build File	D:\Packt\chapter02\maven\Demo\build.xml

5. Save the setting and the new job will be saved. Click on **Build Now**. It will start building the Demo project we created earlier in this chapter. The following is a screenshot of **Console Output**:

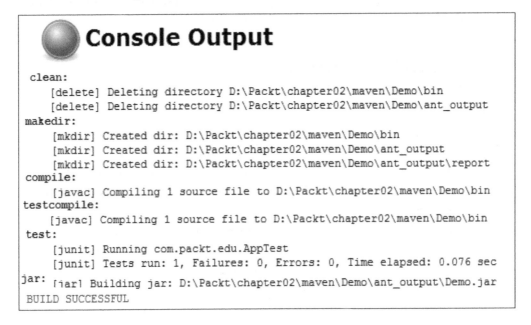

```
Console Output

clean:
    [delete] Deleting directory D:\Packt\chapter02\maven\Demo\bin
    [delete] Deleting directory D:\Packt\chapter02\maven\Demo\ant_output
makedir:
    [mkdir] Created dir: D:\Packt\chapter02\maven\Demo\bin
    [mkdir] Created dir: D:\Packt\chapter02\maven\Demo\ant_output
    [mkdir] Created dir: D:\Packt\chapter02\maven\Demo\ant_output\report
compile:
    [javac] Compiling 1 source file to D:\Packt\chapter02\maven\Demo\bin
testcompile:
    [javac] Compiling 1 source file to D:\Packt\chapter02\maven\Demo\bin
test:
    [junit] Running com.packt.edu.AppTest
    [junit] Tests run: 1, Failures: 0, Errors: 0, Time elapsed: 0.076 sec
jar: [jar] Building jar: D:\Packt\chapter02\maven\Demo\ant_output\Demo.jar
BUILD SUCCESSFUL
```

You can read about securing Jenkins, the post-build action, broken build claim plugins, and the CI game from the Jenkins wiki at `http://jenkins-ci.org/`.

Summary

This chapter covered the concept of CI, explored the build automation tools, and configured Jenkins to accomplish the CI.

The Gradle section covered the environment setup, Gradle tasks, daemons, dependency management, repository setup, Eclipse/Java plugins, and gradually explored the Gradle features. The Maven part demonstrated how to set up Maven, described the POM file, project dependency, and explored the default, clean, and site life cycles. The Ant section described how to write the Ant script to compile and execute JUnit tests. Jenkins covered the build automation setup as well as automated build using Gradle, Maven, and Ant.

By now, the reader will be able to write build scripts using Gradle, Maven, and Ant and configure Jenkins to execute the build scripts.

The next chapter provides an overview of test doubles and different test double types with examples, and includes topics such as dummy, stub, mock, spy, and fake.

3
Test Doubles

This chapter covers the concept of test doubles and explains various test double types, such as mock, fake, dummy, stub, and spy. Sometimes, it is not possible to unit test a piece of code because of unavailability of collaborator objects or the cost of instantiation for the collaborator. Test doubles alleviate the need for a collaborator.

We know about stunt doubles—a trained replacement used for dangerous action sequences in movies, such as jumping out of the Empire State building, a fight sequence on top of a burning train, jumping from an airplane, or similar actions. Stunt doubles are used to protect the real actors or chip in when the actor is not available.

While testing a class that communicates with an API, you don't want to hit the API for every single test; for example, when a piece of code is dependent on database access, it is not possible to unit test the code unless the database is accessible. Similarly, while testing a class that communicates with a payment gateway, you can't submit payments to a real payment gateway to run tests.

Test doubles act as stunt doubles. They are skilled replacements for collaborator objects. Gerard Meszaros coined the term test doubles and explained test doubles in his book *xUnit Test Patterns*, *Pearson Education*.

Test doubles are categorized into five types. The following diagram shows these types:

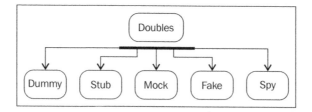

Dummy

An example of a dummy would be a movie scene where the double doesn't perform anything but is only present on the screen. They are used when the actual actor is not present, but their presence is needed for a scene, such as watching the tennis finale of a US Open match.

Similarly, dummy objects are passed to avoid `NullPointerException` for mandatory parameter objects as follows:

```
Book javaBook = new Book("Java 101", "123456");
Member dummyMember = new DummyMember());
javaBook.issueTo(dummyMember);
assertEquals(javaBook.numberOfTimesIssued(),1);
```

In the preceding code snippet, a dummy member was created and passed to a book object to test whether a book can report the number of times it was issued. Here, a member object is not used anywhere but it's needed to issue a book.

Stub

A stub delivers indirect inputs to the caller when the stub's methods are called. Stubs are programmed only for the test scope. Stubs may record other information such as the number of times the methods were invoked and so on.

Account transactions should be rolled back if the ATM's money dispenser fails to dispense money. How can we test this when we don't have the ATM machine, or how can we simulate a scenario where the dispenser fails? We can do this using the following code:

```
public interface Dispenser {
  void dispense(BigDecimal amount) throws DispenserFailed;
}
public class AlwaysFailingDispenserStub implements Dispenser{
  public void dispense(BigDecimal amount) throws DispenserFailed{
    throw new DispenserFailed (ErrorType.HARDWARE,
      "not  responding");
  }
}
class ATMTest...
  @Test
  public void transaction_is_rolledback_when_hardware_fails() {
    Account myAccount = new Account("John", 2000.00);
    TransactionManager txMgr =
      TransactionManager.forAccount(myAccount);
```

```
    txMgr.registerMoneyDispenser(new
      AlwaysFailingDispenserStub());
  WithdrawalResponse response = txMgr.withdraw(500.00);
  assertEquals(false, response.wasSuccess());
  assertEquals(2000.00, myAccount.remainingAmount());
}
```

In the preceding code, `AlwaysFailingDispenserStub` raises an error whenever the `dispense()` method is invoked. It allows us to test the transactional behavior when the hardware is not present.

Mockito allows us to mock interfaces and concrete classes. Using Mockito, you can stub the `dispense()` method to throw an exception.

Fake

Fake objects are working implementations; mostly, the fake class extends the original class, but it usually hacks the performance, which makes it unsuitable for production. The following example demonstrates the fake object:

```
public class AddressDao extends SimpleJdbcDaoSupport{

  public void batchInsertOrUpdate(List<AddressDTO> addressList,
    User user){
    List<AddressDTO> insertList =
      buildListWhereLastChangeTimeMissing(addressList);

    List<AddressDTO> updateList =
      buildListWhereLastChangeTimeValued(addressList);
    int rowCount =   0;

    if (!insertList.isEmpty()) {
      rowCount = getSimpleJdbcTemplate().
        batchUpdate(INSERT_SQL,…);
    }

    if (!updateList.isEmpty()){
      rowCount += getSimpleJdbcTemplate().
        batchUpdate(UPDATE_SQL,…);
    }

    if (addressList.size() != rowCount){
      raiseErrorForDataInconsistency(…);
    }
  }
}
```

`AddressDAO` extends from a Spring framework class and provides an API for mass update. The same method is used to create a new address and update an existing one; if the count doesn't match, then an error is raised. This class cannot be tested directly, and it needs `getSimpleJdbcTemplate()`. So, to test this class, we need to bypass the JDBC collaborator; we can do this by extending the original DAO class but by overriding the collaborator method. The following `FakeAddressDao` class is a fake implementation of `AddressDao`:

```
public class FakeAddressDao extends AddressDao{
  @Override
  public SimpleJdbcTemplate getSimpleJdbcTemplate() {
    return jdbcTemplate;
  }
}
```

`FakeAddressDao` extends `AddressDao` but only overrides `getSimpleJdbcTemplate()` and returns a JDBC template stub. We can use Mockito to create a mock version of the `JdbcTemplate` and return it from the fake implementation. This class cannot be used in production as it uses a mock `JdbcTemplate`; however, the fake class inherits all functionalities of the DAO, so this can be used for testing. The fake classes are very useful for legacy code.

Mock

Mock objects have expectations; a test expects a value from a mock object, and during execution, a mock object returns the expected result. Also, mock objects can keep track of the invocation count, that is, the number of times a method on a mock object is invoked.

The following example is a continuation of the ATM example with a mock version. In the previous example, we stubbed the dispense method of the `Dispenser` interface to throw an exception; here, we'll use a mock object to replicate the same behavior. We'll explain the syntax in *Chapter 4, Progressive Mockito*.

```
public class ATMTest {
  @Mock Dispenser failingDispenser;

  @Before  public void setUp() throws Exception {
    MockitoAnnotations.initMocks(this);
  }

  @Test    public void transaction_is_rolledback_when_
    hardware_fails() throws DispenserFailed {
    Account myAccount = new Account(2000.00, "John");
```

```
    TransactionManager txMgr =
      TransactionManager.forAccount(myAccount);
    txMgr.registerMoneyDispenser(failingDispenser);

    doThrow(new  DispenserFailed()).when(failingDispenser).
      dispense(isA(BigDecimal.class));

    txMgr.withdraw(500);
      assertEquals(2000.00, myAccount.getRemainingBalance());

    verify(failingDispenser, new Times(1)).
      dispense(isA(BigDecimal.class));
  }
}
```

The preceding code is the mock (Mockito) version of the ATM test. The same object can be used in different tests; just the expectation needs to be set. Here, doThrow() raises an error whenever the mock object is called with any BigDecimal value.

Spy

Spy is a variation of a mock/stub, but instead of only setting expectations, spy records the calls made to the collaborator. The following example explains this concept:

```
class ResourceAdapter{
  void print(String userId, String document, Object settings) {
    if(securityService.canAccess("lanPrinter1", userId)) {
      printer.print(document, settings);
    }
  }
}
```

To test the print behavior of the ResourceAdapter class, we need to know whether the printer.print() method gets invoked when a user has permissions. Here, the printer collaborator doesn't do anything; it is just used to verify the ResourceAdapter behavior.

Now, consider the following code:

```
class SpyPrinter implements Printer{
  private int noOfTimescalled = 0;
   @Override
  public void print(Object document, Object settings) {
    noOfTimescalled++;
  }
```

```
    public int getInvocationCount() {
      return noOfTimescalled;
    }
  }
```

SpyPrinter implements the Printer.print() call, increments a noOfTimescalled counter, and getInvocationCount returns the count. Create a fake implementation of the SecurityService class to return true from the canAccess(String printerName, String userId) method. The following is the fake implementation of the SecurityService class:

```
class FakeSecurityService implements SecurityService{
  public boolean canAccess(String printerName, String userId){
    return true;
  }
}
```

The following code snippet verifies the print behavior of the ResourceAdapter class:

```
@Test public void verify() throws Exception {
  SpyPrinter spyPrinter = new SpyPrinter();
  adapter = new ResourceAdapter(
    new FakeSecurityService(), spyPrinter);
  adapter.print("john", "helloWorld.txt", "all pages");
  assertEquals(1, spyPrinter.getInvocationCount());
}
```

Fake SecurityService and a SpyPrinter objects are created and passed to the ResourceAdapter class and then adapter.print is called. In turn, it is expected that the securityService object will return true and the printer will be accessed, and spyPrinter.print(...) will increment the noOfTimescalled counter. Finally, in the preceding code, we verified that the count is 1.

Summary

This chapter provided an overview of test doubles with examples. The following topics covered dummy, stub, mock, fake, and spy. This chapter is a prerequisite for Mockito.

The next chapter will cover the Mockito framework and its advanced uses. Mockito is a mocking framework for Java. It provides the API for mock, spy, and stub creation.

4
Progressive Mockito

This chapter distills the Mockito framework to its main core and provides technical examples. No previous knowledge of mocking is necessary.

The following topics are covered in this chapter:

- Overview of Mockito
- Exploring Mockito APIs
- Advanced Mockito examples
- Behavior-driven development (BDD) with Mockito

Working with Mockito

Mockito is an open source mock unit testing framework for Java. In the previous chapter, we read about test doubles and mock objects. Mockito allows mock object creation, verification, and stubbing.

To find out more about Mockito, visit the following link:

```
http://code.google.com/p/mockito/
```

Why should you use Mockito?

Automated tests are safety nets. They run and notify the user if the system is broken so that the offending code can be fixed very quickly.

If a test suite runs for an hour, the purpose of quick feedback is compromised. Unit tests should act as a safety net and provide quick feedback; this is the main principle of TDD.

I worked with an environment where when a piece of code is checked-in, the automated tests would run and would take hours to complete. So, a developer had to wait for an hour to check-in the new code unless the previous build/test run was complete. A developer can check-in the code in the middle of a build, but the best practice is to monitor the status before signing off; otherwise, the new code can break the next build and cause problem for the other developers. So, the developer has to wait for an additional hour to monitor the next build. This kind of slow build environment blocks the progress of development.

A test may take time to execute due to the following reasons:

- Sometimes a test acquires a connection from the database that fetches/updates data
- It connects to the Internet and downloads files
- It interacts with an SMTP server to send e-mails
- It performs I/O operations

Now the question is do we really need to acquire a database connection or download files to unit test code?

The answer is yes. If it doesn't connect to a database or download the latest stock price, few parts of the system remain untested. So, DB interaction or network connection is mandatory for a few parts of the system, and these are integration tests. To unit test these parts, the external dependencies need to be mocked out.

Mockito plays a key role in mocking out external dependencies. It mocks out the database connection or any external I/O behavior so that the actual logic can be unit tested.

Unit tests should adhere to a number of principles for flexibility and maintainability. The next section will elucidate the principles that we will follow throughout this journey.

Qualities of unit testing

Unit tests should adhere to the following principles:

- **Order independent and isolated**: The `ATest.java` test class should not be dependent on the output of the `BTest.java` test class, or a `when_an_user_is_deleted_the_associated_id_gets_deleted()` test should not depend on the execution of another `when_a_new_user_is_created_an_id_is_returned()` test. The tests shouldn't fail if `BTest.java` is executed after `ATest.java`, or the `when_a_new_user_is_created_an_id_is_returned()` test is executed after `when_an_user_is_deleted_the_associated_id_gets_deleted()`.

- **Trouble-free setup and run**: Unit tests should not require a DB connection or an Internet connection or a clean-up temp directory.

- **Effortless execution**: Unit tests should run fine on all computers, not just on a specific computer.

- **Formula 1 execution**: A test should not take more than a second to finish the execution.

Mockito provides APIs to mock out the external dependencies and achieve the qualities mentioned here.

Drinking Mockito

Download the latest Mockito binary from the following link and add it to the project dependency:

```
http://code.google.com/p/mockito/downloads/list
```

As of February 2014, the latest Mockito version is 1.9.5.

Configuring Mockito

To add Mockito JAR files to the project dependency, perform the following steps:

1. Extract the JAR files into a folder.
2. Launch Eclipse.
3. Create an Eclipse project named Chapter04.
4. Go to the **Libraries** tab in the project build path.
5. Click on the **Add External JARs...** button and browse to the **Mockito JAR** folder.
6. Select all JAR files and click on **OK**.

We worked with Gradle and Maven and built a project with the JUnit dependency. In this section, we will add Mockito dependencies to our existing projects.

The following code snippet will add a Mockito dependency to a Maven project and download the JAR file from the central Maven repository (http://mvnrepository.com/artifact/org.mockito/mockito-core):

```xml
<dependency>
    <groupId>org.mockito</groupId>
    <artifactId>mockito-core</artifactId>
    <version>1.9.5</version>
```

```
    <scope>test</scope>
</dependency>
```

The following Gradle script snippet will add a Mockito dependency to
a Gradle project:

```
testCompile 'org.mockito:mockito-core:1.9.5'
```

Mocking in action

This section demonstrates the mock objects with a stock quote example. In the real
world, people invest money on the stock market—they buy and sell stocks. A stock
symbol is an abbreviation used to uniquely identify shares of a particular stock on a
particular market, such as stocks of Facebook are registered on NASDAQ as FB and
stocks of Apple as AAPL.

We will build a stock broker simulation program. The program will watch the
market statistics, and depending on the current market data, you can perform any
of the following actions:

- Buy stocks
- Sell stocks
- Hold stocks

The domain classes that will be used in the program are `Stock`, `MarketWatcher`,
`Portfolio`, and `StockBroker`.

`Stock` represents a real-world stock. It has a symbol, company name, and price.

`MarketWatcher` looks up the stock market and returns the quote for the stock.
A real implementation of a market watcher can be implemented from `http://www.`
`wikijava.org/wiki/Downloading_stock_market_quotes_from_Yahoo!_finance`.
Note that the real implementation will connect to the Internet and download the
stock quote from a provider.

`Portfolio` represents a user's stock data such as the number of stocks and price
details. `Portfolio` exposes APIs for getting the average stock price and buying and
selling stocks. Suppose on day one someone buys a share at a price of $10.00, and
on day two, the customer buys the same share at a price of $8.00. So, on day two the
person has two shares and the average price of the share is $9.00.

The following screenshot represents the Eclipse project structure. You can download
the project from the Packt Publishing website and work with the files:

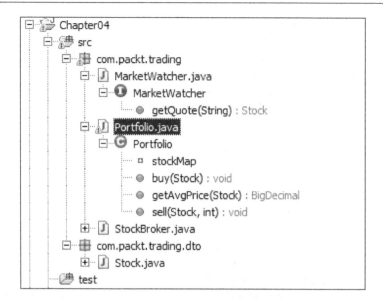

The following code snippet represents the StockBroker class. StockBroker collaborates with the MarketWatcher and Portfolio classes. The perform() method of StockBroker accepts a portfolio and a Stock object:

```java
public class StockBroker {
  private final static BigDecimal LIMIT = new BigDecimal("0.10");

  private final MarketWatcher market;

  public StockBroker(MarketWatcher market) {
    this.market = market;
  }

  public void perform(Portfolio portfolio,Stock stock) {
    Stock liveStock = market.getQuote(stock.getSymbol());
    BigDecimal avgPrice = portfolio.getAvgPrice(stock);
    BigDecimal priceGained =
      liveStock.getPrice().subtract(avgPrice);
    BigDecimal percentGain = priceGained.divide(avgPrice);
    if(percentGain.compareTo(LIMIT) > 0) {
      portfolio.sell(stock, 10);
    }else if(percentGain.compareTo(LIMIT) < 0){
      portfolio.buy(stock);
    }
  }
}
```

Look at the perform method. It takes a portfolio object and a stock object, calls the getQuote method of MarketWatcher, and passes a stock symbol. Then, it gets the average stock price from portfolio and compares the current market price with the average stock price. If the current stock price is 10 percent greater than the average price, then the StockBroker program sells 10 stocks from Portfolio; however, if the current stock price goes down by 10 percent, then the program buys shares from the market to average out the loss.

Why do we sell 10 stocks? This is just an example and 10 is just a number; this could be anything you want.

StockBroker depends on Portfolio and MarketWatcher; a real implementation of Portfolio should interact with a database, and MarketWatcher needs to connect to the Internet. So, if we write a unit test for the broker, we need to execute the test with a database and an Internet connection. A database connection will take time and Internet connectivity depends on the Internet provider. So, the test execution will depend on external entities and will take a while to finish. This will violate the quick test execution principle. Also, the database state might not be the same across all test runs. This is also applicable for the Internet connection service. Each time the database might return different values, and therefore asserting a specific value in your unit test is very difficult.

We'll use Mockito to mock the external dependencies and execute the test in isolation. So, the test will no longer be dependent on real external service, and therefore it will be executed quickly.

Mocking objects

A mock can be created with the help of a static mock() method as follows:

```
import org.mockito.Mockito;

public class StockBrokerTest {
  MarketWatcher marketWatcher =
    Mockito.mock(MarketWatcher.class);
  Portfolio portfolio = Mockito.mock(Portfolio.class);

}
```

Otherwise, you can use Java's static import feature and static import the mock method of the org.mockito.Mockito class as follows:

```
import static org.mockito.Mockito.mock;

public class StockBrokerTest {
```

```
    MarketWatcher marketWatcher = mock(MarketWatcher.class);
    Portfolio portfolio = mock(Portfolio.class);
}
```

There's another alternative; you can use the @Mock annotation as follows:

```
import org.mockito.Mock;

public class StockBrokerTest {
  @Mock
  MarketWatcher marketWatcher;
  @Mock
  Portfolio portfolio;
}
```

However, to work with the @Mock annotation, you are required to call
MockitoAnnotations.initMocks(this) before using the mocks,
or use MockitoJUnitRunner as a JUnit runner.

The following code snippet uses MockitoAnnotations to create mocks:

```
import static org.junit.Assert.assertEquals;
import org.mockito.MockitoAnnotations;

public class StockBrokerTest {

  @Mock
  MarketWatcher marketWatcher;

  @Mock
  Portfolio portfolio;

  @Before
  public void setUp() {
    MockitoAnnotations.initMocks(this);
  }


  @Test
  public void sanity() throws Exception {
    assertNotNull(marketWatcher);
    assertNotNull(portfolio);
  }
}
```

The following code snippet uses the `MockitoJUnitRunner` JUnit runner:

```
import org.mockito.runners.MockitoJUnitRunner;

@RunWith(MockitoJUnitRunner.class)
public class StockBrokerTest {

   @Mock
     MarketWatcher marketWatcher;
   @Mock
     Portfolio portfolio;

   @Test
     public void sanity() throws Exception {
       assertNotNull(marketWatcher);
       assertNotNull(portfolio);
   }
}
```

Before we deep dive into the Mockito world, there are a few things to remember. Mockito cannot mock or spy the following functions: final classes, final methods, enums, static methods, private methods, the `hashCode()` and `equals()` methods, anonymous classes, and primitive types.

PowerMock (an extension of EasyMock) and PowerMockito (an extension of the Mockito framework) allows you to mock static and private methods; even PowerMockito allows you to set expectations on new invocations for private member classes, inner classes, and local or anonymous classes. However, as per the design, you should not opt for mocking private/static properties—it violates the encapsulation. Instead, you should refactor the offending code to make it testable. *Chapter 9, Solving Test Puzzles,* explains the design for the testability concept.

Change the `Portfolio` class, create the `final` class, and rerun the test; the test will fail as the `Portfolio` class is final, and Mockito cannot mock a `final` class.

The following screenshot shows the JUnit output:

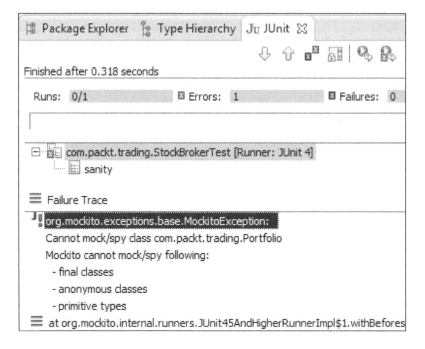

Stubbing methods

We read about stubs in *Chapter 3, Test Doubles*. The stubbing process defines the behavior of a mock method such as the value to be returned or the exception to be thrown when the method is invoked.

The Mockito framework supports stubbing and allows us to return a given value when a specific method is called. This can be done using `Mockito.when()` along with `thenReturn ()`.

The following is the syntax of importing `when`:

```
import static org.mockito.Mockito.when;
```

The following code snippet stubs the `getQuote(String symbol)` method of `MarcketWatcher` and returns a specific `Stock` object:

```
import static org.mockito.Matchers.anyString;
import static org.mockito.Mockito.when;

@RunWith(MockitoJUnitRunner.class)
public class StockBrokerTest {
```

```
@Mock MarketWatcher marketWatcher;
@Mock Portfolio portfolio;

@Test
public void marketWatcher_Returns_current_stock_status() {
  Stock uvsityCorp = new Stock("UV", "Uvsity Corporation",
    new BigDecimal("100.00"));

  when(marketWatcher.getQuote(anyString())).
    thenReturn(uvsityCorp);

  assertNotNull(marketWatcher.getQuote("UV"));
  }

}
```

A uvsityCorp stock object is created with a stock price of $100.00 and the getQuote method is stubbed to return uvsityCorp whenever the getQuote method is called. Note that anyString() is passed to the getQuote method, which means whenever the getQuote method will be called with any String value, the uvsityCorp object will be returned.

The when() method represents the trigger, that is, when to stub.

The following methods are used to represent what to do when the trigger is triggered:

- thenReturn(x): This returns the x value.
- thenThrow(x): This throws an x exception.
- thenAnswer(Answer answer): Unlike returning a hardcoded value, a dynamic user-defined logic is executed. It's more like for fake test doubles, Answer is an interface.
- thenCallRealMethod(): This method calls the real method on the mock object.

The following code snippet stubs the external dependencies and creates a test for the StockBroker class:

```
import com.packt.trading.dto.Stock;
import static org.junit.Assert.assertNotNull;
import static org.mockito.Matchers.anyString;
import static org.mockito.Matchers.isA;
import static org.mockito.Mockito.verify;
import static org.mockito.Mockito.when;

@RunWith(MockitoJUnitRunner.class)
```

```
public class StockBrokerTest {
  @Mock    MarketWatcher marketWatcher;
  @Mock    Portfolio portfolio;
  StockBroker broker;

  @Before public void setUp() {
    broker = new StockBroker(marketWatcher);
  }

  @Test
  public void when_ten_percent_gain_then_the_stock_is_sold() {
    //Portfolio's getAvgPrice is stubbed to return $10.00
    when(portfolio.getAvgPrice(isA(Stock.class))).
      thenReturn(new BigDecimal("10.00"));
    //A stock object is created with current price $11.20
    Stock aCorp = new Stock("A", "A Corp", new
      BigDecimal("11.20"));
    //getQuote method is stubbed to return the stock
    when(marketWatcher.getQuote(anyString())).thenReturn(aCorp);
    //perform method is called, as the stock price increases
    // by 12% the broker should sell the stocks
    broker.perform(portfolio, aCorp);

  //verifying that the broker sold the stocks
  verify(portfolio).sell(aCorp,10);
  }

}
```

> The test method name is when_ten_percent_gain_then_the_
> stock_is_sold; a test name should explain the intention of the
> test. We use underscores to make the test name readable. We will
> use the when_<<something happens>>_then_<<the action is
> taken>> convention for the tests.

In the preceding test example, the getAvgPrice() method of portfolio is stubbed to return $10.00, then the getQuote method is stubbed to return a hardcoded stock object with a current stock price of $11.20. The broker logic should sell the stock as the stock price goes up by 12 percent.

The portfolio object is a mock object. So, unless we stub a method, by default, all the methods of portfolio are autostubbed to return a default value, and for the void methods, no action is performed. The sell method is a void method; so, instead of connecting to a database to update the stock count, the autostub will do nothing.

However, how will we test whether the `sell` method was invoked? We use `Mockito.verify`.

The `verify()` method is a static method, which is used to verify the method invocation. If the method is not invoked, or the argument doesn't match, then the verify method will raise an error to indicate that the code logic has issues.

Verifying the method invocation

To verify a redundant method invocation, or to verify whether a stubbed method was not called but was important from the test perspective, we should manually verify the invocation; for this, we need to use the static `verify` method.

Why do we use verify?

Mock objects are used to stub external dependencies. We set an expectation, and a mock object returns an expected value. In some conditions, a behavior or method of a mock object should not be invoked, or sometimes, we may need to call the method N (a number) times. The `verify` method verifies the invocation of mock objects.

Mockito does not automatically verify all stubbed calls.

If a stubbed behavior should not be called but the method is called due to a bug in the code, `verify` flags the error though we have to verify that manually. The `void` methods don't return values, so you cannot assert the returned values. Hence, `verify` is very handy to test the `void` methods.

Verifying in depth

The `verify()` method has an overloaded version that takes `Times` as an argument. `Times` is a Mockito framework class of the `org.mockito.internal.verification` package, and it takes `wantedNumberOfInvocations` as an integer argument.

If `0` is passed to `Times`, it infers that the method will not be invoked in the testing path. We can pass `0` to `Times(0)` to make sure that the `sell` or `buy` methods are not invoked. If a negative number is passed to the `Times` constructor, Mockito throws `MockitoException` - `org.mockito.exceptions.base.MockitoException`, and this shows the **Negative value is not allowed here** error.

The following methods are used in conjunction with `verify`:

- `times(int wantedNumberOfInvocations)`: This method is invoked exactly *n* times; if the method is not invoked `wantedNumberOfInvocations` times, then the test fails.

- `never()`: This method signifies that the stubbed method is never called or you can use `times(0)` to represent the same scenario. If the stubbed method is invoked at least once, then the test fails.

- `atLeastOnce()`: This method is invoked at least once, and it works fine if it is invoked multiple times. However, the operation fails if the method is not invoked.

- `atLeast(int minNumberOfInvocations)`: This method is called at least *n* times, and it works fine if the method is invoked more than the `minNumberOfInvocations` times. However, the operation fails if the method is not called `minNumberOfInvocations` times.

- `atMost(int maxNumberOfInvocations)`: This method is called at the most n times. However, the operation fails if the method is called more than `minNumberOfInvocations` times.

- `only()`: The `only` method called on a mock fails if any other method is called on the mock object. In our example, if we use `verify(portfolio, only())`. `sell(aCorp,10);`, the test will fail with the following output:

The test fails in line 15 as `portfolio.getAvgPrice(stock)` is called.

- `timeout(int millis)`: This method is interacted in a specified time range.

Verifying zero and no more interactions

The `verifyZeroInteractions(Object... mocks)` method verifies whether no interactions happened on the given mocks.

The following test code directly calls `verifyZeroInteractions` and passes the two mock objects. Since no methods are invoked on the mock objects, the test passes:

```
@Test  public void verify_zero_interaction() {
  verifyZeroInteractions(marketWatcher,portfolio);
}
```

The `verifyNoMoreInteractions(Object... mocks)` method checks whether any of the given mocks has any unverified interaction. We can use this method after verifying a mock method to make sure that nothing else was invoked on the mock.

The following test code demonstrates `verifyNoMoreInteractions`:

```
@Test  public void verify_no_more_interaction() {
  Stock noStock = null;
  portfolio.getAvgPrice(noStock);
  portfolio.sell(null, 0);
  verify(portfolio).getAvgPrice(eq(noStock));
  //this will fail as the sell method was invoked
  verifyNoMoreInteractions(portfolio);
}
```

The following is the JUnit output:

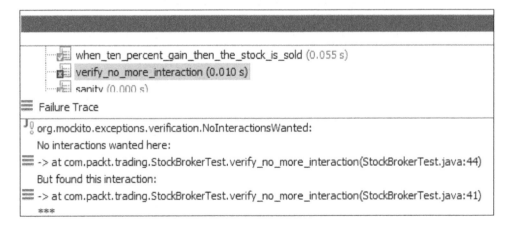

The following are the rationales and examples of argument matchers.

Using argument matcher

`ArgumentMatcher` is a Hamcrest matcher with a predefined `describeTo()` method. `ArgumentMatcher` extends the `org.hamcrest.BaseMatcher` package. It verifies the indirect inputs into a mocked dependency.

The `Matchers.argThat(Matcher)` method is used in conjunction with the `verify` method to verify whether a method is invoked with a specific argument value.

`ArgumentMatcher` plays a key role in mocking. The following section describes the context of `ArgumentMatcher`.

Mock objects return expected values, but when they need to return different values for different arguments, argument matcher comes into play. Suppose we have a method that takes a player name as input and returns the total number of runs (a run is a point scored in a cricket match) scored as output. We want to stub it and return `100` for `Sachin` and `10` for `xyz`. We have to use argument matcher to stub this.

Mockito returns expected values when a method is stubbed. If the method takes arguments, the argument must match during the execution; for example, the `getValue(int someValue)` method is stubbed in the following way:

```
when(mockObject.getValue(1)).thenReturn(expected value);
```

Here, the `getValue` method is called with `mockObject.getValue(100)`. Then, the parameter doesn't match (it is expected that the method will be called with 1, but at runtime, it encounters 100), so the mock object fails to return the expected value. It will return the default value of the return type—if the return type is Boolean, it'll return false; if the return type is object, then null, and so on.

Mockito verifies argument values in natural Java style by using an `equals()` method. Sometimes, we use argument matchers when extra flexibility is required.

Mockito provides built-in matchers such as `anyInt()`, `anyDouble()`, `anyString()`, `anyList()`, and `anyCollection()`.

More built-in matchers and examples of custom argument matchers or Hamcrest matchers can be found at the following link:

```
http://docs.mockito.googlecode.com/hg/latest/org/mockito/Matchers.
html
```

 Examples of other matchers are `isA(java.lang.Class<T> clazz)`, `any(java.lang.Class<T> clazz)`, and `eq(T)` or `eq(primitive value)`.

The `isA` argument checks whether the passed object is an instance of the class type passed in the `isA` argument. The `any(T)` argument also works in the same way.

Why do we need wildcard matchers?

Wildcard matchers are used to verify the indirect inputs to the mocked dependencies. The following example describes the context.

In the following code snippet, an object is passed to a method and then a `request` object is created and passed to `service`. Now, from a test, if we call the `someMethod` method and `service` is a mocked object, then from test, we cannot stub `callMethod` with a specific `request` as the `request` object is local to the `someMethod`:

```
public void someMethod(Object obj){
   Request req = new Request();
   req.setValue(obj);
   Response resp = service.callMethod(req);
}
```

If we are using argument matchers, all arguments have to be provided by matchers.

We're passing three arguments and all of them are passed using matchers:

```
verify(mock).someMethod(anyInt(), anyString(),
   eq("third argument"));
```

The following example will fail because the first and the third arguments are not passed using matcher:

```
verify(mock).someMethod(1, anyString(), "third
   argument");
```

The ArgumentMatcher class

The `ArgumentMatcher` class allows the creation of customized argument matchers. `ArgumentMatcher` is a Hamcrest matcher with the predefined `describeTo()` method.

Use the `Matchers.argThat(org.hamcrest.Matcher)` method and pass an instance of the Hamcrest matcher.

Consider the `MarketWatcher` class; it takes a stock symbol and then gets the quote from the market.

We will create a mock for the `MarketWatcher.getQuote` method that takes a `String` object. We wish to make this method conditional. If a blue chip stock symbol is passed to the method, then the method will return $1000.00; otherwise, it will return $5.00.

How will we identify a blue chip share? A blue chip share is a common stock of a well-known company whose value and dividends are reliable and usually safe for investment. For example, if the stock symbol is FB or AAPL, we will consider the stock as a blue chip stock.

Let us create a custom matcher to identify blue chip stocks. The following code shows a custom argument matcher:

```
class BlueChipStockMatcher extends ArgumentMatcher<String>{
  @Override
  public boolean matches(Object symbol) {
    return "FB".equals(symbol) ||
      "AAPL".equals(symbol);
  }
}
```

The following class extends `BlueChipStockMatcher` and then negates the result to indicate that the stock is not a blue chip stock:

```
class OtherStockMatcher extends BlueChipStockMatcher{
  @Override
  public boolean matches(Object symbol) {
    return !super.matches(symbol);
  }
}
```

The following test uses the custom matchers to sell the shares:

```
@Test
public void argument_matcher() {
    when(portfolio.getAvgPrice(isA(Stock.class))).
      thenReturn(new BigDecimal("10.00"));

    Stock blueChipStock = new Stock("FB", "FB Corp", new
      BigDecimal(1000.00));
    Stock otherStock = new Stock("XY", "XY Corp", new
      BigDecimal(5.00));

    when(marketWatcher.getQuote(argThat(new
      BlueChipStockMatcher()))).thenReturn(blueChipStock);
    when(marketWatcher.getQuote(argThat(new
      OtherStockMatcher()))).thenReturn(otherStock);

    broker.perform(portfolio, blueChipStock);
    verify(portfolio).sell(blueChipStock,10);
```

```
        broker.perform(portfolio, otherStock);
        verify(portfolio, never()).sell(otherStock,10);
    }
```

In the preceding code, marketWatcher is stubbed to return a blue chip share when the stock symbol is FB or AAPL; otherwise, it returns a normal stock.

Throwing exceptions

Unit tests are not meant for only happy path testing. We should test our code for the failure conditions too. Mockito provides an API to raise an error during testing. Suppose we are testing a flow where we compute a value and then print it to a printer. If the printer is not configured, or a network error happens, or a page is not loaded, the system throws an exception. We can test this using Mockito's exception APIs.

How do we test exceptional conditions such as database access failure?

Mockito provides a method called thenThrow(Throwable); this method throws an exception when the stubbed method is invoked.

We will stub the getAvgPrice method to throw an exception when the method is called, as follows:

```
@Test(expected = IllegalStateException.class)
public void throwsException() throws Exception {
  when(portfolio.getAvgPrice(isA(Stock.class))).thenThrow(
    new IllegalStateException("Database down"));

  portfolio.getAvgPrice(new Stock(null, null, null));
}
```

We are stubbing portfolio to throw an exception when getAvgPrice() is invoked. The following is the syntax to throw an exception from a method that returns void:

```
doThrow(exception).when(mock).voidmethod(arguments);
```

The buy method in Portfolio is a void method; we will stub the buy method to throw an exception. The following test code throws IllegalStateException when the buy method is invoked on the portfolio object. Note that doThrow().when() will be used to raise the error from the buy method:

```
@Test(expected = IllegalStateException.class)
public void throwsException_void_methods() throws Exception {
  doThrow(new IllegalStateException()).
    when(portfolio).buy(isA(Stock.class));
  portfolio.buy(new Stock(null, null, null));
}
```

Stubbing consecutive calls

Stubbing a method for consecutive calls is required in the following situations:

- Calling a stubbed method in a loop when you need different results for different calls
- When you need one invocation to throw an exception and other invocations to return a value

We need to test a condition where the first call will return a value, the next call should not find any value, and then again it should return a value.

The varargs version of thenReturn(objects...) takes comma-separated return values and returns the arguments in order such that if we pass two arguments to the thenReturn method, then the first call to the stubbed method will return the first argument. Thereafter, all other calls will return the second argument, as shown in the following code:

```
@Test
public void consecutive_calls() throws Exception {
  Stock stock = new Stock(null, null, null);
  when(portfolio.getAvgPrice(stock)).thenReturn(
    BigDecimal.TEN, BigDecimal.ZERO);
  assertEquals(BigDecimal.TEN, portfolio.getAvgPrice(stock));
  assertEquals(BigDecimal.ZERO, portfolio.getAvgPrice(stock));
  assertEquals(BigDecimal.ZERO, portfolio.getAvgPrice(stock));
}
```

Note that thenReturn takes two values: BigDecimal.TEN and BigDecimal.ZERO. The first call to getAvgPrice will return BigDecimal.TEN, and then each call will return BigDecimal.ZERO.

This can be done in another way — Mockito methods return stub objects and follow a builder pattern to allow a chain of calls.

In the following example, thenReturn and thenThrow are combined to build a chain of response. After the second call, each getAvgPrice invocation will throw an exception:

```
when(portfolio.getAvgPrice(stock)).thenReturn(BigDecimal.TEN).
  thenReturn(BigDecimal.TEN).thenThrow(new
  IllegalStateException())
```

Stubbing with an Answer

Stubbed methods return a hardcoded value but cannot return an on the fly result. The Mockito framework provides the callbacks to compute the on the fly results.

Mockito allows stubbing with the generic `Answer` interface. This is a callback; when a stubbed method on a mock object is invoked, the `answer(InvocationOnMock invocation)` method of the `Answer` object is called. This `Answer` object's `answer()` method returns the actual object.

The syntax of `Answer` is `when(mock.someMethod()).thenAnswer(new Answer() {...})`; or `when(mock.someMethod()).then(answer)`;, which is similar to `thenReturn()` and `thenThrow()`.

The `Answer` interface is defined as follows:

```
public interface Answer<T> {
    T answer(InvocationOnMock invocation) throws Throwable;
}
```

The `InvocationOnMock` argument is an important part of callback. It can return the arguments passed to the method and also return the mock object as follows:

```
Object[] args = invocation.getArguments();
Object mock = invocation.getMock();
```

Add a new method to the `Portfolio` class to return the total stock value. We are using a mock `Portfolio` instance, so we cannot return the total stock value. We can fix this using `Answer` and make the test totally configurable.

When a new stock is bought, we will store the stock in `HashMap`, and when the `getCurrentValue` method will be invoked, we will compute the value dynamically from `HashMap`. So, we need two `Answer` objects, one to store stocks and the other to compute the total.

The following code snippet creates two `Answer` classes. Add `HashMap` to the test class:

```
Map<String, List<Stock>> stockMap = new HashMap<String,
  List<Stock>>();
```

One can buy 10 stocks of Facebook or 10 different stocks. The `stockMap` object stores a key-value pair. The key is the `Stock` symbol and the value is a list of stocks. 10 Facebook stocks will add a single key, `FB`, and a list of 10 Facebook stocks. An Apple stock will add another entry to the map with an `AAPL` key and value and a list with a single Apple stock.

The following `Answer` implementation is called when the `buy` method is invoked. The `invocationOnMock` object returns the arguments, and the `buy` method accepts only one argument, that is, a `Stock` object. So, type casted the 0th argument to `Stock`. Then, insert `Stock` to the `stockMap` object:

```
class BuyAnswer implements Answer<Object>{
  @Override
  public Object answer(InvocationOnMock invocation) throws
    Throwable
  {
    Stock newStock = (Stock)invocation.getArguments()[0];
    List<Stock> stocks = stockMap.get(newStock.getSymbol());
    if(stocks != null) {
      stocks.add(newStock);
    }else {
      stocks = new ArrayList<Stock>();
      stocks.add(newStock);
      stockMap.put(newStock.getSymbol(), stocks);
    }
    return null;
  }
}
```

The following `answer` object implements the total price computation logic:

```
class TotalPriceAnswer implements Answer<BigDecimal>{
  @Override
  public BigDecimal answer(InvocationOnMock invocation)
    throws Throwable  {
    BigDecimal totalPrice = BigDecimal.ZERO;

    for(String stockId: stockMap.keySet()) {
      for(Stock stock:stockMap.get(stockId)) {
        totalPrice = totalPrice.add(stock.getPrice());
      }
    }
    return totalPrice;
  }
}
```

The getCurrentValue() method will be stubbed to return the preceding answer implementation.

The following JUnit test code uses the TotalPriceAnswer method:

```
@Test
  public void answering() throws Exception {
    stockMap.clear();
    doAnswer(new BuyAnswer()).when(portfolio).
      buy(isA(Stock.class));

    when(portfolio.getCurrentValue()).
    then(new TotalPriceAnswer());

    portfolio.buy(new Stock("A", "A", BigDecimal.TEN));
    portfolio.buy(new Stock("B", "B", BigDecimal.ONE));

    assertEquals(new BigDecimal("11"),
      portfolio.getCurrentValue());
}
```

Check that the stockMap object is cleared to remove existing data. Then, the void buy method is stubbed to add stocks to stockMap using the doAnswer method, and then the getCurrentValue method is stubbed to the TotalPriceAnswer answer.

Spying objects

A Mockito spy object allows us to use real objects instead of mocks by replacing some of the methods with the stubbed ones. This behavior allows us to test the legacy code; one cannot mock a class that needs to be tested. Legacy code comes with methods that cannot be tested, but other methods use them; so, these methods need to be stubbed to work with the other methods. A spy object can stub the nontestable methods so that other methods can be tested easily.

Once an expectation is set for a method on a spy object, then spy no longer returns the original value. It starts returning the stubbed value, but still it exhibits the original behavior for the other methods that are not stubbed.

Mockito can create a spy of a real object. Unlike stubbing, when we use spy, the real methods are called (unless a method was stubbed).

Spy is also known as partial mock; one example of the use of spy in the real world is dealing with legacy code.

Declaration of spy is done using the following code:

```
SomeClass realObject = new RealImplemenation();
SomeClass spyObject = spy(realObject);
```

The following is a self-explanatory example of spy:

```
@Test public void spying() throws Exception {
    Stock realStock = new Stock("A",
      "Company A", BigDecimal.ONE);
    Stock spyStock = spy(realStock);
    //call real method from  spy
    assertEquals("A", spyStock.getSymbol());

    //Changing value using spy
    spyStock.updatePrice(BigDecimal.ZERO);

    //verify spy has the changed value
    assertEquals(BigDecimal.ZERO, spyStock.getPrice());

    //Stubbing method
    when(spyStock.getPrice()).thenReturn(BigDecimal.TEN);

    //Changing value using spy
    spyStock.updatePrice(new BigDecimal("7"));

    //Stubbed method value 10.00  is returned NOT 7
    assertNotEquals(new BigDecimal("7"),
      spyStock.getPrice());
    //Stubbed method value 10.00
    assertEquals(BigDecimal.TEN,  spyStock.getPrice());

}
```

Stubbing void methods

In the *Throwing exceptions* section of this chapter, we learned that doThrow is used for throwing exceptions for the void methods. The *Stubbing with an Answer* section of this chapter showed you how to use doAnswer for the void methods.

In this section, we will explore the other void methods: doNothing, doReturn, doThrow, and doCallRealMethod.

The doNothing() API does nothing. By default, all the void methods do nothing. However, if you need consecutive calls on a void method, the first call is to throw an error, the next call is to do nothing, and then the next call to perform some logic using doAnswer() and then follow this syntax:

```
doThrow(new RuntimeException()).
doNothing().
doAnswer(someAnswer).
when(mock).someVoidMethod();

//this call throws exception
mock.someVoidMethod();
// this call does nothing
mock.someVoidMethod();
```

The doCallRealMethod() API is used when you want to call the real implementation of a method on a mock or a spy object as follows:

```
doCallRealMethod().when(mock).someVoidMethod();
```

The doReturn() method is similar to stubbing a method and returning an expected value. However, this is used only when when(mock).thenReturn(return) cannot be used.

The when-thenReturn method is more readable than doReturn(); also, doReturn() is not a safe type. The thenReturn method checks the method return types and raises a compilation error if an unsafe type is passed.

Here is the syntax for using the doReturn() test:

```
doReturn(value).when(mock).method(argument);
```

The following code snippet provides an example of unsafe usage of doReturn:

```
@Test public void doReturn_is_not_type_safe() throws Exception {
    //then return is type safe- It has to return a BigDecimal
    when(portfolio.getCurrentValue()).thenReturn(BigDecimal.ONE);
     //method call works fine
    portfolio.getCurrentValue();

     //returning a String instead of BigDecimal
    doReturn("See returning a String").
      when(portfolio.getCurrentValue());
      //this call will fail with an error
    portfolio.getCurrentValue();
}
```

The following screenshot shows how the test fails:

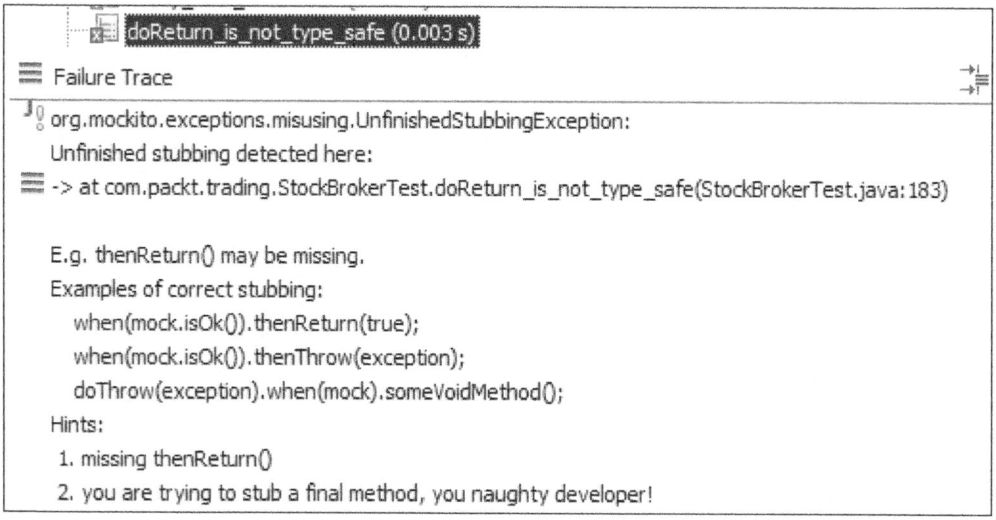

Spying real objects and calling real methods on a spy has side effects; to counter this side effect, use `doReturn()` instead of `thenReturn()`.

The following code describes the side effect of spying and calling `thenReturn()`:

```
@Test
  public void doReturn_usage() throws Exception {
    List<String> list = new ArrayList<String>();
    List<String> spy = spy(list);
    //impossible the real list.get(0) is called and fails
    //with IndexOutofBoundsException, as the list is empty
    when(spy.get(0)).thenReturn("not reachable");
  }
```

In the preceding code, the spy object calls a real method while trying to stub `get(index)`, and unlike the mock objects, the real method was called and it failed with an `ArrayIndexOutOfBounds` error.

The following screenshot displays the failure message:

```
     verify_zero_interaction (0.002 s)
     doReturn_usage (0.085 s)

≡ Failure Trace

  java.lang.IndexOutOfBoundsException: Index: 0, Size: 0
≡ at java.util.ArrayList.RangeCheck(Unknown Source)
≡ at java.util.ArrayList.get(Unknown Source)
≡ at com.packt.trading.StockBrokerTest.doReturn_usage(StockBrokerTest.java:195)
≡ at sun.reflect.NativeMethodAccessorImpl.invoke0(Native Method)
```

This can be protected using doReturn() as shown in the following code, but note that typically we don't mock lists or domain objects; this is just an example:

```
@Test public void doReturn_usage() throws Exception {
  List<String> list = new ArrayList<String>();
  List<String> spy = spy(list);

  //doReturn fixed the issue
  doReturn("now reachable").when(spy).get(0);
  assertEquals("now reachable", spy.get(0));
}
```

Capturing arguments with ArgumentCaptor

ArgumentCaptor is used to verify the arguments passed to a stubbed method. Sometimes, we compute a value, then create another object using the computed value, and then call a mock object using that new object. This computed value is not returned from the original method, but it is used for some other computation.

ArgumentCaptor provides an API to access objects that are instantiated within the method under the test.

The following code snippet explains the problem behind the inaccessibility of the method arguments:

```
public void buildPerson(String firstName, String lastName,
  String middleName, int age){
  Person person = new Person();
  person.setFirstName(firstName);
  person.setMiddleName(middleName);
  person.setLastName(lastName);
  person.setAge(age);
  this,personService.save(person);
}
```

We are passing a first name, middle name, last name, and an age to the `buildPerson` method. This method creates a `Person` object and sets the name and age to it. Finally, it invokes the `personService` class and saves the `person` object to a database.

Here, we cannot stub the `save` behavior of `personService` from a JUnit test with a specific value since the `Person` object is created inside the method. We can mock `save` using a generic matcher object such as `isA(Person.class)` and then verify whether the `Person` object contains the correct name and age using the argument captor.

Mockito verifies argument values in natural Java style by using an `equals()` method. This is also the recommended way of matching arguments because it makes tests clean and simple. In some situations though, it is necessary to assert on certain arguments after the actual verification.

The following code uses two `ArgumentCaptors` and verifies whether it uses a specific stock symbol, `A`, and not any other value while calling the method:

```
@Test
public void argument_captor() throws Exception {
  when(portfolio.getAvgPrice(isA(Stock.class))).thenReturn(
    new BigDecimal("10.00"));
  Stock aCorp = new Stock("A", "A Corp", new
    BigDecimal(11.20));
  when(marketWatcher.getQuote(anyString())).thenReturn(aCorp);
  broker.perform(portfolio, aCorp);

  ArgumentCaptor<String> stockIdCaptor =
    ArgumentCaptor.forClass(String.class);

  verify(marketWatcher).getQuote(stockIdCaptor.capture());
  assertEquals("A", stockIdCaptor.getValue());

  //Two arguments captured
  ArgumentCaptor<Stock>  stockCaptor =
    ArgumentCaptor.forClass(Stock.class);
  ArgumentCaptor<Integer> stockSellCountCaptor =
    ArgumentCaptor.forClass(Integer.class);

  verify(portfolio).sell(stockCaptor.capture(),
    stockSellCountCaptor.capture());
  assertEquals("A", stockCaptor.getValue().getSymbol());
  assertEquals(10, stockSellCountCaptor.getValue().intValue());
}
```

Check that `ArgumentCaptor` takes a `Class` type in the `forClass` method and then the captor is passed to the `verify` method to collect the argument details. The `sell` method takes two arguments, `Stock` and `Integer`. So, two `ArgumentCaptors` are created. The `stockCaptor` object captures the `Stock` argument and `stockSellCountCaptor` captures the stock quantity. Finally, the values are compared to verify whether the correct values were passed to the `sell` method.

Verifying the invocation order

Mockito facilitates verifying if interactions with a mock were performed in a given order using the `InOrder` API. It allows us to create `InOrder` of mocks and verify the call order of all calls of all mocks.

The following test sequentially invokes the `getAvgPrice`, `getCurrentValue`, `getQuote`, and `buy` methods, but verifies whether the `buy()` method is invoked before the `getAvgPrice()` method. So, the verification order is wrong and hence the test fails:

```
@Test public void inorder() throws Exception {
   Stock aCorp = new Stock("A", "A Corp",
     new BigDecimal(11.20));
   portfolio.getAvgPrice(aCorp);
   portfolio.getCurrentValue();
   marketWatcher.getQuote("X");
   portfolio.buy(aCorp);
   InOrder inOrder=inOrder(portfolio,marketWatcher);
   inOrder.verify(portfolio).buy(isA(Stock.class));
   inOrder.verify(portfolio).getAvgPrice(isA(Stock.class));
}
```

The following screenshot shows the error message output:

```
          inorder (0.018 s)
```

≡ Failure Trace

org.mockito.exceptions.verification.VerificationInOrderFailure:
Verification in order failure
Wanted but not invoked:
portfolio.getAvgPrice(
   isA(com.packt.trading.dto.Stock)
);
≡ -> at com.packt.trading.StockBrokerTest.inorder(StockBrokerTest.java:240)
Wanted anywhere AFTER following interaction:
portfolio.buy(
   com.packt.trading.dto.Stock@77158a
);
≡ -> at com.packt.trading.StockBrokerTest.inorder(StockBrokerTest.java:236)

Reordering the verification sequence, we fixed the test as follows:

```
@Test public void inorder() throws Exception {
  Stock aCorp = new Stock("A", "A Corp", new
    BigDecimal(11.20));
  portfolio.getAvgPrice(aCorp);
  portfolio.getCurrentValue();
  marketWatcher.getQuote("X");
  portfolio.buy(aCorp);

  InOrder inOrder=inOrder(portfolio,marketWatcher);
  inOrder.verify(portfolio).getAvgPrice(isA(Stock.class));
  inOrder.verify(portfolio).getCurrentValue();
  inOrder.verify(marketWatcher).getQuote(anyString());
  inOrder.verify(portfolio).buy(isA(Stock.class));
}
```

Changing the default settings

We learned that nonstubbed methods of a mock object return default values such as null for an object and false for a Boolean. However, Mockito allows us to change the default settings.

The following are the allowed settings:

- **RETURNS_DEFAULTS**: This is the default setting. It returns null for object, false for Boolean, and so on.
- **RETURNS_SMART_NULLS**: This returns spy of a given type.
- **RETURNS_MOCKS**: This returns mocks for objects and the default value for primitives.
- **RETURNS_DEEP_STUBS**: This returns a deep stub.
- **CALLS_REAL_METHODS**: This calls a real method.

The following example overrides the default Mockito settings and uses different return types:

```
@Test
  public void changing_default() throws Exception {
    Stock aCorp = new Stock("A", "A Corp", new
      BigDecimal(11.20));
    Portfolio pf = Mockito.mock(Portfolio.class);
    //default null is returned
    assertNull(pf.getAvgPrice(aCorp));
    Portfolio pf1 = Mockito.mock(Portfolio.class,
      Mockito.RETURNS_SMART_NULLS);
    //a smart null is returned
    System.out.println("#1 "+pf1.getAvgPrice(aCorp));
    assertNotNull(pf1.getAvgPrice(aCorp));

    Portfolio pf2 = Mockito.mock(Portfolio.class,
      Mockito.RETURNS_MOCKS);
    //a mock is returned
    System.out.println("#2 "+pf2.getAvgPrice(aCorp));
    assertNotNull(pf2.getAvgPrice(aCorp));

    Portfolio pf3 = Mockito.mock(Portfolio.class,
      Mockito.RETURNS_DEEP_STUBS);
    //a deep stubbed mock is returned
    System.out.println("#3 "+pf3.getAvgPrice(aCorp));
    assertNotNull(pf3.getAvgPrice(aCorp));
  }
```

The following screenshot shows the console output:

```
<terminated> StockBrokerTest [JUnit]
#1 SmartNull returned by this unstubbed method call on a mock:
portfolio.getAvgPrice(
    com.packt.trading.dto.Stock@18dfef8
);
#2 Mock for BigDecimal, hashCode: 2773808
#3 Mock for BigDecimal, hashCode: 14074220
```

Resetting mock objects

A static method reset (T...) enables resetting mock objects. The reset method should be handled with special care; if you need to reset a mock, you will most likely need another test.

A reset method clears the stubs.

The following code snippet stubs the getAvgPrice method to return a value, but reset clears the stub; after reset, the getAvgPrice method returns NULL:

```
@Test
public void resetMock() throws Exception {
   Stock aCorp = new Stock("A", "A Corp", new BigDecimal(11.20));

   Portfolio portfolio = Mockito.mock(Portfolio.class);
   when(portfolio.getAvgPrice(eq(aCorp))).
      thenReturn(BigDecimal.ONE);
   assertNotNull(portfolio.getAvgPrice(aCorp));

   Mockito.reset(portfolio);
   //Resets the stub, so getAvgPrice returns NULL
   assertNull(portfolio.getAvgPrice(aCorp));
}
```

Exploring Mockito annotations

We learned that Mockito supports the @Mock annotation for mocking. Just like @Mock, Mockito supports the following three useful annotations:

- @Captor: This simplifies the creation of ArgumentCaptor, which is useful when the argument to capture is a super generic class, such as List<Map<String,Set<String>>.

- @Spy: This creates a spy of a given object. Use it instead of spy (object).

- @InjectMocks: This injects mock or spy fields into the tested object automatically using a constructor injection, setter injection, or field injection.

Working with inline stubbing

Mockito allows us to create mocks while stubbing it. Basically, it allows creating a stub in one line of code. This can be helpful to keep the test code clean.

For example, some stubs can be created and stubbed at field initialization in a test. We use the Stock objects in almost all tests. We can create a global mock Stock and stub it at definition, as shown in the following code snippet:

```
Stock globalStock =  when(Mockito.mock(Stock.class).getPrice()).
  thenReturn(BigDecimal.ONE).getMock();

@Test
public void access_global_mock() throws Exception {
  assertEquals(BigDecimal.ONE, globalStock.getPrice());
}
```

Determining mocking details

Mockito.mockingDetails identifies whether a particular object is a mock or a spy, as follows:

```
@Test
public void mocking_details() throws Exception {
  Portfolio pf1 = Mockito.mock(Portfolio.class,
    Mockito.RETURNS_MOCKS);

  BigDecimal result = pf1.getAvgPrice(globalStock);
  assertNotNull(result);
  assertTrue(Mockito.mockingDetails(pf1).isMock());
```

```
Stock myStock = new Stock(null, null, null);
Stock spy = spy(myStock);
assertTrue(Mockito.mockingDetails(spy).isSpy());

}
```

Behavior-driven development with Mockito

BDD is a software engineering process based on TDD. BDD combines the best practices of TDD, **domain-driven development (DDD)**, and **object-oriented programming (OOP)**.

In an agile team, scoping a feature is a mammoth task. The business stakeholders talk about business interests, and the development team talks about technical challenges. BDD provides a universal language that allows useful communication and feedback between the stakeholders.

Dan North developed BDD, created the **JBehave** framework for BDD, and proposed the following best practices:

- Unit test names should start with the word *should* and *should* be written in the order of the business value

- **Acceptance tests (AT)** should be written in a user story manner, such as "As a (role) I want (feature) so that (benefit)"

- Acceptance criteria should be written in terms of scenarios and implemented as "Given (initial context), when (event occurs), then (ensure some outcomes)"

Let's write a user story for our stock broker simulation:

Story: A stock is sold

> **In order** to maximize profit
>
> **As a** Stock broker
>
> **I want** to sell a stock **when** the price goes up by 10 percent

The following is a scenario example:

Scenario: 10 percent increase in stock price should sell the stock in the market

> **Given** a customer previously bought FB stocks at $10.00 per share
>
> **And** he currently has 10 shares left in his portfolio
>
> **When** the FB stock price becomes $11.00

Then I should sell all the FB stocks and the portfolio should have zero FB stocks

Mockito supports the BDD style of writing tests using the given-when-then syntax.

Writing tests in BDD style

In BDD, given represents the initial context and when represents the event or condition. However, Mockito already has a when style of (initial context definition) method stubbing; therefore, when doesn't go well with BDD. Thus, the BDDMockito class introduces an alias so that we can stub method calls with the given(object) method.

The following JUnit test is implemented in BDD style:

```
@RunWith(MockitoJUnitRunner.class)
public class StockBrokerBDDTest {
   @Mock MarketWatcher marketWatcher;
   @Mock Portfolio portfolio;

   StockBroker broker;

   @Before public void setUp() {
      broker = new StockBroker(marketWatcher);
   }

   @Test
   public void
      should_sell_a_stock_when_price_increases_by_ten_percent(){
      Stock aCorp = new Stock("FB", "FaceBook", new
         BigDecimal(11.20));
      //Given a customer previously bought 10 'FB' stocks at
      //$10.00/per share
      given(portfolio.getAvgPrice(isA(Stock.class))).
         willReturn(new BigDecimal("10.00"));

      given(marketWatcher.getQuote(eq("FB"))).
         willReturn(aCorp);

      //when the 'FB' stock price becomes $11.00
      broker.perform(portfolio, aCorp);

      //then the 'FB' stocks are sold
      verify(portfolio).sell(aCorp,10);
   }
}
```

Note that the test name starts with a `should` statement. The `given` syntax of `Mockito` is used to set the initial context that the portfolio already has `FB` stocks bought at $10.00 per share and the current `FB` stock price is $11.00 per share.

The following screenshot shows the test execution output:

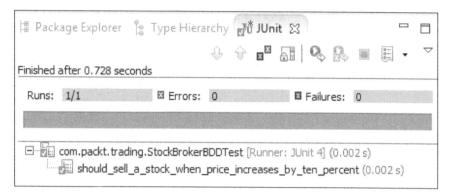

The BDD syntax

The following methods are used in conjunction with `given`:

- `willReturn`(a value to be returned): This returns a given value

- `willThrow`(a throwable to be thrown): This throws a given exception

- `will`(Answer answer) and `willAnswer`(Answer answer): This is similar to `then`(answer) and `thenAnswer`(answer)

- `willCallRealMethod()`: This calls the real method on the mock object or spy

The `jMock` and `EasyMock` frameworks are the other two Java-based unit testing frameworks that support mocking for automated unit tests.

The `jMock` and `EasyMock` frameworks provide mocking capabilities, but the syntax is not as simple as Mockito. You can visit the following URLs to explore the frameworks:

- `http://jmock.org/`
- `http://easymock.org/`

To learn more about BDD and JBehave, visit `http://jbehave.org/`.

Summary

In this chapter, Mockito is described in detail and technical examples are provided to demonstrate the capability of Mockito.

By the end of this chapter, you will be able to use advanced features of the Mockito framework, and start BDD with Mockito.

The next chapter will explain the importance of code coverage, line and branch coverage, how to measure code coverage, Eclipse plugins, setting up Cobertura, and generating coverage report using Ant, Gradle, and Maven.

5
Exploring Code Coverage

This chapter explains the code coverage, coverage tools, and provides step-by-step guidance to generate a coverage report.

The following topics are covered in this chapter:

- Code, branch, and line coverage
- Coverage tools such as Clover, Cobertura, EclEmma, and JaCoCo
- Measuring coverage using Eclipse plugins
- Using Ant, Maven, and Gradle to generate reports

Understanding code coverage

Code coverage is a measurement of percentage of instructions of code being executed while the automated tests are running.

A piece of code with high code coverage implies that the code has been thoroughly unit tested and has a lower chance of containing bugs than code with a low code coverage. You should concentrate on writing meaningful (business logic) unit tests and not on having 100 percent coverage because it's easy to cheat and have 100 percent coverage with completely useless tests.

Numerous metrics can be used to measure the code coverage. The following are the ones that are widely used:

- **Statement or line coverage**: This measures the statements or lines being covered
- **Branch coverage**: This measures the percentage of each branch of each control structure, such as the if else and switch case statements
- **Function or method coverage**: This measures the function execution

The following Java code will elucidate the metrics.

An `absSum` method takes two integer arguments and then returns the absolute sum of the two arguments. An `Integer` type can hold a NULL value, so the method checks for NULL. If both arguments are NULL, then the method returns 0 as given in the following code:

```java
public class Metrics {
  public int absSum(Integer op1, Integer op2) {
    if (op1 == null && op2 == null) {
      return 0;
    }
    if (op1 == null && op2 != null) {
      return Math.abs(op2);
    }
    if (op2 == null) {
      return Math.abs(op1);
    }
    return Math.abs(op1)+Math.abs(op2);
  }
}
```

This example has 10 branches: the first `if(op1 == null && op2 == null)` statement has four branches: `op1 == null`, `op1!= null`, `op2 == null`, and `op2 != null`. Similarly, the second `if` statement has four branches and the last `if (op2 == null)` statement has two branches, `op2== null` and `op2 != null`.

If a test passes two non-null integers to the `absSum` method, then it covers four lines, that is, three `if` statements and the final `return` statement, but the first three `return` statements remain uncovered. It covers three out of ten branches; the first `if` statement covers one out of four branches, that is, `op1 == null`. Similarly, the second `if` statement covers one branch out of four branches, and the last `if` statement covers one branch out of two branches `op2 != null`. So, the branch coverage becomes 30 percent.

To cover all instructions and all branches, the following four input pairs need to be passed to the method: `[null, null]`, `[null, value]`, `[value, null]`, and `[value, value]`.

Learning the inner details of code instrumentation

Coverage is measured by the ratio of basic code branches or instructions that were exercised by some tests to the total number of instructions or branches available in the system under test.

The ratio is measured in a series of steps. First, in a copy of source code, each block of statement is instrumented with an accumulator flag. Then, the tests run on the instrumented code and update the flags. Finally, a program collects the accumulator flags and measures the ratio of the flags turned on versus the total number of flags. Bytecode can be changed on the fly or during compilation. This is actually what test coverage frameworks do under the covers.

Two code instrumentation options are available: source code instrumentation and object code instrumentation. Object code instrumentation modifies the generated bytecode, so it is hard to implement.

The preceding code coverage example has seven lines, but if we expand the branches into lines, then it will result in 14 lines. If a coverage tool needs to instrument the code, then it will modify the source code and initialize an array of length 14 with 0 and set 1 when a line is executed while a test is being run. The following example demonstrates the source code instrumentation:

```java
int[] visitedLines = new int[14];
public int absSumModified(Integer op1 , Integer op2) {
  visitedLines[0] = 1;
  if(op1 == null) {
    visitedLines[1] = 1;
    if(op2 == null) {
      visitedLines[2] = 1;
      return 0;
    }else {
      visitedLines[3] = 1;
    }
  }else {
    visitedLines[4] = 1;
  }

  visitedLines[5] = 1;
  if(op1 == null) {
    visitedLines[6] = 1;
    if(op2 != null) {
      visitedLines[7] = 1;
      return Math.abs(op2);
    }else {
      visitedLines[8] = 1;
    }
  }else {
    visitedLines[9] = 1;
  }
```

```
    visitedLines[10] = 1;
    if(op2 == null) {
      visitedLines[11] = 1;
      return Math.abs(op1);
    }else {
      visitedLines[12] = 1;
    }
    visitedLines[13] = 1;
    return Math.abs(op1)+Math.abs(op2);
  }}
```

After test execution, the coverage tool checks the visitedLines array and computes the ratio of all lines that have visitedLines[index] equal to 1 versus the total number of lines. If we test the method with the input sets [null, null] and [value, value], then the five lines (lines 4, 7, 8, 9, and 12) remain uncovered. To cover 100 percent, we need to test the method with four possible combinations of null and non-null integers.

Configuring the Eclipse plugin

We learned that the coverage tools can either instrument the object code or source code. Java code coverage tools can be categorized into two sections: tools that instrument the source code and tools that instrument the bytecode.

Source code instrumentation is easier but requires source code recompilation. Bytecode instrumentation is complex but doesn't require source code recompilation.

The following are the available Java code coverage tools:

- **Cobertura**: This tool instruments the bytecode offline and is a widely used coverage tool. Cobertura is an open source project (GNU GPL) and is very easy to configure with Eclipse and build tools. Version 1.9, which was released in March 2010, is the latest stable version.

- **EMMA**: This tool instruments the bytecode offline or on the fly and is distributed under the **Common Public License** (CPL). Version 2.1, released in June 2005, is the latest version. **Google CodePro AnalytiX** is based on EMMA.

- **Clover**: This tool instruments the source code and comes with a proprietary Atlassian license, and the latest stable version, 3.2, was released in February 2014.

- **JaCoCo**: This tool is distributed under **Eclipse Public License** (**EPL**). JaCoCo instruments the bytecode on the fly while running the code. The latest stable version, 0.6.4, was released in December 2013. JaCoCo was a replacement of EMMA. EclEmma is a JaCoCo-based Eclipse plugin.

The following section will explore the Eclipse plugins based on the preceding Java-based coverage tools.

Uncovering the Clover plugin

A trial version of the Clover plugin can be installed for a month. You can refer to the installation instruction at `https://confluence.atlassian.com/display/CLOVER/`. The Clover Eclipse plugin supports the site update and manual download installation.

The following are the steps to install and execute the Clover plugin:

1. During installation, Clover shows a list of installable elements. Expand the **Clover** blind and select **Clover 3** and **Clover 3 Ant Support**. The following screenshot displays the details:

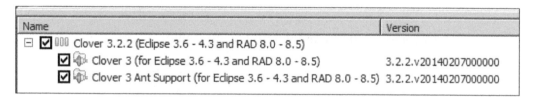

2. Open the **Show View** menu and select all **Clover** views. The following screenshot displays the **Clover** views:

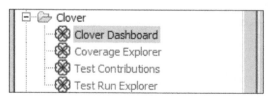

3. Create a new Java project named Chapter05 and add the Metrics.java and MetricsTest.java Java files as designed in the preceding section. Open Clover's **Coverage Explorer** and click on the **Enable or disable Clover on one or more project** button. The following screenshot shows the button details:

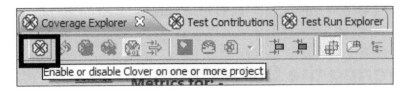

4. Select the Chapter05 project. Clover will enable the source code instrumentation on this project. Right-click on the MetricsTest file and go to **Run With Clover As | JUnit Test**. The following screenshot shows the pop-up menu:

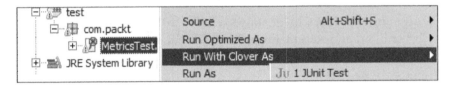

5. Open **Coverage Explorer** and it will show the following coverage output:

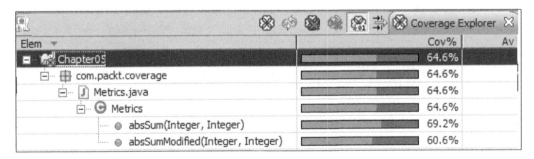

6. Open **Clover Dashboard**. The dashboard will show you the coverage details, test results, complexity, and the least-tested methods. The following screenshot shows the dashboard details:

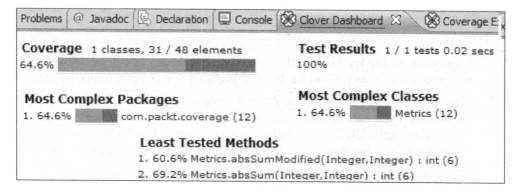

7. Open the source code. The clover plugin decorates the source code; the uncovered lines become red and the covered lines become green. It also shows the execution count against each line. The following is the instrumented source code output:

```
2     public int absSum(Integer op1, Integer op2) {
2         if (op1 == null && op2 == null) {
0             return 0;
2         }
2
2         if (op1 == null && op2 != null) {
1             return Math.abs(op2);
2         }
2
1         if (op2 == null) {
0             return Math.abs(op1);
1         }
```

Working with the EclEmma plugin

EclEmma Version 2.0 is based on the JaCoCo code coverage library. Follow the instructions at http://www.eclemma.org/index.html to install the EclEmma Eclipse plugin. Like Clover, EclEmma supports site update and its manual download.

Once EclEmma is installed, follow the steps to configure and execute tests using EclEmma:

1. Right-click on the test class and go to **Coverage As | 1 JUnit Test**. This will instrument the bytecode on the fly and bring up the coverage report.

2. After EclEmma installation, a new menu button appears under the main menu panel. When you expand this menu, it shows the JUnit tests that have been executed recently. Click on the menu button to generate the coverage report. The following screenshot shows the EclEmma code coverage menu button:

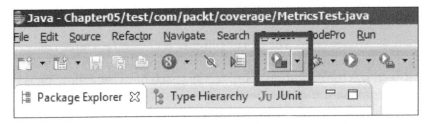

3. When you open the **Coverage** tab, it shows the coverage details. The following screenshot shows the output:

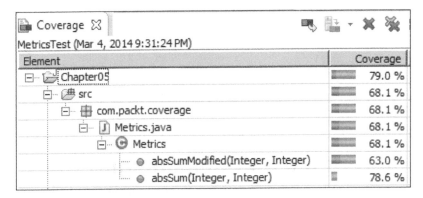

4. The branch coverage report is more prominent in EclEmma. The following screenshot shows the coverage details:

```
if(op1 == null) {
    visitedLine[1] = 1;
    if(op2 == null) {


    if(op2 != null) {
```

A green diamond signifies that the branch is 100 percent covered, a red diamond signifies the branch is not covered, and a yellow diamond signifies that the branch is partially covered.

Examining the eCobertura plugin

eCobertura is a Cobertura-based Eclipse plugin. eCobertura shows the branch coverage in a tabular format. To install the eCobertura plugin, go to `https://marketplace.eclipse.org/content/ecobertura#.UxYBmoVh85w` and drag the **Install** button to your Eclipse workspace that is running. Eclipse will automatically install the plugin for you. The following screenshot shows the Marketplace **Install** button:

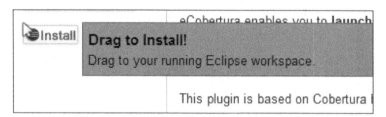

After installation, a new menu button appears under the menu panel for Cobertura, as shown in the following screenshot:

The following are the steps to measure code coverage using eCobertura:

1. Go to **Show View | Other,** and select the **Coverage Session View** option under **eCobertura**.
2. Execute the test and then click on the Cobertura menu button, or from the dropdown, select the test you want to measure.

3. Open the **Coverage Session View** tab. This will show you the following output:

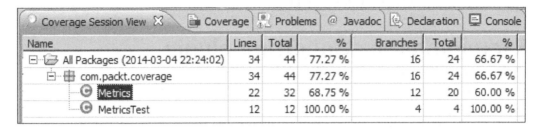

Name	Lines	Total	%	Branches	Total	%
All Packages (2014-03-04 22:24:02)	34	44	77.27 %	16	24	66.67 %
com.packt.coverage	34	44	77.27 %	16	24	66.67 %
Metrics	22	32	68.75 %	12	20	60.00 %
MetricsTest	12	12	100.00 %	4	4	100.00 %

Note that the branch coverage is 60 percent. In the preceding section, we measured 10 branches. Using our custom coverage program, we measured that 4 out of 10 branches were covered. It proves that our custom code coverage program works fine.

Measuring coverage using Gradle

Gradle can be configured to generate coverage reports using JaCoCo. This section will explain how to configure the Gradle JaCoCo plugin in your project.

The following are the steps to configure the Gradle plugin:

1. Create a base folder named Chapter05 under any directory, such as D:/Packt; then, add a lib folder under Chapter05 and copy the JUnit4 and hamcrest JARs to the lib folder. Add another folder named Chapter05 under the base folder Chapter05 for the Java project. As per Gradle conventions, source files are kept under src/main/java and test files are kept under src/test/java. Create the directories under Chapter05\Chapter05.

This Chapter05 naming strategy is used for you to easily track the project and download the code from the Packt Publishing website, but your code should express the intent of the code. The name Chapter05 doesn't make any sense, maybe you can name it something like SimpleGradleProject or GradleCoverageProject.

2. Copy the content of the Eclipse project and the `Metrics` and `MetricsTest` Java files that we created in the *Uncovering the Clover plugin* section to the new directory. Copy the content of the `src` folder to `src/main/java` and the `test` folder to `src/test/java` (as per Gradle conventions).

3. Create a `build.gradle` file directly under `Chapter05\Chapter05`, and add the following code snippet to the file to enable the JaCoCo coverage:

```
apply plugin: 'java'
apply plugin: "jacoco"
repositories {
    flatDir(dir: '../lib', name: 'JUnit Library')
    mavenCentral()
}
dependencies {
    testCompile'junit:junit:4.11', ':hamcrest-core:1.3'}
    jacocoTestReport {
      reports {
        xml.enabled false
        csv.enabled false
        html.destination "${buildDir}/jacocoHtml"
      }
    }
}
```

4. The jaCoCo plugin adds a new task, `jacocoTestReport`. To execute the `jacocoTestReport` task, a `mavenCentral()` repository dependency needs to be added to the `repositories` closure. Gradle downloads the required jaCoCo JARs from the `mavenCentral` repository.

5. Open the command prompt, go to the `Chapter05\Chapter05` directory, and run the `gradle jacocoTestReport` command. This will download the JAR files and generate the coverage report. The following screenshot shows the console output:

```
D:\Packt\Chapter05\Chapter05>gradle jacocoTestReport
:compileJava UP-TO-DATE
:processResources UP-TO-DATE
:classes UP-TO-DATE
:jacocoTestReport
Download http://repo1.maven.org/maven2/org/jacoco/org.
Download http://repo1.maven.org/maven2/org/jacoco/org.
```

6. Open `Chapter05\Chapter05\build\jacocoHtml` and launch the `index.html` file. The following is the JaCoCo coverage report output:

Element	Missed Instructions	Cov.	Missed Branches	Cov.	Missed
☉ Metrics		68%		60%	7
Total	43 of 135	68%	8 of 20	60%	7

▤ Chapter05 > ⊞ com.packt.coverage

com.packt.coverage

Working with the Maven Cobertura plugin

Maven has a Cobertura plugin to measure code coverage; this section will explain how to configure the Cobertura Maven plugin in your project.

Cobertura uses `asm` to instrument the bytecode. The `asm` framework is a Java bytecode manipulation and analysis framework. Visit `http://asm.ow2.org/` for `asm` details. Cobertura modifies the `.class` file, imports `net.sourceforge.cobertura.coveragedata.*`, implements the `HasBeenInstrumented` interface, and adds code to capture coverage, such as `ProjectData.getGlobalProjectData().getOrCreateClassData("com.packt.coverage.Metrics").touch(21);`.

After instrumenting the bytecode, Cobertura creates a `.ser` file and updates the file during test execution. This `.ser` file contains the test coverage details. The instrumented bytecode can be slightly slower than normal without it.

Follow the ensuing steps to configure Maven to generate a Cobertura report:

1. Create a `pom.xml` file and place it under `/Chapter05/Chapter05`.

2. Modify the `pom.xml` file to add the project details as follows:

```
<project xmlns="http://maven.apache.org/POM/4.0.0"
  xmlns:xsi="http://www.w3.org/2001/XMLSchema-instance"
  xsi:schemaLocation="http://maven.apache.org/POM/4.0.0
    http://maven.apache.org/xsd/maven-4.0.0.xsd">
<modelVersion>4.0.0</modelVersion>

<groupId>org.packt</groupId>
<artifactId>Chapter05</artifactId>
```

```
<version>1.0-SNAPSHOT</version>
<packaging>jar</packaging>

<name>Chapter05</name>
<url>http://maven.apache.org</url>
```

3. Add the Cobertura plugin details as follows:

```
<build>
  <plugins>
    <plugin>
      <groupId>org.codehaus.mojo</groupId>
      <artifactId>cobertura-maven-plugin</artifactId>
      <version>2.2</version>
      <configuration>
        <formats>
          <format>html</format>
          <format>xml</format>
        </formats>
      </configuration>
      <executions>
        <execution>
          <phase>package</phase>
          <goals>
            <goal>cobertura</goal>
          </goals>
        </execution>
      </executions>
    </plugin>
  </plugins>
</build>
```

4. Open the command prompt, change the directory to /Chapter05/Chapter05, and issue the mvn cobertura:cobertura command. This will start downloading Cobertura plugin files and start instrumenting the .class files. The following screenshot portrays the Maven console output:

```
[INFO] --- cobertura-maven-plugin:2.2:cobertura (default-cli) @ Chapter05
[INFO] Cobertura 1.9 - GNU GPL License (NO WARRANTY) - See COPYRIGHT file
Cobertura: Loaded information on 1 classes.
Report time: 187ms
[INFO] Cobertura Report generation was successful.
[INFO] Cobertura 1.9 - GNU GPL License (NO WARRANTY) - See COPYRIGHT file
Cobertura: Loaded information on 1 classes.
Report time: 117ms
[INFO] Cobertura Report generation was successful.
[INFO] -----------------------------------------------------------------------
```

5. Open `/Chapter05/Chapter05/target`. The `target` folder contains the following important subfolders:

   ○ `cobertura`: This contains the `cobertura.ser` file

   ○ `generated-classes`: This contains the instrumented bytecode or the `.class` files

   ○ `site`: This contains the coverage report in XML and HTML formats

   ○ `surefire-reports`: This contains the test execution report

The following screenshot shows the coverage report generated in the HTML format in the `site` folder:

Coverage Report - com.packt.coverage

Package	# Classes	Line Coverage		Branch Coverage		Complexity
com.packt.coverage	1	69%	22/32	60%	12/20	8

Classes in this Package	Line Coverage		Branch Coverage		Complexity
Metrics	69%	22/32	60%	12/20	8

Report generated by Cobertura 1.9 on 3/5/14 11:28 PM.

Running the Cobertura Ant task

This section will explain how to configure the Cobertura Ant task in your project.

The following are the steps for configuration:

1. Gradle and Maven can download the coverage tool JARs while running the build, but Ant needs the Cobertura JAR files to the classpath. Download the Cobertura ZIP file from `http://cobertura.github.io/cobertura/`.

2. Extract the ZIP file and copy all JAR files in the downloaded ZIP to `Chapter05\lib`. Include all JARs from the `lib` folder and `cobertura.jar` from the `root` folder.

3. Create a `build.properties` file under `Chapter05\Chapter05` and enter the following information:

```
src.dir=src/main/java
test.dir=src/test/java
# The path to cobertura.jar
cobertura.dir=../lib
classes.dir=classes
```

```
instrumented.dir=instrumented
reports.dir=reports
# Unit test reports from JUnit are deposited into this
  directory
reports.xml.dir=${reports.dir}/junit-xml
reports.html.dir=${reports.dir}/junit-html
coverage.xml.dir=${reports.dir}/cobertura-xml
coverage.summaryxml.dir=${reports.dir}/cobertura-summary-xml
coverage.html.dir=${reports.dir}/cobertura-html
```

The `src.dir` attribute represents the source folder location and `test.dir` represents the test file location. The `cobertura.dir` attribute refers to the Cobertura library or JAR files. The coverage tool needs to access the Cobertura library files. The other entries are required for report generation and bytecode instrumentation.

4. Create a `build.xml` file under `Chapter05\Chapter05`, and add targets for Cobertura instrumentation and JUnit test to update the `.ser` file and generate the report. Download the `build.xml` file from the Packt Publishing website (the `Chapter05` code). The important targets are `init`, `compile`, `testcompile`, `instrument`, `test`, `coverage-report`, `summary-coverage-report`, `alternate-coverage-report`, and `clean`.

5. Open the command prompt, change the directory to `Chapter05\Chapter05`, and issue the `ant` command. This will generate the report. The following is the console output of the command:

```
D:\Packt\Chapter05\Chapter05>ant
Buildfile: build.xml

instrument:
    [delete] Deleting: D:\Packt\Chapter05\Chapter05\cobertura.ser
    [delete] Deleting directory D:\Packt\Chapter05\Chapter05\instrum
[cobertura-instrument] Cobertura null - GNU GPL License (NO WARRANT
[cobertura-instrument] Mar 06, 2014 10:24:53 PM net.sourceforge.cob
[cobertura-instrument] INFO: Cobertura: Saved information on 1 clas
test:
[junitreport] Processing D:\Packt\Chapter05\Chapter05\reports\junit
[junitreport] Loading stylesheet jar:file:/D:/Software/apache-ant-1
```

Cobertura generates the report in `Chapter05\Chapter05\reports`. The `reports` folder contains various reports in XML and HTML formats.

> Code coverage is not a silver bullet that can deliver zero-defect software! The most important thing is writing effective tests and unit testing the logic. Writing tests for getters and setters or constructor doesn't add value.

Summary

In this chapter, code coverage is described in depth and examples are provided to measure code coverage using Eclipse plugins and various coverage tools, such as Clover, JaCoCo, EclEmma, and Cobertura. We have also configured Ant, Maven, and Gradle to generate code coverage reports using coverage tools.

By the end of this chapter, you should be able configure Eclipse plugins and build scripts to measure code coverage.

The next chapter covers the static code analysis, code metrics, and various open source tools. It configures and uses PMD, Checkstyle, and FindBugs to analyze code quality and explores the Sonar code quality dashboard.

6
Revealing Code Quality

"Testing by itself does not improve software quality. Test results are an indicator of quality, but in and of themselves, they don't improve it. Trying to improve software quality by increasing the amount of testing is like trying to lose weight by weighing yourself more often. What you eat before you step onto the scale determines how much you will weigh, and the software development techniques you use determine how many errors testing will find. If you want to lose weight, don't buy a new scale; change your diet. If you want to improve your software, don't test more; develop better."

— Steve McConnell

A poorly developed system generates more bugs than a well-designed system. Manual testing can identify software bugs but cannot improve the quality of the system; however, TDD and JUnit tests are considered as automated unit testing frameworks, and they indeed help in improving the quality of the system. Static code quality analysis exposes quality issues in the code and provides suggestions for improvement, and continuous health monitoring keeps the system healthy.

The following topics will be covered in this chapter:

- Code quality metrics
- Static code analysis using PMD, Checkstyle, and FindBugs
- The SonarQube dashboard
- The SonarQube runner
- Code quality analysis using Ant, Maven, and Gradle

Understanding the static code analysis

Static code analysis is the process of analyzing code without executing it. Code review is also a sort of static code analysis but is performed with humans or team members. Generally, static code analysis is performed by an automated tool.

Usually, a static analysis includes the following metrics:

- Violation of coding best practices such as long method body, long parameter list, large classes, and variable names.

- Cohesion represents responsibility of a single module (class). If a module or class possesses too many responsibilities, such as tax calculation, sending e-mails, and formatting user inputs, the class or module is less cohesive. Performing multiple dissimilar tasks introduces complexity and maintainability issues. High cohesion means performing only a particular type of task.

  Suppose a person is assigned to handle customer tickets, code new features, design the architecture, organize the annual office party, and so on; this person will be over occupied and is bound to make mistakes. It will be very difficult for him or her to manage all the responsibilities.

  In refactoring terms, if a class performs too many tasks, the class is called a GOD object or class.

- Coupling measures the dependency on other modules or code. Low dependency enforces high cohesion. If module C depends on two other modules, A and B, any change in the APIs of A or B will force C to change.

  Event-driven architecture is an example of loose coupling. In an event-driven system when something changes, an event is published to a destination without any knowledge of who will process the event; the event consumers consume the event and take action(s). This decouples the event publisher from the event consumers. So, any change in the consumer doesn't force the publisher to change.

- Cyclomatic complexity measures the complexity of a program. In 1976, Thomas J. McCabe, Sr. developed cyclomatic complexity. It measures the number of linearly independent paths in a program. This is not restricted to a program-level complexity, but it can also be applied to individual functions, modules, methods, or classes within a program.

Cyclomatic complexity of a program is defined with a control flow graph of the program. Complexity is represented as $M = E-N+2P$, where M is complexity, E is the number of edges of the graph, N is the number of nodes of the graph, and P is the number of connected components. Any method with a complexity greater than 10 has a serious problem.

A method that has no conditional statements has a cyclomatic complexity of 1. The following diagram represents the directed graph and complexity:

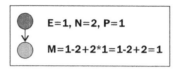

A method with a single condition (an IF) or a single loop (a FOR) has a complexity of 2. The following diagram explains the calculation:

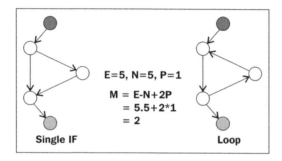

The following is the corresponding code:

```
public void trim(String input){
    if(input != null){
       return input.trim();
    }
    return null;
}
```

Various automated tools are available for static code analysis. In addition, the built-in Eclipse compiler can already perform a lot of static code analysis. The following are the widely used ones:

- **Checkstyle**: This tool performs static code analysis, and it can also be used to show violations of a configured coding standard. It comes under a GNU General Public License. You can check it out at the following link: http://checkstyle.sourceforge.net.

- **FindBugs**: This is an open source static bytecode analyzer for potential Java errors. Plugins are available for Eclipse, NetBeans, and IntelliJ IDEA. It comes under a GNU General Public License. FindBugs can be configured with Jenkins. The following is the link for the FindBugs website: `http://findbugs.sourceforge.net`.

- **PMD**: This is a static ruleset based on the Java source code analyzer that identifies potential problems. PMD has an Eclipse plugin that shows an error icon in the editor, but PMD errors are not true errors; rather, they're the result of inefficient code.

In the next section, we will examine the static analysis tools.

Working with the Checkstyle plugin

This section covers the Checkstyle static analysis tool and how to configure Eclipse with Checkstyle. Checkstyle verifies the following rules:

- Missing Javadoc comments
- The use of magic numbers
- Naming conventions of variables and methods
- Method's argument length and line lengths
- The use of imports
- The spaces between some characters
- The good practices of class construction
- Duplicated code

The Checkstyle plugin can be downloaded from `http://sourceforge.net/projects/eclipse-cs/`, or you can install it through Eclipse Marketplace. Just search for Checkstyle.

Perform the following steps to configure the Checkstyle Eclipse plugin:

1. Click on the **Install New Software** menu; Eclipse will open a new wizard.
2. Click on the **Add** button and a new **Add Repository** pop up will appear.
3. Click on the **Archive...** button and browse to the downloaded ZIP file's location.
4. Select defaults, finish installation, and restart Eclipse.

The following screenshot shows the Checkstyle components to be installed:

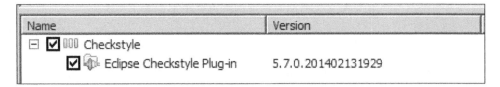

Now that installation has finished, it's time to examine the Checkstyle capabilities. Create a Java project named `CodeQualityChapter06` (create a `chapter06` folder under a directory named `packt` and save the project in `\Packt\chapter06`), add a Java class named `Calculator.java`, and add the following code snippet to `Calculator.java`:

```java
package com.packt.code.quality;
public class Calculator<T extends Number> {
  public String add(T... numbers) {
    T result = null;
    int x =0;
    for(T t:numbers) { x++;
      if(result == null) {
        if(t instanceof Integer) {
          result = (T) new Integer("0");
        }else if(t instanceof Short) {
          result = (T) new Short("0");
        }else if(t instanceof Long) {
          result = (T) new Long("0");
        }else if(t instanceof Float) {
          result = (T) new Float("0.0");
        }else if(t instanceof Double) {
          result = (T) new Double("0.0");
        }
      }
      if(t instanceof Integer) {
        Integer val = ((Integer)result + (Integer)t);
        result =(T)val;
      }else if(t instanceof Short) {
        Short val = (short) ((Short)result + (Short)t);
        result =(T)val;
      }else if(t instanceof Long) {
        Long val =  ((Long)result + (Long)t);
        result =(T)val;
      }else if(t instanceof Float) {
        Float val =  ((Float)result + (Float)t);
```

```
        result =(T)val;
      }else if(t instanceof Double) {
        Double val =  ((Double)result + (Double)t);
        result =(T)val;
      }
      if(x == 1045) {
        System.out.println("warning !!!");
      }
    }
    return result.toString();
  } }
```

This class, `Calculator.java`, calculates the sum of a list of numbers. It's a generic class; we can calculate the sum of integers or doubles or any number.

Right-click on `CodeQualityChapter06` and enable **Checkstyle**. The following screenshot displays the Checkstyle pop-up menu:

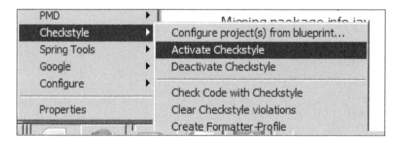

This action will trigger the Checkstyle validation. It will open the **Checks** tab (if the **Checks** tab is not opened automatically, then open the view from the show views menu) and show a graphical view of violations. The following screenshot displays the graphical violation pie chart:

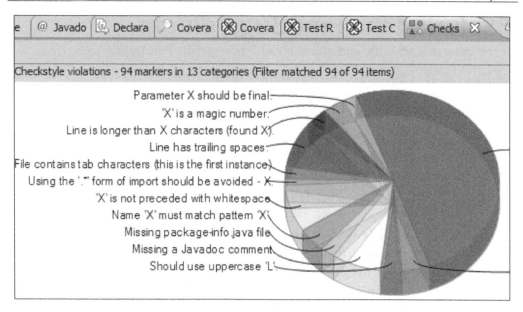

Another view shows the violations in a tabular format. The following screenshot displays the violations in a tabular format:

Overview of Checkstyle violations - 94 markers in 13 categories (Filter matched 94 of 94 items)	
Checkstyle violation type	Marker count
⚠ File contains tab characters (this is the first instance).	2
⚠ Parameter X should be final.	2
⚠ Should use uppercase 'L'.	3
⚠ Line is longer than X characters (found X).	3
⚠ 'X' is a magic number.	3
⚠ Method 'X' is not designed for extension - needs to be abstract, final or empty.	4
⚠ Name 'X' must match pattern 'X'.	4
⚠ Missing a Javadoc comment.	7
⚠ 'X' is not preceded with whitespace.	8
⚠ Line has trailing spaces.	8
⚠ 'X' is not followed by whitespace.	47

Exploring the FindBugs plugin

This section describes the configuration and usage of the FindBugs plugin.

FindBugs works with three types of errors. You can visit `http://findbugs.sourceforge.net/bugDescriptions.html` for the FindBugs error details. The following are the FindBugs-supported error categories and errors:

- **Correctness bug:** This is an apparent coding mistake that results in code that was probably not what the developer intended; for example, a method ignores the return value of a self-assigned field. The following are a few examples of a correctness bug:

    ○ The class defines `tostring()` but it should be `toString()`

    ○ A value is checked here to see whether it is null, but this value can't be null because it was previously dereferenced, and if it were null, a null pointer exception would have occurred at the earlier dereference

    ○ The method in the subclass doesn't override a similar method in a superclass because the type of a parameter doesn't exactly match the type of the corresponding parameter in the superclass

    ○ Class defines `equal(Object)` but it should be `equals(Object)`

- **Bad practice:** This includes violations of recommended best practices and essential coding practice. The following are the examples of bad practices:

    ○ **Hash code and equals problems**:

        ○ Class defines `hashCode()` but it should be `equals()` and `hashCode()`

        ○ Class defines `equals()` but it should be `hashCode()`

        ○ Class defines `hashCode()` and uses `Object.equals()`

        ○ Class defines `equals()` and uses `Object.hashCode()`

    ○ **Cloneable idiom**:

        ○ Class defines `clone()` but doesn't implement `Cloneable`

    ○ **Serializable problems**:

        ○ Class is `Serializable`, but doesn't define `serialVersionUID`

        ○ Comparator doesn't implement `Serializable`

        ○ Non serializable class has a `serializable` inner class

○ **Dropped exceptions**: Here, an exception is created and dropped rather than thrown, such as the following example, where the exception was created but not thrown:

```
if (x < 0)
    new IllegalArgumentException("x must be nonnegative");
```

○ **Misuse of finalize**:

  ○ Explicit invocation of finalize

  ○ Finalizer does not call the superclass finalizer

- **Dodgy errors**: This kind of code is confusing, anomalous, or written in a way that leads to errors. Examples include the following:

  ○ **Dead store of class literal**: An instruction assigns a class literal to a variable and then never uses it.

  ○ **Switch fall through**: A value stored in the previous switch case is overwritten here due to a switch fall through. It is likely that you forgot to put a break or return at the end of the previous case.

  ○ **Unconfirmed type casts** and **redundant null check**: This error occurs when a value is null, for example, consider the following code:

```
Object x = null;
Car myCar = (Car)x;
if(myCar != null){
  //...
}
```

The following is the update site URL for the FindBugs Eclipse plugin: `http://findbugs.cs.umd.edu/eclipse`.

You can also install it through Eclipse Marketplace.

Install FindBugs and then add the following code to the `CodeQualityChapter06` project for verification:

```
public class Buggy implements Cloneable {
    private Integer magicNumber;
    public Buggy(Integer magicNumber) {
        this.magicNumber = magicNumber;
    }
    public boolean isBuggy(String x) {
        return "Buggy" == x;
    }
    public boolean equals(Object o) {
        if (o instanceof Buggy) {
```

```
                   return ((Buggy) o).magicNumber == magicNumber;
              }
          if (o instanceof Integer) {
                   return magicNumber == ((Integer) o);
              }
          return false;
      }
     Buggy() { }
     static class MoreBuggy extends Buggy {
          static MoreBuggy singleton = new MoreBuggy();
      }
     static MoreBuggy foo = MoreBuggy.singleton;
  }
```

Right-click on the project and click on the **Find Bugs** menu. The following is the pop-up menu displayed:

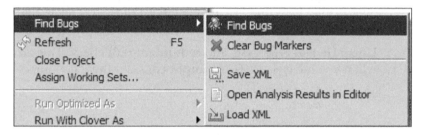

Open the source file; it shows the bug icons. The following screenshot displays the bugs:

```
    public boolean isBuggy(String x) {
        return "Buggy" == x;
    }

    public boolean equals(Object o) {
        if (o instanceof Buggy) {
            return ((Buggy) o).magicNumber == magicNumber;
        }
        if (o instanceof Integer) {
            return magicNumber == ((Integer) o);
        }
```

The following screenshot displays the bugs in a tabular format with the error categories:

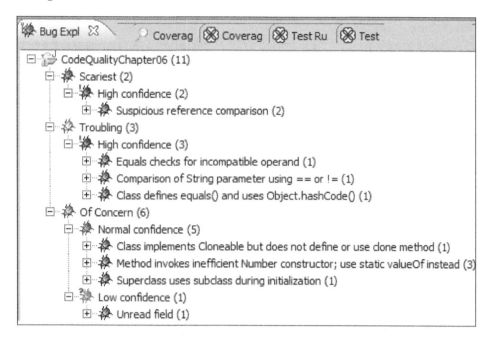

Working with the PMD plugin

PMD can find duplicate code, dead code, empty if/while statements, empty try/catch blocks, complicated expressions, cyclomatic complexity, and so on.

The following is the update site URL for Eclipse: `http://sourceforge.net/projects/pmd/files/pmd-eclipse/update-site/`. You can also install it through Eclipse Marketplace.

After installation, right-click on the `CodeQualityChapter06` project and select the **Toggle PMD Nature** menu item. It will enable the project for PMD analysis. The following screenshot demonstrates the PMD pop-up menu options:

PMD shows the errors in the **Problems** tab. The following screenshot shows the PMD violations in the **Problems** tab:

i	Infos (11 items)
i	A method should have only one exit point, and that should be the last statement in the method
i	A method should have only one exit point, and that should be the last statement in the method
i	Avoid empty catch blocks
i	Document empty constructor
i	Each class should declare at least one constructor
i	Ensure you override both equals() and hashCode()
i	Found non-transient, non-static member. Please mark as transient or provide accessors.
i	It is a good practice to call super() in a constructor
i	Parameter 'x' is not assigned and could be declared final
i	Use explicit scoping instead of the default package private level
i	Use explicit scoping instead of the default package private level

The next section will describe the SonarQube dashboard and analyze projects using the SonarQube runner, Ant, Gradle, and Maven.

Monitoring code quality with SonarQube

SonarQube is a web-based open source continuous quality assessment dashboard. It comes with a GNU General Public License and supports cross-platform, so it can be installed on many popular operating systems. SonarQube is developed in Java. As of March 2014, the latest version is 4.1.2.

SonarQube exhibits the following features:

- It is a web-based code quality dashboard that can be accessed from anywhere.
- It supports numerous languages. The languages and coding platforms supported in Version 4.1.2 are ABAP, Android, C/C++, C#, COBOL, Erlang, Flex/ActionScript, Groovy, Java, JavaScript, Natural, PHP, PL/I, PL/SQL, Python, VB.NET, Visual Basic 6, Web (analysis of HTML included in pages on HTML, JSP, JSF, Ruby, PHP, and so on), and XML.
- It offers the following metrics:
  - Bugs and potential bugs
  - Breach in coding standards
  - Duplications
  - Lack of unit tests

- ° Bad distribution of complexities
- ° Spaghetti design
- ° Not enough or too many comments

- It records history in a database and provides chronological graphs of quality metrics.

- It can be expanded using numerous plugins.

- It supports continuous automated inspection using Ant/Maven/Gradle and CI tools such as Jenkins, CruiseControl, and Bamboo.

- It integrates with Eclipse.

The following section covers the SonarQube installation and usage.

Running SonarQube

The following are the SonarQube configuration steps:

1. Download SonarQube from `http://www.sonarqube.org/downloads/`.

2. Uncompress the downloaded file into the directory of your choice. We'll refer to it as `<sonar_install_directory>` or `SONAR_HOME` in the next steps.

3. Open the `<sonar_install_directory>/bin` directory. The `bin` directory lists the SonarQube-supported operating systems. Go to a specific OS directory such as open `windows-x86-64` for a Windows 64-bit machine.

4. Run a shell script or batch file to start Sonar. The following screenshot shows the command prompt output of a Windows 64-bit machine. Note that the server logs the **Web server is started** information when the web server is started:

```
Sonar
wrapper  | --> Wrapper Started as Console
wrapper  | Launching a JVM...
jvm 1    | Wrapper (Version 3.2.3) http://wrapper.tanukisoft
jvm 1    |   Copyright 1999-2006 Tanuki Software, Inc.  All
jvm 1    |
jvm 1    | 2014.03.16 20:46:24 INFO  Web server is started
```

5. Open Internet Explorer and type in `http://localhost:9000`. This will launch the SonarQube dashboard. Initially, the dashboard shows an empty project list. First, we need to analyze the projects to get them displayed in the dashboard. The following is the SonarQube dashboard on display:

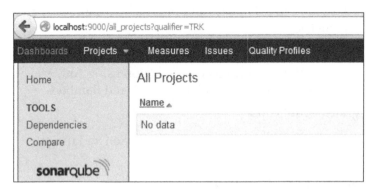

Installation is complete. Next, we need to analyze a project using SonarQube.

Analyzing code with the SonarQube runner

This section configures the SonarQube runner and analyzes a project. SonarQube supports numerous project analysis options, and the SonarQube runner is the prescribed one. The following are the steps to analyze a project using the SonarQube runner:

1. Download the runner from `http://repo1.maven.org/maven2/org/codehaus/sonar/runner/sonar-runner-dist/2.3/sonar-runner-dist-2.3.zip`.

2. Unzip the downloaded file into the directory of your choice. We'll refer to it as `<runner_install_directory>` in the next steps.

3. Open `sonar.properties` from the `<sonar_install_directory>/conf/sonar.properties` installation directory. Sonar stores data in a database; if not specified, then by default, it stores data in an embedded H2 database. The following `jdbc.url` command should be present in the properties file: `sonar.jdbc.url=jdbc:h2:tcp://localhost:9092/sonar`.

4. Open `<runner_install_directory>/conf/sonar-runner.properties` and change the `sonar.host.url` property to `http://localhost:9000`, and copy `sonar.jdbc.url` from the `<sonar_install_directory>/conf/sonar.properties` file.

The following is the code snippet taken from the `sonar-runner.properties` file. Check whether `sonar.host.url` and `sonar.jdbc.url` are enabled:

```
#----- Default SonarQube server
sonar.host.url=http://localhost:9000
#----- H2
sonar.jdbc.url=jdbc:h2:tcp://localhost:9092/sonar
```

5. Create a new `SONAR_RUNNER_HOME` environment variable, which is set to `<runner_install_directory>`.

6. Add the `<runner_install_directory>/bin` directory to your `Path` variable.

7. Open command prompt and check whether the runner is installed. Issue the `sonar-runner -h` command, and you will get the following output:

```
C:\Users\achasu00>sonar-runner -h
D:\SoftWare\sonar-runner-2.3
INFO:
INFO: usage: sonar-runner [options]
INFO:
INFO: Options:
INFO:   -D,--define <arg>      Define property
INFO:   -e,--errors            Produce execution error messages
INFO:   -h,--help              Display help information
INFO:   -v,--version           Display version information
INFO:   -X,--debug             Produce execution debug output
```

8. Go to the `CodeQualityChapter06` project folder, create a properties file named `sonar-project.properties`, and add the following lines to the file:

```
# Required metadata
sonar.projectKey=packt:CodeQualityChapter06
sonar.projectName=CodeQualityChapter06
sonar.projectVersion=1.0
#source file location
sonar.sources=src/main/java
# The value of the property must be the key of the
  language.
sonar.language=java
# Encoding of the source code
sonar.sourceEncoding=UTF-8
```

9. Open the command prompt, change the directory to `CodeQualityChapter06`, and issue the `sonar-runner` command; this will start the project analysis. Sonar will download JAR files and store the analysis data into an H2 database. Once the analysis is over, open `http://localhost:9000`; this will launch the SonarQube dashboard.

The metrics displayed in the dashboard are technical debt, code details, documentation, code duplication, complexity, and coverage.

The following screenshot shows the **Technical Debt** metric:

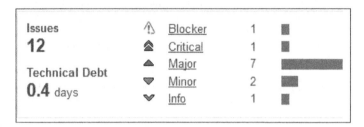

The following screenshot shows the code details metric:

Lines of code	Classes
37	**3**
93 lines	1 packages
11 statements	6 functions
2 files	0 accessors

The following screenshot shows the **Documentation** metric:

Documentation	Comments
0.0% docu. API	**50.0%**
6 public API	37 lines
6 undocu. API	

The following screenshot shows the cyclomatic **Complexity** metric:

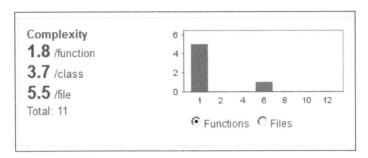

10. Click on the **Issues 12** hyperlink in the **Technical Debt** metric; this will open an issue's details with a severity legend. The following is the **Severity** legend:

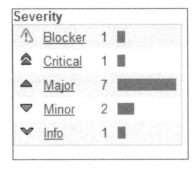

The following screenshot shows the issue details:

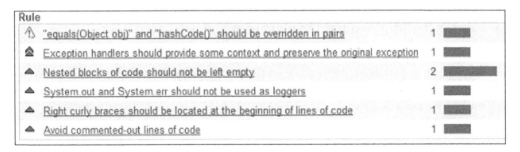

11. Click on any of the three complexity hyperlinks. Sonar will open the files and show the complexity details.

The following is an example of the complexity of `Buggy.java`:

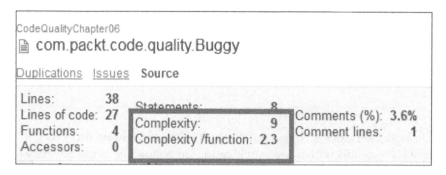

The **Hotspot** view displays the pain areas of the project, such as hotspots by duplicate lines, major violations, most violated rules, and the most violated resources.

The **Time Machine** view displays the chronological view of the project, such as a graphical day- or month-wise comparison of code complexity or code coverage.

Improving quality with the Sonar Eclipse plugin

Sonar provides an Eclipse plugin for accessing and fixing the Sonar-reported code issues in the Eclipse editor. The plugin can be downloaded from http://www.sonarsource.com/products/plugins/developer-tools/eclipse/.

Once the plugin is installed, right-click on the project, open the **Configure** menu, and click on the **Associate with Sonar...** menu item. The following screenshot shows the **Configure** menu details:

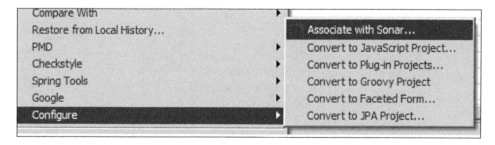

In the `sonar-project.properties` file, we stored the `sonar.projectKey=packt:C odeQualityChapter06` project key.

In the Sonar wizard, enter `GroupId=packt` and `ArtifactId= CodeQualityChapter06`. Click on **Find on server** and then click on **Finish**. This will connect to the local Sonar server and bring the issue details into the **Problems** tab.

The following is the Sonar wizard's screenshot:

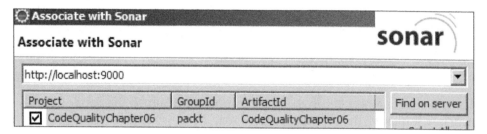

The following are the violations from the Sonar repository:

Description	Type	Reso... ▲
⊟ ⚠ Warnings (11 items)		
"equals(Object obj)" and "hashCode()" should be overridden in pairs : T	Sonar Violation	Buggy.java
Exception handlers should provide some context and preserve the origi	Sonar Violation	Buggy.java
Nested blocks of code should not be left empty : Either remove or fill th	Sonar Violation	Buggy.java
Nested blocks of code should not be left empty : Either remove or fill th	Sonar Violation	Buggy.java
Right curly braces should be located at the beginning of lines of code :	Sonar Violation	Buggy.java
Strings should be compared using equals() : Replace "==" and "!=" by	Sonar Violation	Buggy.java
The members of an interface declaration or class should appear in a pre	Sonar Violation	Buggy.java
TODO tags should be handled : Complete the task associated to this TC	Sonar Violation	Buggy.java
Avoid commented-out lines of code : This block of commented-out lines	Sonar Violation	Calculator.java
Method names should comply with a naming convention : Rename this r	Sonar Violation	Calculator.java
System.out and System.err should not be used as loggers : Replace thi	Sonar Violation	Calculator.java

Click on any problem, and it will take you to the source code's line and show a tooltip of the problem. The following screenshot shows the blocker violation that the `hashCode()` method is not implemented:

```
    public boolean isBuggy(String x) {
        return "Buggy" == x;
    }
```

Multiple markers at this line
- "equals(Object obj)" and "hashCode()" should be overridden in pairs : This class overrides "equals()" and should therefore also override "hashCode()".
- overrides java.lang.Object.equals

Add a `hashCode` method, rerun the Sonar runner, and launch the Sonar Eclipse wizard; it will remove the blocking issue.

Monitoring quality with Gradle and SonarQube

This section covers the Gradle integration with Sonar. Gradle has an inbuilt Sonar plugin. Create a `build.gradle` file under `/Packt/Chapter06/ CodeQualityChapter06`. Add the following lines to the `build.gradle` file and the Sonar lines are highlighted:

```
apply plugin: 'java'
apply plugin: 'sonar-runner'
apply plugin: "jacoco"

repositories {
    flatDir(dir: '../lib', name: 'JUnit Library')
    mavenCentral()
}

dependencies {
    testCompile'junit:junit:4.11', ':hamcrest-core:1.3'
}
```

```
jacocoTestReport {
    reports {
        xml.enabled false
        csv.enabled false
        html.destination "${buildDir}/jacocoHtml"
    }
}
sonarRunner {
    sonarProperties {
        property "sonar.projectName", "CodeQualityChapter06"
        property "sonar.projectKey", "packt:CodeQualityChapter06"
        property "sonar.jacoco.reportPath",
            "${project.buildDir}/jacoco/test.exec"
    }
}
```

Note that `sonar.projectKey` refers to `packt:CodeQualityChapter06`. Open the command prompt and issue the `gradle sonarRunner` command. This will start building the project. The following is the console output:

```
23:48:09.089 INFO  - Store results in database
23:48:09.169 INFO  - ANALYSIS SUCCESSFUL, you can browse
23:48:09.208 INFO  - Executing post-job class org.sonar.plugins
23:48:09.220 INFO  - Executing post-job class org.sonar.plugins
23:48:09.242 INFO  - Executing post-job class org.sonar.plugins
23:48:09.253 INFO  - -> Keep one snapshot per day
23:48:09.257 INFO  - -> Keep one snapshot per week
23:48:09.259 INFO  - -> Keep one snapshot per month
23:48:09.263 INFO  - -> Delete data prior to: 2009-03-22
23:48:09.268 INFO  - -> Clean CodeQualityChapter06 [id=1]
23:48:09.275 INFO  - <- Clean snapshot 7

BUILD SUCCESSFUL

Total time: 23.639 secs
```

Open the Sonar URL, and it will show the coverage computed by the JaCoCo plugin. The following is the code coverage and the technical debt output. Note that the **+8** new issues are added to the project. Technical debt is increased from 0.4 days to 1.2 days:

Unit Tests Coverage	Unit test success
53.5%	0 tests (+0)
54.0% line coverage	
52.8% branch coverage	

Issues			
20 (+8)	⚠ Blocker	1 (+0)
Added: 9	⬆ Critical	1 (+0)
Removed: 1	▲ Major	15 (+8)
	▼ Minor	2 (+0)
Technical Debt	⌄ Info	1 (+0)
1.2 days (+0.8)		
Added: 0.9		
Removed: 0.1		

Monitoring quality with Maven and SonarQube

This section describes how to integrate Maven with SonarQube. We will use the `CodeQualityChapter06` Eclipse project for the analysis. Maven has a plugin for Sonar. Create a `pom.xml` file under `/Packt/Chapter06/CodeQualityChapter06`. Add the following lines to the `pom.xml` file:

```xml
<project xmlns="http://maven.apache.org/POM/4.0.0"
    xmlns:xsi="http://www.w3.org/2001/XMLSchema-instance"
    xsi:schemaLocation="http://maven.apache.org/POM/4.0.0
    http://maven.apache.org/xsd/maven-4.0.0.xsd">
    <modelVersion>4.0.0</modelVersion>
    <groupId>packt</groupId>
    <artifactId>Chapter06</artifactId>
    <version>1.0-SNAPSHOT</version>
    <packaging>jar</packaging>
    <name>Chapter06</name>
    <url>http://maven.apache.org</url>
    <properties>
        <project.build.sourceEncoding>UTF-8
        </project.build.sourceEncoding>
    <sonar.language>java</sonar.language>
    </properties>
```

```
<dependencies>
  <dependency>
    <groupId>junit</groupId>
    <artifactId>junit</artifactId>
    <version>4.11</version>
    <scope>test</scope>
  </dependency>
</dependencies>
```

Open the command prompt, go to the project base folder, and issue the `mvn sonar:sonar` command. This command will download the SonarQube version of JAR files from the repository and start analyzing the project. Note the highlighted section `<sonar.language>java<...>` in the preceding script. This `<sonar.language>` tag signifies that the Maven will analyze a `java` project.

In the Gradle script or Sonar runner, we didn't mention a project version; here in Maven, as per the Maven project convention, we have to specify a `<version>1.0-SNAPSHOT</version>` version in the `POM.xml` file.

SonarQube uniquely identifies a project using a key (`GroupId` or `ArtifactId`) and a version. So, Maven analysis will create a new project statistics in the Sonar server as the version number is supplied in Maven, but not in Gradle and Sonar runner.

The following screenshot displays the **Projects** section on the Sonar dashboard. Note that the Maven analysis created **Version 1.0-SNAPSHOT**, whereas the Gradle and Sonar runner both updated an **unspecified** version of the project:

A	Name	Version	LOCs	Technical Debt	Last Analysis
	Chapter06	1.0-SNAPSHOT	73	0.4	00:15
	CodeQualityChapter06	unspecified	73	1.2	Mar 16 2014

Monitoring quality with Ant and SonarQube

This section describes how to configure Ant to integrate with Sonar. An Ant target needs a task to perform a build step. SonarQube provides an Ant task for project analysis. The Ant task JAR needs to be downloaded from `http://repository.codehaus.org/org/codehaus/sonar-plugins/sonar-ant-task/2.1/sonar-ant-task-2.1.jar`.

We will analyze the `CodeQualityChapter06` project with Ant. Copy the downloaded JAR file in `\Packt\chapter06\lib` and create a `build.xml` file directly under `CodeQualityChapter06`. You can copy the existing `build.xml` file that we used in *Chapter 5, Code Coverage*, or download the code for this chapter.

> XML namespaces act like Java packages and provide a qualified name for an XML element or attribute and avoid name collision. The namespace is defined by the `xmlns` attribute at the start tag of an element. The namespace declaration has the `xmlns:prefix="URI"` syntax.

To access a Sonar task, we will refer to a namespace `sonar` defined in the `antlib:org.sonar.ant` URI. We will define the URI in `taskdef`.

Modify the `build.xml` file and add the `sonar` namespace and the following snippet (excluding the common tasks, compilation task, and test tasks for the space economy):

```
<project name="chapter06" default="coverage" basedir="."
  xmlns:sonar="antlib:org.sonar.ant">
  <property name="sonar.projectKey" value="packt:chapter06_ant" />
  <property name="sonar.projectName" value="Chapter06" />
  <property name="sonar.projectVersion" value="2.0" />
  <property name="sonar.language" value="java" />
  <property name="sonar.sources" value="src/main/java" />
  <property name="sonar.binaries" value="target" />
  <property name="sonar.sourceEncoding" value="UTF-8" />
  <target name="sonar" depends="compile">
    <taskdef uri="antlib:org.sonar.ant"
      resource="org/sonar/ant/antlib.xml">
      <classpath path="${lib.dir}/sonar-ant-task-2.1.jar" />
    </taskdef>
    <sonar:sonar />
  </target>
```

Note that the `sonar.projectKey`, `sonar.projectName`, `sonar.projectVersion`, and `sonar.language` properties are defined in the preceding XML code. The Sonar task uses these attributes to uniquely identify a project and project language. Also note that a `taskdef` URI, `uri="antlib:org.sonar.ant"`, is defined to locate an `org/sonar/ant/antlib.xml` XML resource in the `${lib.dir}/sonar-ant-task-2.1.jar` classpath. The `sonar-ant-task` JAR contains the XML file.

Open the command prompt, change the directory to `CodeQualityChapter06`, and issue the `ant sonar` command. This will execute the Sonar task and start analyzing the project.

The following is the SonarQube dashboard output. The second row with **Version 2.0** and key **packt:chapter06_ant** is the Ant analysis result:

A Name ▲	Version	LOCs	Technical Debt	Last Analysis
📄 Chapter06	1.0-SNAPSHOT	73	0.4	00:15
📄 Chapter06	2.0	73	0.4	00:41
📄 Co[packt:chapter06_ant]	unspecified	73 ✎	1.2 ✎	Mar 16 2014

Getting familiar with false positives

This section deals with the false positives. In general, a static code analysis tool analyzes a source code against a set of rules and reports a violation when it finds a violation pattern in the source code. However, when we review the pattern and find that the violation is not correct in the context, then the reported violation is a false positive.

Static analysis tools report violations, but we have to filter out correct rule sets and remove the false positive rules. The SonarQube manual code review feature enables you to review code, add comments, and flag violations as false positives. The following Sonar URL describes how to review violations and flag violations as false positives: `http://www.sonarqube.org/sonar-2-8-in-screenshots/`.

Summary

This chapter explained the static code analysis and code quality attributes in depth. It covered the SonarQube code quality dashboard, static code analysis using Eclipse plugins, the Sonar runner and build scripts such as Ant, Maven, and Gradle, and code quality tools such as PMD, Checkstyle, and FindBugs.

By now, the reader will be able to configure the Sonar dashboard, set up Eclipse plugins, and configure Sonar runner and build scripts to analyze code quality using PMD, FindBugs, and Checkstyle.

The next chapter will cover the unit testing web tier code with mock objects.

7
Unit Testing the Web Tier

"If you don't like unit testing your product, most likely your customers won't like to test it either."

— Anonymous

Enterprise applications follow the **N-tier architecture model** to handle numerous nonfunctional concerns such as upgradability, scalability, and maintainability. The best design approach is to decouple the tiers from each other; this allows scaling out a tier without affecting another tier, or refactoring code in one tier without affecting the other tiers. Usually, any web application contains three tiers: presentation, business logic, and a database tier. This chapter deals with unit testing the web tier or presentation layer. The next chapters cover the application and database layers.

The following topics will be covered in this chapter:

- Unit testing a servlet controller in MVC
- Understanding what to test in the presentation layer

Unit testing servlets

Model View Controller (MVC) is a widely used web development pattern. MVC pattern defines three interconnected components: model, view, and controller.

The model represents the application data, logic, or business rules.

A view is a representation of information or model. A model can have multiple views; for example, the marks of a student can be represented in a tabular format or on a graphical chart.

The controller accepts the client request and initiates commands to either update the model or change the view.

The controller controls the flow of the application. In JEE applications, a controller is usually implemented as a servlet. A controller servlet intercepts requests and then maps each request to an appropriate handler resource. In this section, we will build a classic MVC front controller servlet to redirect requests to views.

Requests with only a context path, such as `http://localhost:8080/context/`, are routed to the `login.jsp` page, all home page requests (with URL `/home.do`) are routed to the `home.jsp` page, and all other requests are routed to the `error.jsp` page.

Building and unit testing a J2EE web application

Follow the ensuing steps to build a web application and test the controller logic:

1. Create a dynamic web project named `DemoServletTest` in Eclipse.

2. Create a controller servlet named `com.packt.servlet.DemoController`, and add the following lines to the `doGet` method:

```
protected void doGet(HttpServletRequest req,
  HttpServletResponse res) throws ServletException, IOException {
  String urlContext = req.getServletPath();
  if(urlContext.equals("/")) {
    req.getRequestDispatcher("login.jsp").forward(req, res);
  }else if(urlContext.equals("/home.do")) {
    req.getRequestDispatcher("home.jsp").forward(req, res);
  }else {
    req.setAttribute("error",
      "Invalid request path '"+urlContext+"'");
    req.getRequestDispatcher("error.jsp").forward(req, res);
  }
}
```

This method gets the servlet path from the request and matches the path with / tokens. When no match is found, then the `doGet` method sets an error attribute to the request.

3. Create three JSP files: `login.jsp`, `home.jsp`, and `error.jsp`. Modify the `error.jsp` file, and add the following scriptlet to display the error message:

```
<body>
  <font color="RED"><%=request.getAttribute("error") %></font>
</body>
```

4. Modify the `web.xml` file to map all requests to `DemoController`. Add the following lines of code to the `web.xml` file:

```
<web-app xmlns:xsi="http://www.w3.org/2001/XMLSchema-
   instance" xmlns="http://java.sun.com/xml/ns/javaee"
   xmlns:web="http://java.sun.com/xml/ns/javaee/web-
   app_2_5.xsd" xsi:schemaLocation="http://java.sun.com/xml/
   ns/javaee
   http://java.sun.com/xml/ns/javaee/web-app_3_0.xsd"
   id="WebApp_ID" version="3.0">
 <display-name>DemoServletTest</display-name>
 <servlet>
   <servlet-name>demo</servlet-name>
   <servlet-class>com.packt.servlet.DemoController
   </servlet-class>
 </servlet>
 <servlet-mapping>
   <servlet-name>demo</servlet-name>
   <url-pattern>/</url-pattern>
 </servlet-mapping>
</web-app>
```

The `demo` servlet maps the `url-pattern` tag.

The application is ready, but how do we unit test the controller logic?

We cannot instantiate the `HttpServletRequest` or `HttpServletResponse` objects. We can mock the `HttpServletRequest` or `HttpServletResponse` objects using Mockito.

Create a test class named `DemoControllerTest` and add the following code snippet:

```
@RunWith(MockitoJUnitRunner.class)
public class DemoControllerTest {
    @Mock    HttpServletRequest req;
    @Mock    HttpServletResponse res;
    @Mock    RequestDispatcher dispatcher;
    DemoController controllerServlet;

    @Before
    public void setup() {
      controllerServlet = new DemoController();
      when(req.getRequestDispatcher(anyString())).
        thenReturn(dispatcher);
    }

    @Test
    public void when_servlet_path_is_empty_then_opens_login_page(){
```

```
      when(req.getServletPath()).thenReturn("/");
      controllerServlet.doGet(req, res);
      ArgumentCaptor<String> dispatcherArgument =
        ArgumentCaptor.forClass(String.class);
      verify(req).getRequestDispatcher(
        dispatcherArgument.capture());
      assertEquals("login.jsp", dispatcherArgument.getValue());
    }

    @Test
    public void when_home_page_request_then_opens_home_page(){
      when(req.getServletPath()).thenReturn("/home.do");
      controllerServlet.doGet(req, res);

      ArgumentCaptor<String> dispatcherArgument =
        ArgumentCaptor.forClass(String.class);
      verify(req).getRequestDispatcher(
        dispatcherArgument.capture());
      assertEquals("home.jsp", dispatcherArgument.getValue());
    }

    @Test
    public void when_invalid_request_then_opens_error_page(){
      when(req.getServletPath()).thenReturn("/xyz.do");
      controllerServlet.doGet(req, res);
      ArgumentCaptor<String> dispatcherArgument =
        ArgumentCaptor.forClass(String.class);
      verify(req).getRequestDispatcher(
        dispatcherArgument.capture());
      assertEquals("error.jsp", dispatcherArgument.getValue());
    }
  }
}
```

Note that the `request` and `response` objects are mocked using mockito and then expectations are set to get `ServletPath`, and `verify` is used to check the view name returned by the controller. We added three tests to verify the controller logic: one to check the default context path, one to check the `home.do` URL, and the other to verify the error condition.

Create a Tomcat server instance from the server view (right-click on the server view and create a new server; from the server wizard choose Tomcat and set the runtime configuration) and run the application. Open the browser and go to `http://localhost:8080/DemoServletTest/`, and check that the application opens the **Login page**. The following is the browser output:

Go to `http://localhost:8080/DemoServletTest/home.do`; it will open the **Home page**. The following is the browser output:

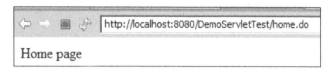

Go to any other URL, such as `http://localhost:8080/DemoServletTest/abc`. It will open an error page and display an error message. The following is the error output:

The results of the preceding browser verify that our JUnit tests work fine.

`DemoServletTest` acts as a **front controller**. A front controller is a design pattern where a single servlet handles all web requests and routes them to other controllers or handlers for actual processing. All dynamic web applications written in the Java or Servlet API need a front controller servlet to handle HTTP requests, so all projects write logically duplicate code to handle requests through the front controller servlets.

Spring MVC was built to provide a flexible framework for web application developers. Spring's `DispatcherServlet` acts as the front controller; similar to the `DemoServletTest` test, it receives all incoming requests and delegates the processing of the requests to handlers. It allows developers to concentrate on business logic rather than work on the boilerplate of a custom front controller. The next section describes the Spring MVC architecture and how web applications can be unit tested using Spring MVC.

Playing with Spring MVC

In Spring MVC, the following is a pattern of a simplified request handling mechanism:

1. `DispatcherServlet` receives a request and confers the request with handler mappings to find out which controller can handle the request, and then passes the request to that controller.

2. The controller performs the business logic (can delegate the request to a service or business logic processor) and returns some information back to `DispatcherServlet` for user display or response. Instead of sending the information (model) directly to the user, the controller returns a view name that can render the model.

3. `DispatcherServlet` then resolves the physical view from the view name and passes the model object to the view. This way, `DispatcherServlet` is decoupled from the view implementation.

4. The view renders the model. A view could be a JSP page, a servlet, a PDF file, an excel report, or any presentable component.

The following sequence diagram represents the flow and interaction of Spring MVC components:

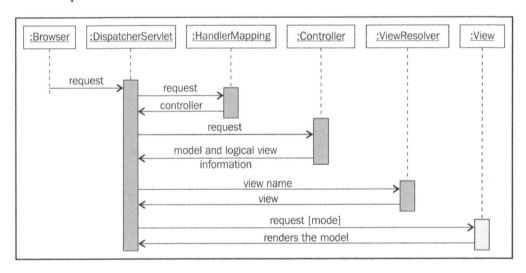

We will build a Spring web application and unit test the code using JUnit. The following are the steps to be performed:

1. Launch Eclipse and create a dynamic web project named `SpringMvcTest`.

2. Open `web.xml` and enter the following lines:

```
<display-name>SpringMVCTest</display-name>
<servlet>
  <servlet-name>dispatcher</servlet-name>
  <servlet-class>
    org.springframework.web.servlet.DispatcherServlet
  </servlet-class>
  <load-on-startup>1</load-on-startup>
</servlet>
<servlet-mapping>
  <servlet-name>dispatcher</servlet-name>
  <url-pattern>/</url-pattern>
</servlet-mapping>
<context-param>
  <param-name>contextConfigLocation</param-name>
  <param-value>
    /WEB-INF/dispatcher-servlet.xml
  </param-value>
</context-param>
</web-app>
```

The dispatcher is named `DispatcherServlet`, and it maps all requests.
Note the `contextConfigLocation` parameter. This indicates that the Spring
beans are defined in `/WEB-INF/dispatcher-servlet.xml`.

3. Create an XML file named `dispatcher-servlet.xml` in `WEB-INF` and add
the following lines:

```
<?xml version="1.0" encoding="UTF-8"?>
<beans xmlns="http://www.springframework.org/schema/beans"
  xmlns:context=
  "http://www.springframework.org/schema/context"
  xmlns:xsi="http://www.w3.org/2001/XMLSchema-instance"
  xsi:schemaLocation="
  http://www.springframework.org/schema/beans
  http://www.springframework.org/schema/beans/spring-
  beans-3.0.xsd
  http://www.springframework.org/schema/context
  http://www.springframework.org/schema/context/
  spring-context-3.0.xsd">
  <context:component-scan base-package="com.packt" />
  <bean class= "org.springframework.web.servlet.view.
    InternalResourceViewResolver">
  <property name="prefix">
    <value>/WEB-INF/pages/</value>
```

```
      </property>
      <property name="suffix">
          <value>.jsp</value>
        </property>
      </bean>
  </beans>
```

This XML defines a Spring view resolver. Any view will be found under the /WEB-INF/pages location with the .jsp suffix, and all beans are configured under the com.packt package with Spring annotations.

4. Create a class named LoginInfo in the com.packt.model package. This class represents the login information. Add two private String fields, userId and password, and generate the getters and setters.

5. Create a JSP page named login.jsp under /WEB-INF/view, and add the following lines to create a form using the Spring tag library. Modify the form and add normal HTML input for username and password:

```
<%@ taglib prefix="sf" uri="http://www.springframework.org/tags/
form"%>
<sf:form method="POST" modelAttribute=
  "loginInfo" action="/onLogin">

</sf:form>
```

6. Create a controller class named com.packt.controller.LoginController to handle login requests. Add the following lines:

```
@Controller
@Scope("session")
public class LoginController implements Serializable {
  @RequestMapping({ "/", "/login" })
  public String onStartUp(ModelMap model) {
    model.addAttribute("loginInfo", new LoginInfo());
    return "login";
  }
}
```

The @Controller annotation indicates that the class is a Spring MVC controller class. In smap1-servlet.xml, we defined <context:component-scan base-package="com.packt" />, so Spring will scan this @Controller annotation and create a bean. The @RequestMapping annotation maps any request with the default path /SpringMvcTest/ or /SpringMvcTest/login to the onStartUp method. This method returns a logical view name login. The view resolver defined in the XML file will map the login request to the physical view login.jsp page under /WEB-INF/pages.

7. Create another method in the `Login` class to handle the login and submit requests, as follows:

```
@RequestMapping({ "/onLogin" })
public String onLogin(@ModelAttribute("loginInfo")
  LoginInfo loginInfo, ModelMap model) {
  if(!"junit".equals(loginInfo.getUserId())) {
    model.addAttribute("error", "invalid login name");
    return "login";
  }
  if(!"password".equals(loginInfo.getPassword())) {
    model.addAttribute("error", "invalid password");
    return "login";
  }
  model.addAttribute("name", "junit reader!");
  return "greetings";
}
```

The `onLogin` method is mapped with `/onLogin`. The `@ModelAttribute("loginInfo")` method is the model submitted from the `login.jsp` form. This method checks whether the username is `junit` and password is `password`. If the user ID or password does not match, then an error message is shown on the login page, otherwise, the `greetings` view is opened.

8. Change the content of the `login.jsp` file to submit the form to `/SpringMvcTest/onLogin` and the `modelattribute` name to `loginInfo`, as follows:

```
<sf:form method="POST" modelAttribute="loginInfo" action=
  "/SpringMvcTest/onLogin">
```

Also, add the `<h1>${error}</h1>` JSTL expression to display the error message.

9. Create a JSP file named `greetings.jsp` and add the following lines:

```
<h1>Hello :${name}</h1>
```

10. In the browser, enter `http://localhost:8080/SpringMvcTest/`; this will open the login page. On the login page, do not enter any value and just click on **Submit**. It will show the **invalid login name** error message. Now, enter `junit` in the **User Id** field and `password` in the **Password** field and hit *Enter*. The application will greet you with the message shown in the following screenshot:

We can unit test the `controller` class. The following are the steps:

1. Create a `LoginControllerTest.java` class in `com.packt.controller`.

2. Using the following code, add a test to check that when the user ID is null, the error message is thrown:

```
public class LoginControllerTest {
  LoginController controller = new LoginController();
  @Test
  public void when_no_name_entered_shows_error_message(){
    ModelMap model = new ModelMap();
    String viewName = controller.onLogin(
      new LoginInfo(), model);
    assertEquals("login", viewName);
    assertEquals("invalid login name", model.get("error"));
  }
}
```

3. Add another test to check invalid passwords, as follows:

```
@Test
public void when_invalid_password_entered_shows_
  error_message()     {
  ModelMap model = new ModelMap();
  LoginInfo loginInfo = new LoginInfo();
  loginInfo.setUserId("junit");
  String viewName =controller.onLogin(loginInfo, model);
  assertEquals("login", viewName);
  assertEquals("invalid password", model.get("error"));
}
```

4. Add a `happyPath` test, as follows:

```
@Test    public void happyPath(){
  loginInfo.setUserId("junit");
  loginInfo.setPassword("password");
  String viewName =controller.onLogin(loginInfo, model);
  assertEquals("greetings", viewName);
}
```

This is just an example of Spring MVC, so we checked the username and password with the hardcoded constants. In the real world, a service looks up the database for the user and returns an error message; the service can be autowired to the controller. This way, we can unit test the controller and the service layer.

Summary

This chapter explained the unit testing strategy for the presentation layer and provided examples on front controller servlets and Spring MVC.

By now, you should be able to unit test the web tier components and isolate the view components from the presentation logic.

The next chapter will cover the unit testing of the database layer.

8
Playing with Data

"Any program is only as good as it is useful."

– Linus Torvalds

Enterprise applications store, retrieve, transmit, manipulate, and analyze data. Storing, processing, and analyzing data is very critical to any business. The **Business Intelligence (BI)** process transforms data into meaningful information for business. BI analyzes statistical data and helps with decision making and predictions for businesses, such as risk assessment, planning and forecasting, and analyzing buying trends. Information can be stored in a file or to a database. Querying and accessing data from a relational database is easier than the file system. This chapter covers the unit testing of the database layer. The following topics are covered in depth:

- Separation of concerns
- Unit testing the persistence layer
- Writing clean data access code using Spring JDBC
- Integration testing of JDBC code
- Integration testing of Spring JDBC

Separating concerns

This section elaborates on the separation of concerns. Enterprise application information can be represented using the following building blocks:

- **What**: This represents the information to store. We cannot store everything; so, categorization of the data to be stored is very important.

- **Who**: This represents the actors. Information is a sensitive thing and it's important to control access across users; for example, an employee should not be able to access the salary information of another employee, but a manager or member of HR staff can access salary data of the staff.

- **Data store**: This represents information and its accessibility.

- **Process**: This represents the processing of data. Any information doesn't make any sense unless some action is performed on it.

The following diagram describes the key information blocks of an enterprise application:

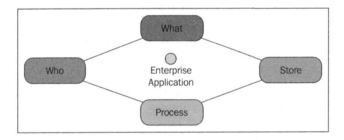

This section covers the **Store** block and unit testing the data access layer.

The following diagram represents the components of a loosely coupled application:

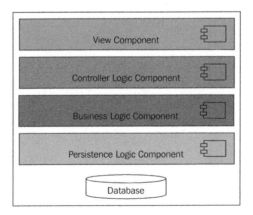

The view component represents the JSPs, taglibs, widgets, and so on. Writing automated JUnit tests for the view components is not easy and requires manual effort. We'll skip the view components in this chapter.

We unit tested the controller logic component in *Chapter 7, Unit Testing the Web Tier*.

Controller logic component accesses the business logic component. The business logic component performs the business logic and delegates data access to the persistence logic component. We'll cover the unit testing of business logic in the forthcoming chapters. Mock objects are used to mimic the persistence or data access layer.

The persistence logic layer or database client layer is responsible for managing the database connection, retrieving data from a database, and storing data back in the database. Unit testing the data access layer is very important; if anything goes wrong in this layer, the application will fail. We can unit test the data access logic in isolation from the database, and perform the integration test to verify the application and database integrity.

You can have 100 percent test coverage of your database access code. However, if this code is misused by the controllers and/or the view layer, the whole application is useless. You need integration tests to verify the wiring, which will be covered later.

Databases represent a data store or a relational database.

Separating the data access layer from the business logic layer helps us to make changes to the database without affecting the business logic layer, and it allows us to unit test the business logic layer in isolation from the database. Suppose you are using the MySQL database and you want to migrate to SQL server. Then, in that case, you don't have to touch the business logic layer.

Unit testing the persistence logic

In this section, we'll build a Phonebook application and store phone numbers. We'll use the **Apache Derby** database for persistence. Derby can be downloaded from `http://db.apache.org/derby/`.

You can use better built-in databases such as H2. It has more features and is less restrictive than Derby; however, we're using Derby for simplicity.

The following are the steps to run Derby:

1. Download the binary media file and extract the media to a preferred location. We'll refer to it as DERBY_HOME in the next steps.

2. On a Windows machine, go to DERBY_HOME\bin and execute the startNetworkServer.bat file.

3. It will launch a command prompt and print a message to the console that the database server has started, such as **started and ready to accept connections on port 1527**.

We will create a Java project to test the Phonebook application. Follow the ensuing steps to build the application:

1. Launch Eclipse and create a Java project named **DatabaseAccess**.

2. Add a `PhoneEntry` class to store phone details. The following are the class details:

```
package com.packt.database.model;

public class PhoneEntry implements Serializable {

  private static final long serialVersionUID = 1L;

  private String phoneNumber;
  private String firstName;
  private String lastName;

  // getters and setters
}
```

3. Create a data access interface for Phonebook. The following are the API details:

```
package com.packt.database.dao;

import java.util.List;
import com.packt.database.model.PhoneEntry;

public interface PhoneBookDao {
  boolean create(PhoneEntry entry);

  boolean update(PhoneEntry entryToUpdate);

  List<PhoneEntry> searchByNumber(String number);

  List<PhoneEntry> searchByFirstName(String firstName);

  List<PhoneEntry> searchByLastName(String lastName);

  boolean delete(String number);
}
```

4. Create a database access interface implementation to communicate with the database. The following are the data access object details:

```
public class PhoneBookDerbyDao implements PhoneBookDao {

  private String driver =
    "org.apache.derby.jdbc.EmbeddedDriver";
  private String protocol = "jdbc:derby:";
  private String userId = "dbo";
  private String dbName = "phoneBook";

  public PhoneBookDerbyDao() {
    loadDriver();
  }

  protected void loadDriver() {
    try {
      Class.forName(driver).newInstance();
    } catch (ClassNotFoundException cnfe) {
      cnfe.printStackTrace(System.err);
    } catch (InstantiationException ie) {
      ie.printStackTrace(System.err);
    } catch (IllegalAccessException iae) {
      iae.printStackTrace(System.err);
    }
  }

  protected Connection getConnection() throws SQLException {
    Connection conn = null;
    Properties props = new Properties();
    props.put("user", userId);
    conn = DriverManager.getConnection(protocol +
      dbName + ";create=true",props);
    conn.setAutoCommit(false);
    return conn;
  }
}
```

Note that the PhoneBookDerbyDao class is a Derby implementation of the dao. It has configuration attributes such as driver, protocol, and dbName, and getters or setters. The loadDriver() method loads the database driver and gets invoked from the PhoneBookDerbyDao constructor. The getConnection() method connects to a Derby database and establishes a connection.

5. Implement the create behavior, as follows:

```
@Override
public boolean create(PhoneEntry entry) {
  PreparedStatement preparedStmt = null;
  Connection conn = null;
  try {
  conn = getConnection();
  preparedStmt = conn
    .prepareStatement("insert into PhoneBook values
    (?,?,?)");

  preparedStmt.setString(1, entry.getPhoneNumber());
  preparedStmt.setString(2, entry.getFirstName());
  preparedStmt.setString(3, entry.getLastName());
  preparedStmt.executeUpdate();
  // Note that it can cause problems on some dbs if
  //autocommit mode is on
  conn.commit();
    return true;
  } catch (SQLException e) {
    e.printStackTrace();
  } finally {

    if (preparedStmt != null) {
      try {
        preparedStmt.close();
      } catch (SQLException e) {
        e.printStackTrace();
      }
    }

    if (conn != null) {
      try {
        conn.close();
      } catch (SQLException e) {
        e.printStackTrace();
      }
    }
  }

  return false;
}
```

The `create` method first acquires a database connection and creates a prepared statement from `connection`. Then, it populates the prepared statement with the `PhoneEntry` values, executes the prepared statement, and then commits the connection. The `finally` block closes the resources. Then, the prepared statement is closed and the connection is closed.

6. We need to unit test the JDBC API call since we didn't configure the database yet. We'll unit test the `create()` behavior in isolation from the database. Create a `PhoneBookDerbyDaoTest` JUnit test under the `test\` `com.packt.database.dao` package. To run the test in isolation from the database, we need to bypass the `loadDriver` and `getConnection` methods. So, we need a fake object to test the class and need mock objects to mock out the JDBC configuration classes, such as `Connection`, `ResultSet`, and `PreparedStatement`.

   `TestablePhoneBookDerbyDao` is the fake object implementation of the dao. We created a mock `Connection` object and returned from the fake object's `getConnection` method. The following is the JUnit test for the dao class:

```
@RunWith(MockitoJUnitRunner.class )
public class PhoneBookDerbyDaoTest {
  @Mock
  Connection connection;


  class TestablePhoneBookDerbyDao extends
    PhoneBookDerbyDao{
    protected void loadDriver() {
    }

    protected Connection getConnection() throws
      SQLException {
      return connection;
    }
  }
}
```

7. `PhoneBookDerbyDao` needs `PreparedStatement` to pass the `PhoneEntry` details to the database. Create the mock `PreparedStatement` and `connection` methods. Update the test class and add the following lines:

```
@Mock
 Connection connection;
@Mock
PreparedStatement statement;
```

```
PhoneBookDerbyDao dao;


@Before
public void setUp(){
  dao = new TestablePhoneBookDerbyDao();
}
```

Invoke the `create` method with `PhoneEntry` and verify whether the `PhoneEntry` detail was passed to the `statement` object. Finally, verify whether `connection` was committed, and `statement` and `connection` were closed, as follows:

```
@Test
public void creates_phone_entry() throws Exception {
  //Setting up sample object
  PhoneEntry johnDoe= new PhoneEntry();
  johnDoe.setFirstName("John");
  johnDoe.setLastName("Doe");
  johnDoe.setPhoneNumber("123");

  //Stubbing the connection obj to return the mocked
    statement
  when(connection.prepareStatement(anyString())).
    thenReturn(statement;

  //Calling the actual method
  boolean succeed = dao.create(johnDoe);
  assertTrue(succeed);

  //Creating argument captors
  ArgumentCaptor<String> stringArgCaptor =
    ArgumentCaptor.forClass(String.class);
  ArgumentCaptor<Integer> intArgCaptor =
    ArgumentCaptor.forClass(Integer.class);

  //verifying that the mocked statement's setString is
  //invoked 3 times for firstName, lastName and
  //phoneNumber
  verify(statement, new Times(3)).setString(intArgCaptor.
  capture(), stringArgCaptor.capture());

  //Verify the arguments passed to the statement object
  assertEquals("123",
    stringArgCaptor.getAllValues().get(0));
  assertEquals("John",
```

```
    stringArgCaptor.getAllValues().get(1));
  assertEquals("Doe",
    stringArgCaptor.getAllValues().get(2));

  verify(connection).prepareStatement
    (stringArgCaptor.capture());
  assertEquals(PhoneBookDerbyDao.INSERT_INTO_PHONE_
    BOOK_VALUES    stringArgCaptor.getValue());

  //verify that the mock resources were used and closed
  verify(statement).executeUpdate();
  verify(connection).commit();
  verify(statement).close();
  verify(connection).close();

}
```

[

Overuse of argument captors can lead to fragile tests because your system under test is no longer a black box.
]

8.   We'll verify the data retrieval logic and enhance the searchByNumber() method to retrieve PhoneEntry by number. The following is the logic:

```
@Override
public List<PhoneEntry> searchByNumber(String number) {
  PreparedStatement preparedStmt = null;
  Connection conn = null;
  ResultSet resultSet = null;
  List<PhoneEntry> entries = new ArrayList<PhoneEntry>();
  try {
    conn = getConnection();
    preparedStmt = conn
      .prepareStatement("SELECT * FROM
      PhoneBook where num=?");

    preparedStmt.setString(1, number);
    resultSet = preparedStmt.executeQuery();
    while (resultSet.next()) {
      PhoneEntry entry = new PhoneEntry();
      entry.setFirstName
        (resultSet.getString("fname"));
      entry.setLastName
        (resultSet.getString("lname"));
      entry.setPhoneNumber
        (resultSet.getString("num"));
```

```
      entries.add(entry);
    }
    return entries;
  } catch (SQLException e) {
    e.printStackTrace();
  } finally {

    try {
      if (resultSet != null) {
        resultSet.close();
        resultSet = null;
      }
    } catch (SQLException e) {
      e.printStackTrace();
    }

    if (preparedStmt != null) {
      try {
        preparedStmt.close();
      } catch (SQLException e) {
        e.printStackTrace();
      }
    }

    if (conn != null) {
      try {
        conn.close();
      } catch (SQLException e) {
        e.printStackTrace();
      }
    }
  }
  return null;
}
```

In the preceding code, the following statements are executed in sequence:

1. A database `Connection` is acquired. Then, `PreparedStatement` is created from the `Connection` object.

2. After this, `PreparedStatement` is populated.

3. Now, `PreparedStatement` is executed and `ResultSet` is returned.

4. `ResultSet` is iterated and the `PhoneEntry` objects are populated from `ResultSet`.

5. Finally, the JDBC resources are closed.

9. To unit test this logic, we need mock `ResultSet`, `PreparedStatement`, and `Connection` objects. The `ResultSet` object will be stubbed to return a `PhoneEntry` object, the `PreparedStatement` object will be stubbed to return the mock `ResultSet` object, and the `Connection` object will be stubbed to return the mock `PreparedStatement` object.

In a persistence logic unit test, the following things are verified:

- The JDBC API call sequence, such as connection, was committed
- Resources were closed or cleaned up
- Mapping `ResultSet` to model object (POJO)

The following is the test code to verify the logic:

```
@Test
public void retrieves_phone_entry() throws Exception {

    //Stub JDBC resources to return mock objects
    when(mockConn.prepareStatement(anyString())).
        thenReturn(mockPrepStmt);
    when(mockPrepStmt.executeQuery()).
        thenReturn(mockResultSet);
    when(mockResultSet.next()).thenReturn(true).
        thenReturn(false);

    //Stub the resultSet to return value
    when(mockResultSet.getString("fname")).
        thenReturn("John");
    when(mockResultSet.getString("lname")).
        thenReturn("Doe");
    when(mockResultSet.getString("num")).
        thenReturn("123");

    //Execute
    List<PhoneEntry> phoneEntries =
        dao.searchByNumber("123");

    assertEquals(1, phoneEntries.size());
    PhoneEntry johnDoe = phoneEntries.get(0);

    //verify mapping
    assertEquals("John", johnDoe.getFirstName());
    assertEquals("Doe", johnDoe.getLastName());
```

```
        assertEquals("123", johnDoe.getPhoneNumber());
        //Verify Resource Clean up
        verify(mockResultSet).close();
        verify(mockPrepStmt).close();
        verify(mockConn).close();
    }
```

We should write a unit test for `update`, `delete`, and `serachByXXX` behaviors.

Simplifying persistence with Spring

Look at the `PhoneBookDerbyDao` class. It has 398 lines to support create, read, update, and delete (CRUD) operations. Every method performs almost similar tasks. The following tasks are invoked from the CRUD methods:

- Passing connection parameters
- Opening a connection
- Creating a statement
- Preparing the statement
- Executing the statement
- Iterating through the results (only in the read method)
- Populating the model objects (only in the read method)
- Processing any exception
- Handling transactions
- Closing the ResultSet (only in the read method)
- Closing the statement
- Closing the connection

The Spring framework provides APIs to reduce JDBC code duplication. Spring JDBC hides the low-level details and allows us to concentrate on business logic. We'll implement `PhoneBookDao` using Spring JDBC.

Download the latest version of JDBC JAR and its dependencies from `http://maven.springframework.org/release/org/springframework/spring/`.

Follow the ensuing steps to implement Spring JDBC and simplify the code:

1. Launch Eclipse, open the `DatabaseAccess` project, and edit `.classpath` to add the following Spring dependencies shown in the screenshot:

2. Create a `PhoneBookDerbySpringDao` class that implements the `PhoneBookDao` interface. The following is the Spring implementation of the `create` method:

```
public class PhoneBookDerbySpringDao  implements
  PhoneBookDao {

private final JdbcTemplate jdbcTemplate;

  public PhoneBookDerbySpringDao(JdbcTemplate
    jdbcTemplate) {
  this.jdbcTemplate = jdbcTemplate;
  }

  @Override
  public boolean create(PhoneEntry entry) {
    int rowCount = jdbcTemplate.update("insert into
      PhoneBook values (?,?,?)",
    new Object[]{entry.getPhoneNumber(),
      entry.getFirstName(),
        entry.getLastName()
    });
    return rowCount == 1;
  }
}
```

JdbcTemplate simplifies the use of JDBC; it handles the resources and helps to avoid common errors such as not closing the connection. It creates and populates the statement object, iterates through the ResultSet object, which leaves the application code to provide SQL, and extracts results. PhoneBookDerbySpringDao contains a JdbcTemplate instance and delegates the database tasks to the jdbcTemplate.

JdbcTemplate has an update method for insert and update operations. It takes a SQL query and parameters. The new Spring version of the create() method invokes the update() method on jdbcTemplate and passes PhoneEntry details. Now the create method looks simple, just two lines of code. The Spring framework handles the resource life cycle.

3. Create a JUnit class named PhoneBookDerbySpringDaoTest for unit testing. We'll create a jdbcTemplate mock and pass it to dao. The following is the JUnit implementation:

```
@RunWith(MockitoJUnitRunner.class)
public class PhoneBookDerbySpringDaoTest {

  @Mock
  JdbcTemplate mockJdbcTemplate;

  PhoneBookDerbySpringDao springDao;

  @Before
  public void init() {
    springDao = new
      PhoneBookDerbySpringDao(mockJdbcTemplate);
  }

  @Test
  public void creates_PhoneEntry() throws Exception {
    //create PhoneEntry
    String charlsPhoneNumber = "1234567";
    String charlsFirstName = "Charles";
    String charlsLastName = "Doe";

    PhoneEntry charles = new PhoneEntry();
    charles.setFirstName(charlsFirstName);
    charles.setLastName(charlsLastName);
    charles.setPhoneNumber(charlsPhoneNumber);

    //Stub jdbcTemplate's update to return 1
    when(mockJdbcTemplate.update(anyString(),
```

```
        anyObject(), anyObject(), anyObject())).thenReturn(1);

    //Execute
    assertTrue(springDao.create(charles));

    //Create argument capture
    ArgumentCaptor<Object> varArgs =
      ArgumentCaptor.forClass(Object.class);

    ArgumentCaptor<String> strArg =
      ArgumentCaptor.forClass(String.class);

    //Verify update method was called and capture args
    verify(mockJdbcTemplate).update(strArg.capture(),
       varArgs.capture(),varArgs.capture(),
       varArgs.capture());

    //Verify 1st dynamic argument was the phone number
    assertEquals(charlsPhoneNumber,
      varArgs.getAllValues().get(0));
    //Verify the name arguments
    assertEquals(charlsFirstName,
      varArgs.getAllValues().get(1));
    assertEquals(charlsLastName,
      varArgs.getAllValues().get(2));
  }
}
```

Look at the new Spring dao; it is only 54 lines long. The class looks neat, simple, and readable. It doesn't handle resources, it rather concentrates on data access.

Verifying the system integrity

Integration tests let us find bugs that unit testing couldn't catch. We have unit tested the JDBC API usages in isolation from the database, but we need to test the integration of data and data access API, such as the JDBC driver, connection, and rollback. In this section, we'll test the data access layer with a database.

We need to create the database table before we start writing tests. Download the code from the Packt Publishing website and import the project `DatabaseAccess` in your Eclipse workspace, go to the `com.packt.database.util` package and run the `DatabaseManager` class. It will create the table. The following is the fairly simple table creation code:

```
conn = DriverManager.getConnection(url, props);
conn.setAutoCommit(false);
statement = conn.createStatement();
statement.execute("create table PhoneBook
  (num varchar(50), fname varchar(40),lname varchar(40))");
conn.commit();
```

The following are the steps to test the JDBC code:

1. Create a source folder named `integration` for the database centric tests, such as `src` or `test`.

2. Create a new JUnit test named `PhoneBookDerbyJdbcDaoIntegrationTest` and add the following lines to test the create, search, update, and delete functionalities:

```
public class PhoneBookDerbyJdbcDaoIntegrationTest {
  PhoneBookDerbyDao jdbcDao;

  @Before
  public void init() {
    jdbcDao = new PhoneBookDerbyDao();
  }

  @Test
  public void integration() throws Exception {
    PhoneEntry entry = new PhoneEntry();
    entry.setFirstName("john");
    entry.setLastName("smith");
    entry.setPhoneNumber("12345");

    assertTrue(jdbcDao.create(entry));
    List<PhoneEntry> phoneEntries =
    jdbcDao.searchByFirstName("john");

    //verify create
    assertFalse(phoneEntries.isEmpty());

    //modify last name
```

```
entry.setLastName("doe");

//update
assertTrue(jdbcDao.update(entry));

//retrieve
phoneEntries = jdbcDao.searchByFirstName("john");

//verify update
assertFalse(phoneEntries.isEmpty());
assertEquals("doe", phoneEntries.get(0).getLastName());

//delete
jdbcDao.delete(entry.getPhoneNumber());

//retrieve
phoneEntries = jdbcDao.searchByFirstName("john");

//verify delete
assertTrue(phoneEntries.isEmpty());
   }


}
```

The integration test creates a `PhoneBookDerbyJdbcDao` instance and calls the `PhoneBookDerbyJdbcDao` method to assert results.

Writing integration tests with Spring

Spring provides the module or utility library for integration tests. The following are the steps to write JUnit tests using the Spring transaction management API and `SpringJUnit4ClassRunner`:

1. Spring supports XML-based configuration and wiring beans. Create an XML file named `integration.xml` in the `integration` source package. Modify the XML file and define the `dataSource`, `transactionManager`, and `JdbcTemplate` Spring beans. The following is the XML body:

    ```
    <beans xmlns="http://www.springframework.org/schema/beans"
      xmlns:xsi="http://www.w3.org/2001/XMLSchema-instance"
      xsi:schemaLocation="
        http://www.springframework.org/schema/beans
        http://www.springframework.org/schema/beans/spring-
        beans-3.0.xsd">
    ```

```
<bean id="dataSource" class=
  "org.springframework.jdbc.datasource.
  DriverManagerDataSource">
  <property name="driverClassName"
    value="org.apache.derby.jdbc.EmbeddedDriver"/>
  <property name="url" value=
    "jdbc:derby:derbyDB;create=true"/>
  <property name="username" value="dbo"/>
</bean>

<bean id="transactionManager" class=
  "org.springframework.jdbc.datasource.
  DataSourceTransactionManager">
  <constructor-arg ref="dataSource"/>
</bean>

<bean id="jdbcTemplate" class=
  "org.springframework.jdbc.core.JdbcTemplate">
  <property name="dataSource" ref="dataSource"/>
</bean>
</beans>
```

 To find out more about Spring beans, visit `http://docs.spring.io/spring/docs/1.2.9/reference/beans.html`.

A `dataSource` bean is defined with `driverClassName`, `url`, and `username`. The `dataSource` reference is passed to the `jdbcTemplate` and `transactionManager` beans.

2. Spring supports automatic transaction rollback after test execution. It helps us to shield the development database against getting corrupted. The test runner needs to have a reference to a transaction manager bean before test execution. `SpringJUnit4ClassRunner` handles the integration tests. Add a `PhoneBookDerbySpringDaoIntegrationTest` JUnit test and add the following lines to it:

```
@ContextConfiguration({ "classpath:integration.xml" })
@TransactionConfiguration(transactionManager =
  "transactionManager", defaultRollback = true)
@Transactional
@RunWith(SpringJUnit4ClassRunner.class)
public class PhoneBookDerbySpringDaoIntegrationTest {

  @Autowired
  JdbcTemplate jdbcTemplate;
```

```java
    PhoneBookDerbySpringDao springDao;

    @Before
    public void init() {
      springDao = new PhoneBookDerbySpringDao(jdbcTemplate);
    }

    @Test
    public void integration() throws Exception {
      PhoneEntry entry = newEntry("12345", "John", "Smith");

      //create
      assertTrue(springDao.create(entry));

      //retrieve
      List<PhoneEntry> phoneEntries =
        springDao.searchByFirstName("John");

      //verify create
      assertFalse(phoneEntries.isEmpty());

      //modify last name
      entry.setLastName("Kallis");

      //update
      assertTrue(springDao.update(entry));

      //retrieve
      phoneEntries = springDao.searchByFirstName("John");

      //verify update
      assertFalse(phoneEntries.isEmpty());
      assertEquals("Kallis",
        phoneEntries.get(0).getLastName());

      //delete
      springDao.delete(entry.getPhoneNumber());

      //retrieve
      phoneEntries = springDao.searchByFirstName("John");

      //verify delete
      assertTrue(phoneEntries.isEmpty());
    }
}
```

The @ContextConfiguration({ "classpath:integration.xml" }) annotation instructs the JUnit runner to load Spring beans from a classpath location. It will load three beans from the integration.xml file.

The class level @Transactional annotation makes all methods transactional.

The @TransactionConfiguration(transactionManager = "transactionManager", defaultRollback = true) annotation defines the transaction manager, and the defaultRollback attribute tells the transaction manager to roll back all transactions after the end of a given test.

The following things happen when the JUnit test is run:

- Spring beans are loaded from the integration.xml file.
- A transaction manager is configured to roll back all transactions.
- The jdbcTemplate bean is automatically wired to the test class member jdbcTemplate.
- The init method creates a new instance of the dao class and passes the jdbcTemplate bean to the dao.
- The test first executes and then creates, updates, and deletes PhoneEntry.
- After test execution, the transaction manager rolls back the transaction. No data is created or modified or deleted from or to the PhoneBook table.

When the JUnit test runs, the following Spring console log is shown:

```
INFO: Began transaction (1): transaction manager [org.springframework.
jdbc.datasource.DataSourceTransactionManager@569c60]; rollback [true]

Apr 11, 2014 10:02:25 PM org.springframework.test.context.transaction.
TransactionalTestExecutionListener endTransaction

INFO: Rolled back transaction after test execution for test context
[[TestContext@134eb84 testClass = PhoneBookDerbySpringDaoIntegrationTest,
testInstance = com.packt.database.dao.PhoneBookDerbySpri
ngDaoIntegrationTest@1522de2, testMethod = integration@
PhoneBookDerbySpringDaoIntegrationTest, testException = [null],
mergedContextConfiguration = [MergedContextConfiguration@425743
testClass = PhoneBookDerbySpringDaoIntegrationTest, locations =
'{classpath:integration.xml}', classes = '{}', activeProfiles =
'{}', contextLoader = 'org.springframework.test.context.support.
DelegatingSmartContextLoader']]]
```

The log shows that a transaction has begun, and finally the transaction is rolled back. However, the transaction was not rolled back due to any exception, rather it got rolled back due to the transactional setting [defaultRollback = true]. The log shows that testException is equal to null, which implies that no exception was thrown.

Summary

This chapter explained the unit testing strategy for the database layer; it provided an example of unit testing in isolation from the database, writing clean JDBC code with Spring, and writing integration tests with database. We also learned about the configured automatic transaction rollback in Spring JDBC integration tests.

You should now be able to unit test the data access layer components in isolation from the database, write neat JDBC code using Spring, and write integration tests using Spring API.

The next chapter covers the service layer and testing legacy code testing.

9

Solving Test Puzzles

"We make a living by what we get, but we make a life by what we give."

— Winston Churchill

You may have worked in greenfield development projects that were written using **test-driven development** (**TDD**) and also in brownfield development or maintenance projects that were not written with TDD. You must have noticed that the test-first code written with TDD is easier to extend than the code with no unit test or unit tests written after coding.

 A greenfield project starts building from scratch and doesn't consider any prior work.

A brownfield project is an extension of prior work or rebuilding a project from an existing project.

This chapter covers the importance of unit testing in greenfield and brownfield projects. The following topics are covered in depth:

- Working with legacy code
- Designing for testability
- Working with greenfield code

The *Working with legacy code* section covers the legacy code and explains how to unit test and refactor the legacy code. The *Designing for testability* section explains how to design for testability. The *Working with greenfield code* section elaborates on TDD, the TDD life cycle, refactoring, and concludes with an example of TDD.

Working with the legacy code

The term **legacy** is frequently used, as slang, to describe complex code, which is difficult to understand, is rigid and fragile in nature, and is almost impossible to enhance.

However, the fact is that any code with no automated unit tests is legacy code. A piece of code can be well written. It can also follow coding guidelines, might be easy to understand, can be clean, loosely coupled, and very easy to extend. However, if it doesn't have automated unit tests, then it is legacy code.

Statistically, fixing bugs or adding new features to a legacy project is quite difficult than doing the same to a greenfield project. In legacy code, either automated unit tests do not exist or very few tests are written; the code is not designed for testability.

We inherit legacy code from some other source, maybe from a very old project, from another team that cannot maintain the code, or we acquire it from another company, but it is our duty to improve the quality.

Unit tests give us some level of assurance that our code is doing what the code is expected to do, and they allow us to change the code quickly and verify the change faster.

In general, legacy code is not testable and requires changes to the code structure (refactoring) to make it testable. However, the dilemma, most of the time, is that the legacy system is so crucial to the business that no one dares to touch the code. It makes no sense to modify an existing crucial module unless something is seriously wrong. Stalemate! You cannot refactor the code unless you have the automated test suite, and you cannot write tests as the code needs refactoring.

Sometimes it feels as though the legacy code, even with unit tests, are hard to understand, maintain, and enhance; hence, we need to be careful to make our tests readable and to avoid close coupling with the actual implementation details.

Working with testing impediments

This section explains the nature or quality of code that makes unit testing difficult. Automated tests help us develop software quickly even when we have a large code base to work on. However, automated tests should be executed very fast so that tests can give us quick feedback. We cannot unit test code when it exhibits any of the following features:

- It performs long running operations
- It connects to a database and modifies database records

- It performs remote computing
- It looks up JNDI resources or web/app server objects
- It accesses the filesystem
- It works with native objects or graphical widgets (UI components, alert, Java Swing components, and so on)
- It accesses network resources such as the LAN printer and downloads data from the Internet

Unit tests should not wait for a long running process to complete; it will defeat the purpose of quick feedback.

Unit tests should be reliable, and they should fail if and only if the production code is broken. However, if your unit test verifies an I/O operation, such as connecting to a LAN printer, which is slow, error prone, and unpredictable, then your unit test may fail due to some network issue, but it will incorrectly signal that the code is broken. So, unit testing a network operation defeats the test reliability principle.

Unit tests run automatically, so it doesn't make any sense to open a modal dialog or show an alert message during test execution because the test will wait, unless the UI dialog or the alert is closed.

So, the preceding features in the production code are barriers during unit testing. The following example shows how to avoid test impediments:

```java
public class MovieTicketPro {

  public void book(Movie movie, ShowTime time, int noOfTickets) {
    MovieDao dao = new MovieDao();
    MovieHall hall = dao.findMovie(movie, time);
    if (hall != null) {
      List<String> seats = dao.getAvilableSeats(movie,
        time);
      if (seats.size() < noOfTickets) {
        BookingErrorController.
          createAndShowTicketNotAvailableError();
        return;
      }
      int booked = 0;
      String bookedSeats = "";
      for (String aSeat : seats) {
        try {
          dao.book(hall, time, aSeat);
          bookedSeats += " " + aSeat;
          booked++;
```

```
        if (booked == noOfTickets) {
          BookingErrorController.
            createAndShowBookedMsg(bookedSeats);
          break;
        }
      } catch (BookingException e) {
        if (e.getType().equals(ErrorType.SeatAlreadyBooked))
          {
          BookingErrorController.
            createAndShowTicketNotAvailableError();
          if (BookingErrorController.
           createAndShowAdjacentSeatsNotAvaialble())
            {
            continue;
          }
          break;
        }
      } catch (Exception e) {
        BookingErrorController.
          createAndShowDatabaseSaveError();
        break;
      }
    }
  }else{
    BookingErrorController.
      createAndShowMovieOrShowTimeNotAvailableError();
  }
}
```

The book() method in the preceding example takes a movie, a show time, and the number of tickets to book, and it books the tickets or shows an error message. If an invalid movie or show time is passed to the book method, it shows an error message that states the movie or show time is not available. The following is the ticket booking logic:

1. First, the book method finds a movie hall for the movie and the movie's show time, for example, the movie *The HOBBIT*, with show time *Evening* is being screened in *SCREEN 2*. If the movie is not being played, an error message is shown.

2. It then retrieves the available seats, for example, 40 seats are available in *SCREEN 2* in the evening.

3. If the requested numbers of seats are greater than the available number of seats, an error message is shown, for example, request for 10 tickets but only two seats available.

4. If the seats requested are available, then it loops through the seats and books them.

5. If any error occurs during seat booking, such as someone concurrently books the seat or some runtime error occurs, the relevant error message is displayed.

The BookingErrorController class is responsible for displaying error messages. The following is the BookingErrorController class:

```
public class BookingErrorController {
    public static void createAndShowTicketNotAvailableError() {
        JOptionPane.showMessageDialog(null,
          "Ticket is not available","Booking message",
          JOptionPane.WARNING_MESSAGE);
    }

    public static void createAndShowDatabaseSaveError() {
        JOptionPane.showMessageDialog(null,
          "Could not book ticket",  "Booking Error",
          JOptionPane.ERROR_MESSAGE);
    }

    public static void createAndShowBookedMsg(String seats) {
        JOptionPane.showMessageDialog(null,
          "Following tickets" + seats+ " Booked",
          "Booking Info", JOptionPane.ERROR_MESSAGE);
    }
    //other methods are ignored for brevity
}
```

Each method calls JOptionPane to display messages. JOptionPane shows the modal dialog box, and the user has to click on the close button or the **Yes/No** button to close the dialog. If the user doesn't close the dialog box, the program keeps waiting for the user action.

So, you cannot unit test the movie ticket booking logic unless you separate the error message display from the code logic.

The second thing to note is the MovieDao creation constructor:

```
MovieDao dao = new MovieDao();
```

The `book()` method instantiates a database access object and invokes methods on it. We should separate the direct database access object creation from code so that we can pass a mock data access object and stub out the database calls; otherwise, the `book()` method will instantiate the real `MovieDao` object and the test will take time to execute. For now, we'll unit test the code with the real data access logic and later refactor the code to separate the `MovieDao` object instantiation.

Create a `MovieTicketProTest` test class and add a sanity check method to call the `book` method with null objects. The following is the code snippet:

```
public class MovieTicketProTest {
   MovieTicketPro movieTicketPro= new MovieTicketPro();

   @Test
   public void sanity() throws Exception {
      movieTicketPro.book(null, null, 1);
   }

}
```

When we execute the test in Eclipse, it shows an error message pop up, and the test waits for user action. The following is the Eclipse output, and you can see that the test is waiting for the pop up:

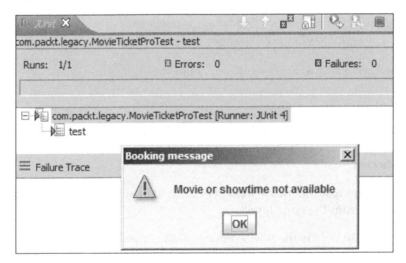

If we include the test on our automation suite, the automation suite will run forever and wait for user intervention. We can localize the problem; extract the protected methods for each `BookingErrorController` method call. This change will allow us to create a `MovieTicketPro` fake object and replace the protected methods with empty implementations. However, the problem is how do we verify the error conditions? We can extract an error message interface, create a generic error message method, and pass and refactor the `BookingErrorController` class to implement the interface. The following are the interface details:

```
package com.packt.legacy;

public interface ErrorMessageDisplayer {
    void showMessage(String title, String message,
        int messageType);
    boolean showConfirmMessage(String title, String message);
}
```

Modify the `BookingErrorController` class to implement the interface. The following is the implementation:

```
public class BookingErrorController implements
    ErrorMessageDisplayer{

    @Override
    public void showMessage(String title, String message,
        int messageType) {
        JOptionPane.showMessageDialog(null, message, title,
            messageType);
    }

    @Override
    public boolean showConfirmMessage(String title,
        String message) {
        int output = JOptionPane.showConfirmDialog(null,
            message, title, JOptionPane.YES_NO_OPTION);
        return output == JOptionPane.YES_OPTION;
    }
    //other methods are ignored for brevity
}
```

Modify the `MovieTicketPro` class and, inline, all the `BookingErrorController` calls. The following is an example of such a change:

```
} catch (Exception e) {
    JOptionPane.showMessageDialog(null, "Could not book ticket",
        "Booking Error", JOptionPane.ERROR_MESSAGE);
    break;
    }
}
}else {
    JOptionPane.showMessageDialog(null,
        "Movie or showtime not available",
        "Booking message", JOptionPane.WARNING_MESSAGE);
}
```

Note that the `BookingErrorController.createAndShowDatabaseSaveError()` and `BookingErrorController.createAndShowMovieOrShowTimeNotAvailableError()` methods are replaced by the original method content.

Now remove the static error message methods from the `BookingErrorController` class. You should not get any compilation errors.

Create a getter method in `MovieTicketPro` to return an implementation of `ErrorMessageDisplayer`. The following is the method body:

```
protected ErrorMessageDisplayer getErrorMessageDisplayer() {
  return new BookingErrorController();
}
```

Replace all contents of the `JOptionPane.showMessageDialog` code with `getErrorMessageDisplayer()`. The following is the modified code:

```
public class MovieTicketPro {
  public void book(Movie movie, ShowTime time, int noOfTickets) {
    MovieDao dao = new MovieDao();
    MovieHall hall = dao.findMovie(movie, time);
    if (hall != null) {
      List<String> seats = dao.getAvilableSeats(movie,
        time);
      if (seats.size() < noOfTickets) {
        getErrorMessageDisplayer().showMessage("Booking message",
          "Ticket is not available", JOptionPane.WARNING_MESSAGE);
       return;
      }
      int booked = 0;
      String bookedSeats = "";
      for (String aSeat : seats) {
        try {
          dao.book(hall, time, aSeat);
          bookedSeats += " " + aSeat;
          booked++;
          if (booked == noOfTickets) {
            getErrorMessageDisplayer().showMessage("Booking Info",
            "Following tickets" + bookedSeats + " Booked",
            JOptionPane.ERROR_MESSAGE);

            break;

          }
        } catch (BookingException e) {
          if (e.getType().equals(ErrorType.SeatAlreadyBooked)) {
```

```
        getErrorMessageDisplayer().showMessage(
          "Booking message", "Ticket is not available",
          JOptionPane.WARNING_MESSAGE);

        boolean yes = getErrorMessageDisplayer().
          showConfirmMessage("Booking message",
          "Adjacent seats not available.
          Can I book any other seat?");

        if (yes) {
          getErrorMessageDisplayer().showMessage(
            "Booking information","Going to auto allocate
            seats.", JOptionPane.INFORMATION_MESSAGE);
          break;
        }


      }
    } catch (Exception e) {
      getErrorMessageDisplayer().showMessage
        ("Booking Error","Could not book ticket",
        JOptionPane.ERROR_MESSAGE);
      break;
    }
  }
} else {
  getErrorMessageDisplayer().showMessage("Booking message",
    "Movie or showtime not available",
    JOptionPane.WARNING_MESSAGE);
  }
}


protected ErrorMessageDisplayer getErrorMessageDisplayer() {
  return new BookingErrorController();
  }
}
```

We can unit test the code as shown in the following code snippet. Create a
fake object and override the `getErrorMessageDisplayer()` method to return
a `ErrorMessageDisplayer` mock. We can verify the error messages indirectly
from the mock object arguments:

```
@RunWith(MockitoJUnitRunner.class)
public class MovieTicketProTest {
  @Mock    ErrorMessageDisplayer messageDisplayer;

  MovieTicketPro movieTicketPro = new MovieTicketPro() {
```

```
        protected ErrorMessageDisplayer
          getErrorMessageDisplayer() {
          return messageDisplayer;
        }
    };
    @Test    public void when_invalid_movie_shows_error_message(){
        movieTicketPro.book(null, null, 1);
        ArgumentCaptor<String> stringArgCaptor = ArgumentCaptor.
          forClass(String.class);
        ArgumentCaptor<Integer> intArgCaptor = ArgumentCaptor.
          forClass(Integer.class);

        verify(messageDisplayer).showMessage(stringArgCaptor.capture(),
          stringArgCaptor.capture(), intArgCaptor.capture());
        assertEquals("Movie or showtime not available",
          stringArgCaptor.getAllValues().get(1));
    }
}
```

We need to separate the database access, create a getter method to return the
MovieDao object, and call the getter method from the book method. From test,
we can create a fake object and override the getMovieDao() method to return
a mock data access object.

The following are the changes in the code:

```
    protected MovieDao getMovieDao() {
        return new MovieDao();
    }
    public void book(Movie movie, ShowTime time, int noOfTickets) {
        MovieDao dao = getMovieDao();
        //code ignored for brevity
    }
```

The following is the modified test:

```
    @RunWith(MockitoJUnitRunner.class)
    public class MovieTicketProTest {
      @Mock ErrorMessageDisplayer messageDisplayer;
      @Mock MovieDao movieDao;

      MovieTicketPro movieTicketPro = new MovieTicketPro() {
        protected ErrorMessageDisplayer
          getErrorMessageDisplayer() {
          return messageDisplayer;
        }
```

```
    protected MovieDao getMovieDao() {
      return movieDao;
    }
  };
}
```

After this change, the test execution finishes very quickly. The following is the test execution output:

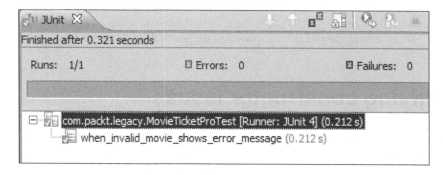

The next section covers designing for testability.

Designing for testability

We learned about testing impediments and how to refactor them. We cannot unit test code when testing impediments are present; we refactor the code and move the impediments out (to another class or methods), and during testing, the impediments are replaced with mock objects.

However, sometimes we cannot mock out the external dependencies because of testing an unfriendly design. This section covers the design for testability, or rather matters to avoid in code. The following Java constructs go up against mocking the testing impediments:

- Constructors initialize testing impediments
- Class-level variable declaration and initialization
- The private methods
- The final methods
- The static methods
- The final classes
- Use of new

- Static variable declaration and initialization
- Static initialization blocks

You cannot unit test the legacy code because either it is tightly coupled or testing unfavorable language constructs hide the testing impediments. The following section explains the testing unfavorable constructs.

 To show a testing impediment, we'll throw a special runtime exception `TestingImpedimentException`. If your test fails with a `TestingImpedimentException`, then that means you cannot automate the test as your code has unfavorable features for testing.

Identifying constructor issues

To build a test, we need to instantiate the class in the test harness, but the problem with legacy code is that it is difficult to break dependency and instantiate a class in a test harness. One such example is in a constructor, where the class instantiates many objects, reads from the properties file, or even creates a database connection. There can be many callers of the class, so you cannot change the constructor to pass dependencies; otherwise, it will cause a series of compilation errors.

We will take a look at a sample legacy code and try to write a test for the class.

Suppose we have a `TestingUnfavorableConstructor` class with two external dependencies `DatabaseDependency` and `FileReadDependency`. Both the dependencies are slow in nature and are testing impediments. `TestingUnfavorableConstructor` creates dependencies in the constructor. Ideally, the dependencies represent the database access and the file reads from the `TestingUnfavorableConstructor` constructor. The following is the `TestingUnfavorableConstructor` class:

```
public class TestingUnfavorableConstructor {
  private DatabaseDependency dependency1;
  private FileReadDependency dependency2;

  public TestingUnfavorableConstructor() {
    this.dependency1 = new DatabaseDependency();
    this.dependency2 = new FileReadDependency();
  }
```

```
public Object testMe(Object arg) {
    return arg;
}

}
```

If we want to unit test the `testMe()` behavior of the class, then we need to create an object of the `TestingUnfavorableConstructor` class. However, when we try to create an instance in a unit test, the class fails to indicate that the class cannot be instantiated from an automated test suite. The following is the output:

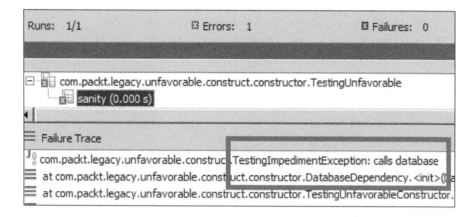

To overcome this, you should inject the dependencies through a constructor instead of creating them in a constructor.

We cannot modify the default constructor because the class is invoked from many other clients. We cannot break the clients. The other two options are as follows:

- Keep the default constructor as it is. Create another constructor and inject dependencies through this new constructor; from test, we can call this new constructor.

- Create a protected method, move the dependency instantiation to that method, create two setter methods, and initialize the dependencies through the setter injection. In the test, create a fake object of the main class and override the protected method to do nothing, and pass the dependencies through the setter methods.

The first option is relatively straight forward. We'll apply the second approach.

The following is the modified code:

```java
public class TestingUnfavorableConstructor {
  private DatabaseDependency dependency1;
  private FileReadDependency dependency2;

  public TestingUnfavorableConstructor() {
    createDependencies();
  }

  protected void createDependencies() {
    this.dependency1 = new DatabaseDependency();
    this.dependency2 = new FileReadDependency();
  }

  public void setDependency1(DatabaseDependency dependency1) {
    this.dependency1 = dependency1;
  }

  public void setDependency2(FileReadDependency dependency2) {
    this.dependency2 = dependency2;
  }

  public Object testMe(Object arg) {
    return arg;
  }
}
```

The following unit test overrides the TestingUnfavorableConstructor and provides an empty implementation of the createDependencies() method, creates mock dependencies, and calls setter methods to set the mock dependencies:

```java
@RunWith(MockitoJUnitRunner.class)
public class TestingUnfavorableConstructorTest {
  @Mock DatabaseDependency dep1;
  @Mock FileReadDependency dep2;
  TestingUnfavorableConstructor unfavorableConstructor;
  @Before  public void setUp() {
    unfavorableConstructor= new TestingUnfavorableConstructor() {
      protected void createDependencies() {
      }
    };

    unfavorableConstructor.setDependency1(dep1);
    unfavorableConstructor.setDependency2(dep2);
```

```
    }

    @Test    public void sanity() throws Exception {
    }
}
```

 Do not instantiate dependencies in the constructor; the dependencies may exhibit testing impediments and make the class nontestable. Instead of instantiating the dependencies in the constructor, you can pass the real implementations (real dependencies) to the constructor or the setter method of the code under the test.

Realizing initialization issues

Class-level variable declaration and object instantiation at the same time creates problems. You don't get the chance to mock out the variable. The following example explains the problem:

The `VariableInitialization` class has a database dependency, and the dependency is instantiated where it is declared, as follows:

```
Public class VariableInitialization {
    DatabaseDependency dependency1 = new DatabaseDependency();
    public void testMe(Object obj) {

    }
}
```

When you instantiate the `VariableInitialization` class in test, the test fails. The following is the output:

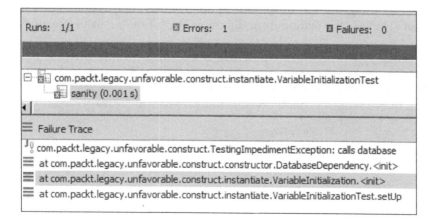

The following is the test class:

```
public class VariableInitializationTest {
  VariableInitialization initialization;

  @Before public void setUp() throws Exception {
    initialization = new VariableInitialization();
  }
  @Test    public void sanity() throws Exception {
  }
}
```

To overcome the class-level variable initialization, you can try out the following options:

- Add a default constructor and move the dependency instantiation to the default constructor. Create another constructor and inject the dependencies through this new constructor; from test, we can call this the new constructor.

- Add a default constructor, and move the dependency instantiation to a protected method and call the method from the default constructor. Create a setter method and initialize the dependency through a setter injection. In the test, create a fake object of the main class and override the protected method to do nothing, and pass the dependencies through the setter methods.

[Do not instantiate variables at the class level.]

Working with private methods

The private methods are useful for hiding the internal state and encapsulation, but they can also hide the testing impediments. The following example explains the details:

The PrivateMethod class has a private method named showError(). This private method hides a test impediment. When we unit test the validate() method with a null object, the validate() method calls the showError message, as follows:

```
public class PrivateMethod {
  public Object validate(Object arg) {
    if(arg == null) {
      showError("Null input");
    }
    return arg;
```

```
    }

    private void showError(String msg) {
      GraphicalInterface.showMessage(msg);
    }
  }
```

The following is the test output:

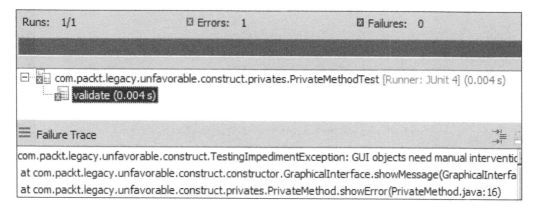

You can extract the testing impediments to a protected method, or you can separate the concern. Create a new class, move the testing impediment to that class, and inject the new class as a dependency.

[Do not hide testing impediments in private methods.   ]

The following code refactors the testing impediments and makes the class unit testable:

```
public class PrivateMethodRefactored {
  public Object validate(Object arg) {
    if(arg == null) {
      showError("Null input");
    }

    return arg;
  }

  protected void showError(String msg) {
    GraphicalInterface.showMessage(msg);
  }
}
```

The `showError` method's access specifier is changed to `protected`.

The following test code extends the class with an anonymous implementation, and it overrides the protected method with an empty implementation. The test code invokes the `validate()` method on the new anonymous implementation of the `PrivateMethodRefactored` class. In turn, the polymorphic behavior will call the empty implementation. Hence, the test will always bypass the testing impediments by calling the overridden empty implementation of the testing impediment, but the real production code will always invoke the protected method:

```
public class PrivateMethodRefactoredTest {

    PrivateMethodRefactored privateMethod;

    @Before
    public void setUp() {
        privateMethod = new PrivateMethodRefactored() {
            protected void showError(String msg) {

            }
        };
    }

    @Test
    public void validate() throws Exception {
        privateMethod.validate(null);
    }
}
```

> This approach of bypassing the testing impediments with overridden versions of the testing impediments is known as faking or fake object. If the code under test contains many testing impediments, then it is not possible to override all of them in an anonymous class. Instead, we can create an inner class, and extend the code under test and override all the testing unfriendly methods.

Working with final methods

When a method is final, you cannot override it. If the final method hides any testing impediment, you cannot unit test the class. The following example explains the issue:

The `FinalDependency` class has a final method named `doSomething`. This method hides a testing unfriendly feature. The following is the class definition:

```
public class FinalDependency {

  public final void doSomething() {
    throw new TestingImpedimentException(
      "Final methods cannot be overriden");
  }
}
```

The `FinalMethodDependency` class has a dependency on `FinalDependency`, and in the `testMe` method, it calls the `doSomething` method as follows:

```
public class FinalMethodDependency {

  private final FinalDependency dependency;

  public FinalMethodDependency(FinalDependency dependency) {
    this.dependency = dependency;
  }
  public void testMe() {
    dependency.doSomething();
  }
}
```

In the test, we'll mock the dependency and unit test the code as follows:

```
@RunWith(MockitoJUnitRunner.class)
public class FinalMethodDependencyTest {
  @Mock
  FinalDependency finalDependency;
  FinalMethodDependency methodDependency;

  @Before
  public void setUp() {
    methodDependency = new
      FinalMethodDependency(finalDependency);
  }

  @Test
  public void testSomething() throws Exception {
    methodDependency.testMe();
  }
}
```

When we run the test, the test still accesses the testing impediment, as the mock object cannot stub a final method. When we try to stub the method, we get an error. The following test stubs the final method call:

```
@Test
public void testSomething() throws Exception {
    doNothing().when(finalDependency).doSomething();
    methodDependency.testMe();
}
```

When we run the test, we get the following error message thrown by the Mockito framework:

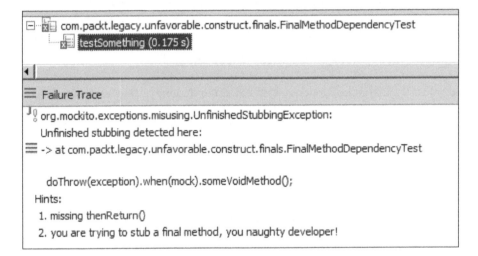

Do not hide the testing impediments in final methods. You cannot override or stub a final method.

The only possible way to overcome this is extracting the content of the final method to a protected method; call the protected method from the final method, and override the protected method in test. Otherwise, you can use the PowerMock or PowerMockito framework if you cannot touch the class at all; for example, when you only have a JAR file.

Exploring static method issues

The `static` methods are good for utility classes, but unnecessary use of `static` can hide the testing impediments and create problems in unit testing. The following example sheds light on the issue:

The `SingletonDependency` class is an implementation of the **Gang of Four (GoF)** singleton design pattern. It has a `private` constructor and a static `getInstance()` method to create only a single instance of the class. The static `callMe()` method hides a testing impediment. Note that the GoF singleton pattern doesn't define methods as `static`, but in this example, we are defining the `callMe()` method as `static` to display a drawback of the `static` methods. The following is the singleton implementation:

```
public class SingletonDependency {
   private static SingletonDependency singletonDependency;

   private SingletonDependency() {
   }

   public synchronized static SingletonDependency getInstance() {
      if (singletonDependency == null) {
        singletonDependency = new SingletonDependency();
      }

      return singletonDependency;
   }

   Public static void callMe() {
      throw new TestingImpedimentException("we dont
         need singleton");
   }
}
```

The `VictimOfAPatternLover` class has a dependency on `SingletonDependency`. The following are the class details:

```
public class VictimOfAPatternLover {
   private final SingletonDependency dependency;

   public VictimOfAPatternLover(SingletonDependency dependency) {
      this.dependency = dependency;
   }

   public void testMe() {
      dependency.callMe();
   }
}
```

Mockito cannot stub a static method. When we try to stub the static `callMe()` method, it still calls the original method and fails for the testing impediment. You cannot stub a `static` method.

[🔦 Do not hide testing impediments in static methods.
You cannot stub static methods.]

The only way to overcome this issue is to create a `protected` method and wrap the `static` call. From the code, call the wrapped method and from the test, override the `protected` method.

Add a `static` wrapper method in the dependency class and call the `static` method from it, as shown in the following code:

```
public static void callMe() {
    throw new TestingImpedimentException("Common we dont
        need singleton");
}

protected void wrapper() {
    callMe();
}
```

In the code, call the `wrapper` method as follows:

```
public void testMe() {
    dependency.wrapper();
}
```

Stub the `wrapper` method in the test as follows:

```
@Test
    public void testMe() throws Exception {
        Mockito.doNothing().when(dependency).wrapper();
        aPatternLover.testMe();
    }
```

Working with final classes

You cannot override a `final` class, so you can hide testing unfavorable features in a `final` class. The following example explains the problem:

The final class hides a testing impediment as follows:

```
public final class FinalDepencyClass {

  public void poison() {
    throw new TestingImpedimentException("Finals cannot
      be mocked");
  }
}
```

The code under test has a dependency on the final class as follows:

```
public class FinalClassDependency {
  private final FinalDepencyClass finalDepencyClass;

  public FinalClassDependency(FinalDepencyClass
    finalDepencyClass) {
    this.finalDepencyClass = finalDepencyClass;
  }

  public void testMe() {
    finalDepencyClass.poison();
  }
}
```

In test, we'll try to stub the `poison` method as follows:

```
@RunWith(MockitoJUnitRunner.class)
public class FinalClassDependencyTest {
  @Mock
  FinalDepencyClass finalDependency;

  FinalClassDependency test;

  @Before
  public void setUp() {
    test = new FinalClassDependency(finalDependency);
  }
  @Test
  public void testMe() throws Exception {
    Mockito.doNothing().when(finalDependency).poison();
    test.testMe();
  }
}
```

The test fails with a **MockitoException** as Mockito cannot mock a final class. The following is the JUnit output:

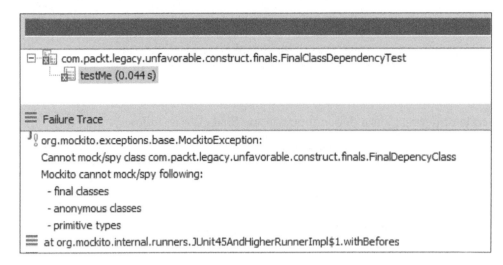

 Do not hide testing impediments in final classes. You cannot mock a final class.

Final classes are important for framework or architecture design so that no one can hack the behavior, but it can create a serious problem for unit testing. Consider it before you choose to make a class final.

Learning the new attribute

Java instantiates classes using the new operator, but a new operator can create problems for unit testing.

The following example explains the issue. The PoisonIvy constructor has a testing impediment such as calls fetch data from a database table or reads from a filesystem; we represented the testing impediment with the TestingImpedimentException:

```
public class PoisonIvy {

  public PoisonIvy() {
    throw new TestingImpedimentException(
      "Do not instantiate concrete class,
      use interfaces");
  }
}
```

```
    public void poison() {

    }
}
```

The following is the code that calls the `PoisonIvy` constructor:

```
public class NewExpressionDependency {

    public void testMe() {
        PoisonIvy ivy = new PoisonIvy();
        ivy.poison();
    }
}
```

When we unit test the `testMe()` code, it fails. The `testMe()` method directly creates an instance of dependency and calls the `poison()` method. You cannot override this `new` expression. If we want to unit test the `testMe()` method, first we need to move the `new` operator outside of `testMe()` as we cannot instantiate the `PoisonIvy` class. The constructor of `PoisonIvy` throws an exception. Hence, we cannot unit test the `testMe` behavior unless we move the object creation out of `testMe`. Instead of creating a new instance of `PoisonIvy` inside `testMe()`, we can pass an instance of `PoisonIvy` as a method argument, or create a class-level dependency and pass `PoisonIvy` as the constructor or setter dependency argument.

> Program to an interface, not to an implementation. Rather than hardcoding the instantiation of the subtype into the code, assign the concrete implementation object at runtime.

What is "program to an interface, not to an implementation"?

This means program to a supertype rather than a subtype. You can interchange the implementation at runtime. In the collection framework, we have the `List` interface and its many implantations. In your class, always define a variable of the `List` type and not `ArrayList`; at runtime, you can assign any implementation you want.

In this example, you can pass `PoisonIvy` as a constructor or setter dependency, and at runtime (during testing), you can pass a mock or a fake implementation to suppress the testing impediments.

Exploring static variables and blocks

Static initializations and `static` blocks are executed during class loading. You cannot override them. If you initialize a testing impediment in a `static` block, then you cannot unit test the class. The following example explains the issue:

The `StaticBlockOwner` class has a static variable named `StaticBlockDependency`, and it initializes the variable in a `static` block. The following is the class:

```
public class StaticBlockOwner {
  private static StaticBlockDependency blockDependency;
  static {
    blockDependency = new StaticBlockDependency();
    blockDependency.loadTime = new Date();
  }
  public void testMe() {
  }
}
```

When we unit test the class, it fails. The following is the unit test:

```
public class StaticBlockOwnerTest {
  StaticBlockOwner owner;
  @Before public void setUp()  {
    owner = new StaticBlockOwner();
  }
  @Test   public void clean() throws Exception {
    owner.testMe();
  }
}
```

The test fails with a `java.lang.ExceptionInInitializationError`, as it tries to instantiate the dependency in a `static` block and the dependency throws an exception.

[Do not instantiate dependencies in the static block.
You cannot override the testing impediments.]

The book *Working Effectively with Legacy Code*, *Pearson Education*, by Michael Feathers explains the legacy code and how effectively you can refactor the legacy code. You can read the e-book at `http://www.amazon.com/Working-Effectively-Legacy-Michael-Feathers/dp/0131177052`.

Working with greenfield code

This section illustrates the three-step rhythm of writing a failing test, coding enough to make it work, and then refactoring it. This is implied greenfield coding as opposed to working with an existing legacy code.

TDD is an evolutionary development approach. It offers test-first development where the production code is written only to satisfy a test, and the code is refactored to improve the code quality. In TDD, unit tests drive the design. You write the code to satisfy a failing test, so it limits the code you write to only what is needed. The tests provide fast automated regression for refactoring and new enhancements.

Kent Beck is the originator of Extreme Programming and TDD. He has authored many books and papers. Visit `http://en.wikipedia.org/wiki/Kent_Beck` for details.

The following diagram represents the TDD life cycle:

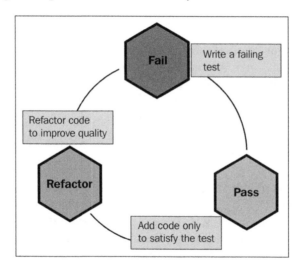

First, we write a failing test, then add code to satisfy the failing test, and then refactor the code and again start with another test.

The following section provides an example of TDD. We'll build a program to conduct an election survey and forecast the result. The program will compile the survey result and display the opinion poll.

The result should present the zone-wise (geographically) poll opinion and overall opinion, such as if there are two zones, east and west, then the result will be presented in the following format:

OVERALL
A 39%, B 31%, C 20% , D 10%
EAST ZONE
A 50%, B 40%, C 10%
WEST ZONE
A 40%, B 60%

Let's look at the following steps:

1. Create a test class named `SurveyResultCompilerTest` and add a `when_one_opinion_then_result_forecasts_the_opinion()` test to compile the overall survey result.

 We'll follow this convention for the test method names, for example, `when_some_condition_then_this_happens`. We will use the underscore symbol as a separator.

2. In this new test method, type in `SurveyResultCompiler()`. The compiler will complain that the `SurveyResultCompiler` class doesn't exist. Hover the mouse over `SurveyResultCompiler`; Eclipse will suggest a quick fix for you. Choose **Create class 'SurveyResultCompiler'**, and create the class in the `com.packt.tdd.survey` package under the `src` source folder, as shown in the following screenshot:

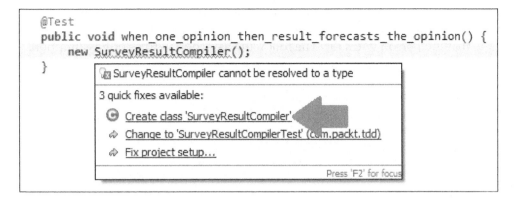

```
@Test
public void when_one_opinion_then_result_forecasts_the_opinion() {
    new SurveyResultCompiler();
}
```

3. SurveyResultCompiler is ready. We need to pass an opinion to SurveyResultCompiler so that it can compile a result. Modify the test to call willVoteFor and pass an opinion. The compiler will complain that the method doesn't exist. Add the method to SurveyResultCompiler by following the quick fix options. The following is the test method:

```
@Test
public void when_one_opinion_then_result_forecasts_the_opinion()
{
    new SurveyResultCompiler().willVoteFor("Party A");
}
```

4. We need a compiled result after the survey. The result should give us the party name and winning percentage. We can think of a Map data type. Modify the test again to obtain the result. The following is the modified test:

```
@Test
public void when_one_opinion_then_result_forecasts_the_opinion()
{
    SurveyResultCompiler surveyResultCompiler = new
        SurveyResultCompiler();
    surveyResultCompiler.willVoteFor("Party A");
    Map<String, BigDecimal> result
      =surveyResultCompiler.forecastResult();
}
```

5. Add the forecastResult method to the SurveyResultCompiler class. The following is the SurveyResultCompiler class:

```
public class SurveyResultCompiler {
  public void willVoteFor(String opinion) {
  }
  public Map<String, BigDecimal> forecastResult() {
    return null;
  }
}
```

6. Verify that when only one person participates in a survey, then the survey result should return a 100 percent winning chance for the political party that the person votes for. The following assertion verifies our assumption:

```
@Test
public void
  when_one_opinion_then_result_forecasts_the_opinion() {
  SurveyResultCompiler surveyResultCompiler = new
    SurveyResultCompiler();
  String opinion = "Party A";
  surveyResultCompiler.willVoteFor(opinion);

  Map<String, BigDecimal> result
    =surveyResultCompiler.forecastResult();

  assertEquals(new BigDecimal("100"),
    result.get(opinion));
}
```

7. When we run the test, it fails with a `NullPointerException`. We need to modify the code as follows to return a result:

```
public Map<String, BigDecimal> forecastResult() {
  Map<String, BigDecimal> result = new HashMap<String,
    BigDecimal>();
  return result;
}
```

8. Rerun the test. It fails for an `AssertionError`. The following is the output:

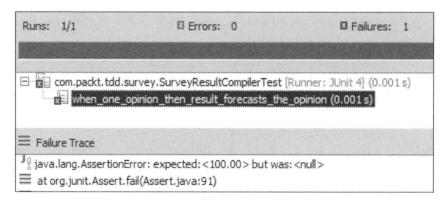

9. We need to modify the code to return 100 percent for `Party A`. The following is the modified code:

```
public Map<String, BigDecimal> forecastResult() {
  Map<String, BigDecimal> result = new HashMap<String,
    BigDecimal>();
  result.put("Party A", new BigDecimal("100"));
  return result;
}
```

10. Rerun the test. It will show you a green bar. The following is the output:

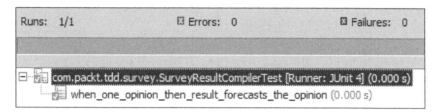

11. Now we need to add another test to verify that when two persons participate in a poll, and they vote for two different political parties, then the result should portray 50 percent chance for each party. Add a `when_different_opinions_then_forecasts_50_percent_chance_for_each_party` test, and add the following lines to verify the assumption:

```
@Test    public void
  when_different_opinions_then_forecasts_50_percent_
  chance_for_each_party() {
  SurveyResultCompiler surveyResultCompiler = new
    SurveyResultCompiler();
  String opinionA = "Party A";
  surveyResultCompiler.willVoteFor(opinionA);
  String opinionB = "Party B";
  surveyResultCompiler.willVoteFor(opinionB);
  Map<String, BigDecimal> result =
    surveyResultCompiler.forecastResult();
  assertEquals(new BigDecimal("50"),
    result.get(opinionA));
  assertEquals(new BigDecimal("50"),
    result.get(opinionB));
}
```

12. When we run the test, it fails. It expects 50 percent but gets 100 percent, as shown in the following screenshot:

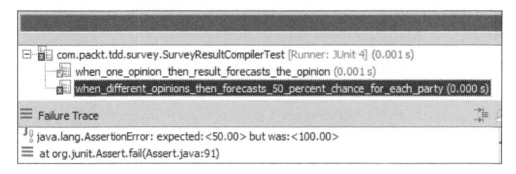

13. We need to modify the code to return 50 percent for `Party A` and 50 percent for `Party B`. The following is the modified code:

```
public Map<String, BigDecimal> forecastResult() {
    Map<String, BigDecimal> result = new HashMap<String,
      BigDecimal>();
    result.put("Party A", new BigDecimal("50"));
    result.put("Party B", new BigDecimal("50"));
    return result;
}
```

14. Rerun the test. The second test passes but the first test fails, as shown in the following screenshot:

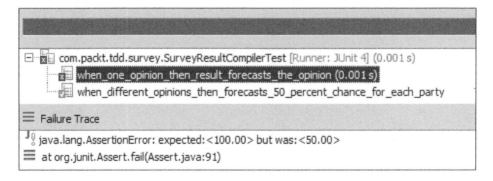

15. We broke the first test. Now we need to revert the changes, but then the second test will fail. We need an algorithm to calculate the percentage. First, we need to store the opinions. Add a `List` to the `SurveyResultCompiler` class and store each opinion. The following is the code:

```
public class SurveyResultCompiler {
  List<String> opinions = new ArrayList<String>();

  public void willVoteFor(String opinion) {
    opinions.add(opinion);
  }
  //the result method is ignored for brevity
}
```

16. Now we need to modify the `forecastResult` method to calculate the percentage. First, loop through the opinions to get the party-wise vote count, such as 10 voters for `Party A` and 20 voters for `Party B`. Then, we can compute the percentage as *vote count * 100 / total votes*. The following is the code:

```
public Map<String, BigDecimal> forecastResult() {

  Map<String, BigDecimal> result = new HashMap<String,
    BigDecimal>();
  Map<String, Integer> countMap = new HashMap<String,
    Integer>();
  for(String party:opinions) {
    Integer count = countMap.get(party);
    if(count == null) {
      count = 1;
    }else {
      count++;
    }
    countMap.put(party, count);
  }

  for(String party:countMap.keySet()) {
    Integer voteCount = countMap.get(party);
    int totalVotes = opinions.size();
    BigDecimal percentage = new
      BigDecimal((voteCount*100)/totalVotes);
    result.put(party, percentage);
  }

  return result;
}
```

17. Rerun the test. You will get a green bar, as shown in the following screenshot:

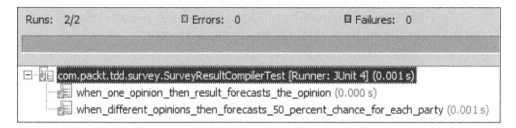

18. Now add a test for three participants. The following is the test:

```
@Test
public void
  when_three_different_opinions_then_forecasts_33_
  percent_chance_for_each_party() {
  SurveyResultCompiler surveyResultCompiler = new
    SurveyResultCompiler();
  String opinionA = "Party A";
  surveyResultCompiler.willVoteFor(opinionA);
  String opinionB = "Party B";
  surveyResultCompiler.willVoteFor(opinionB);
  String opinionC = "Party C";
  surveyResultCompiler.willVoteFor(opinionC);
  Map<String, BigDecimal> result =
    surveyResultCompiler.forecastResult();
  assertEquals(new BigDecimal("33"),
    result.get(opinionA));
  assertEquals(new BigDecimal("33"),
    result.get(opinionB));
  assertEquals(new BigDecimal("33"),
    result.get(opinionC));
}
```

19. Look at the test class, and you will find the duplicate code in each test method; clean them. Move the `SurveyResultCompiler` object instantiation to a `setUp` method instead of instantiating the class in each test method. Inline are the `opinion` variables, such as `opinionA`. The following is the refactored test class:

```
public class SurveyResultCompilerTest {

  SurveyResultCompiler surveyResultCompiler;

  @Before
  public void setUp() {
```

```java
    surveyResultCompiler = new SurveyResultCompiler();
}

@Test public void
  when_one_opinion_then_result_forecasts_the_opinion() {

    surveyResultCompiler.willVoteFor("Party A");
    Map<String, BigDecimal> result =
      surveyResultCompiler.forecastResult();
    assertEquals(new BigDecimal("100"),
      result.get("Party A"));
}

@Test public void
  when_two_different_opinions_then_forecasts_50_
  percent_chance_for_each_party() {

    surveyResultCompiler.willVoteFor("Party A");
    surveyResultCompiler.willVoteFor("Party B");

    Map<String, BigDecimal> result =
      surveyResultCompiler.forecastResult();

    assertEquals(new BigDecimal("50"),
      result.get("Party A"));
    assertEquals(new BigDecimal("50"),
      result.get("Party B"));
}

@Test public void
  when_three_different_opinions_then_forecasts_
  33_percent_chance_for_each_party() {

    surveyResultCompiler.willVoteFor("Party A");
    surveyResultCompiler.willVoteFor("Party B");
    surveyResultCompiler.willVoteFor("Party C");

    Map<String, BigDecimal> result =
      surveyResultCompiler.forecastResult();

    assertEquals(new BigDecimal("33"),
      result.get("Party A"));
    assertEquals(new BigDecimal("33"),
      result.get("Party B"));
    assertEquals(new BigDecimal("33"),
      result.get("Party C"));
  }
}
```

20. The test class looks clean now. Rerun the test to make sure nothing is broken. The following is the test output:

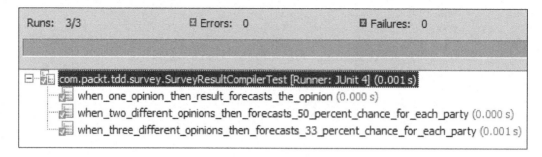

21. Revisit the `SurveyResultCompiler` class. It works with a `List` and two `Map` attributes. Do we really need to keep the `List` attribute? Instead of calculating the votes from `List`, we can directly store the opinions in `Map` and keep the opinion count up to date. The following is the refactored code:

```java
public class SurveyResultCompiler {
  private Map<String, Integer> opinions =
    new HashMap<String, Integer>();
  private long participationCount = 0;
  public void willVoteFor(String opinion) {
    Integer sameOpinionCount = opinions.get(opinion);
    if (sameOpinionCount == null) {
      sameOpinionCount = 1;
    } else {
      sameOpinionCount++;
    }
    opinions.put(opinion, sameOpinionCount);
    participationCount++;
  }

  public Map<String, BigDecimal> forecastResult() {
    Map<String, BigDecimal> result = new HashMap<String,
      BigDecimal>();

    for (String opinion : opinions.keySet()) {
      Integer sameOpinionCount =
        opinions.get(opinion);
      BigDecimal opinionPercentage = new BigDecimal(
        (sameOpinionCount * 100) / participationCount);
      result.put(opinion, opinionPercentage);
    }
    return result;
  }
}
```

22. Rerun the test to make sure nothing is broken. If anything breaks, then immediately revert the changes. The tests should run fine, so we are good to go.

23. One feature is complete. Now we need to develop a new feature — zone-wise calculation. The existing test cases will safeguard our code. If you break any existing test, immediately revisit your change.

What we just completed is TDD. It has the following benefits:

- TDD gives us clean, testable, and maintainable code.

- We document and update the code, but we forget to update the documentation; this creates confusion. You can document your code and keep it updated, or write your code and unit tests in such a way that anybody can understand the intent. In TDD, tests are written to provide enough documentation of code. So, the test is our documentation, but we need to clean the tests too to keep them readable and maintainable.

- We can write many tests with boundary value conditions, null, zero, negative numbers, and so on, and verify our code. And by passing these boundary values, you're trying to break your own code. No need to package the whole application and ship it to **Quality Assurance (QA)** or the customer to discover issues.

- You also avoid over engineering the classes you write. Just write what's needed to make all tests green.

- Another benefit to incrementally build your code is that your API is easier to work with because the code is written and used at the same time.

Summary

This chapter explained the unit testing strategy for the legacy code and new development. It covered the legacy code issues, refactored the legacy code, illustrated design for testability, described the TDD concepts and TDD life cycle, demonstrated TDD examples, and refactoring.

Now the reader should be able to write unit tests for legacy code, refactor the legacy code to improve the design of the existing code, and start writing simple, clean, and maintainable code that follows TDD, and refactor the code to improve its quality.

The next chapter covers the best practices of unit testing.

10
Best Practices

"It is insanity to keep doing things the same way and expect things to improve."

– Anonymous

Writing clean, readable, and maintainable JUnit test cases, just like writing clean code, is an art. A well-written unit test can prevent maintenance nightmare and acts as a system documentation; however, if not used carefully, it can produce meaningless boilerplate test cases. Mistakes are part of the learning process as long as you aren't making them repeatedly. JUnit is not rocket science, so we can practice, follow guidelines, and learn from others to make it perfect.

This chapter covers JUnit guidelines and best practices. The following categories are covered in depth:

- Writing meaningful tests
- Test automation
- Test configuration
- Assertion convention
- Exception handling
- Test smells and refactoring test smells

Writing meaningful tests

The common understanding of unit testing is testing the smallest possible part of software, specifically a method. In reality, we do not test methods; rather, we test a logical unit or the behavior of the system.

Logical units can extent to a single method, to an entire class, or a collaboration of multiple classes. For example, a standard calculator program can have an add method for adding two numbers. We can verify the add behavior by invoking the add method, or we can design the calculator program to have a simple calculate API that can take two numbers and an operation (add, subtract, divide, and so on), and depending on the operand type (integer, double, and so on), the calculator may delegate the calculation to a collaborator class, such as a double calculator or a long calculator. We can still unit test the add behavior, but now multiple classes are involved. We can call this new test an integration test.

A unit test verifies an assumption about the behavior of the system. In addition to this, if a test tests the entire system, it can't be a unit test—we call these tests **confederation** tests because they set up the entire ecosystem, including setting up the necessary components.

The following section elaborates on writing meaningful tests.

Improving readability

Martin Fowler said *Any fool can write code that a computer can understand. Good programmers write code that humans can understand.* Writing obscure code can be fashionable for old timers but it's not a standard Java practice. We should write readable and maintainable code such that anybody can understand the purpose of the code and enhance or maintain the code in future.

JUnit tests are written to test logical units. A test method name should portray the intention of the test so that a reader can understand what is being tested, such as the condition and the expectation or action.

Suppose you are writing a test for a role-based system and the system denies unauthorized access. You can use the following patterns, but if you choose to follow one pattern, it's best to stick to it:

- `testDenialOfUnauthorizedAccess()`
- `when_unauthorized_user_then_denies_the_access()`
- `should_deny_access_for_unauthorized_users()`

I prefer the underscore (_) pattern as it's more readable.

For boundary value conditions, you can follow these patterns:

- `testRegisteringNullUser()`
- `should_not_register_a_null_user()`

- should_throw_exception_when_a_null_user_is_registered()
- when_null_user_then_registrar_throws_exception()

Likewise, a test class should portray the intention of the tests. Usually, we follow two conventions, Test<class name> or <class name>Test. Suppose you are testing the UserRegistration behavior. You can use UserRegistrationTest or TestUserRegistration. Several test coverage tools fail to recognize classes without the Test suffix. So, UserRegistrationTest is a safe choice.

Breaking everything that could possibly break

An Extreme Programming concept is *test everything that could possibly break*. This means trying all different combinations of inputs to make sure we don't miss any combination that can cause the class to generate an error. However, this is an impossible thing to do in practice. We can test boundary value conditions. We can even cover all branches and lines, but we cannot test all input combinations. Suppose a method adds two integers. We can pass NULL, 0, Integer.MAX_VALUE, negative numbers, and so on, but we literally cannot test the method with all possible integer values.

Ignoring simple test cases

Writing trivial JUnits (such that for getter and setter) is mostly a waste of time and money. We don't have the luxury to write infinite tests as it can eat our development time, application build time, and reduce test maintainability. If we start writing tests for getter/setters, we may miss more useful test cases. Usually, unit tests are automated and run during a build process. A build is required to finish early providing feedback, but the process will be delayed if we keep adding trivial tests. Unit tests are system documentation, so they portray the system behavior; however, if we keep adding tests for trivial things, then it defeats the purpose. Write tests that will pay you back with information.

Verifying invalid parameters

Test invalid parameters to every method. Your code needs to recognize and handle invalid data. The tests that pass using incorrect data and boundary value conditions provide comprehensive API documentation.

Suppose you are writing a test for an add method. It takes two integers and returns an integer. The following is the Adder class:

```
public class Adder {
  public Integer add(Integer first, Integer second) {
    if (first == null || second == null) {
```

```
        throw new IllegalArgumentException("Invalid inputs
          first=[" + first+ "], second=[" + second + "]");
    }

    return first + second;
  }
}
```

The boundary values that can be tested are null, zero, negative numbers, and overflow conditions, as follows:

```
public class AdderTest {
  Adder adder = new Adder();

  @Test(expected=IllegalArgumentException.class)
  public void should_throw_exception_when_encounters_a_NULL_input(){
    adder.add(null, 1);
  }

  @Test(expected=IllegalArgumentException.class)
  public void should_throw_exception_when_second_input_is_NULL(){
    adder.add(2, null);
  }

  @Test
  public void should_return_zero_when_both_inputs_are_zero(){
    int actual =adder.add(0, 0);
    assertEquals(0, actual);
  }

  @Test
  public void
    should_return_first_input_when_second_input_is_zero()  {
    int actual =adder.add(1, 0);
    assertEquals(1, actual);
  }

  @Test
  public void
    should_return_second_input_when_first_input_is_zero()  {
    int actual =adder.add(0, 2);
    assertEquals(2, actual);
  }

  @Test
```

```
public void should_return_zero_when_summation_is_zero(){
  int actual =adder.add(5, -5);
  assertEquals(0, actual);
}

@Test public void
  should_return_a_negative_when_both_inputs_are_negative() {
  int actual =adder.add(-8, -5);
  assertTrue(actual < 0);
}


@Test
public void
  should_overflow_when_summation_exceeds_integer_limit() {
  int actual =adder.add(Integer.MAX_VALUE, 1);
  assertTrue(actual< 0);
}
}
```

Your class may have a public API that accepts user input and delegates input formatting to a dependent class or method. You should verify the user input in the public API only, not on all methods or dependent classes.

Suppose the class A has a doSomething(String input) method. A calls B to format the input. If clients can call only class A, then you should not worry about validating the null input in class B. However, if both A and B are exposed, then B definitely should check for the NULL values. Checking NULL everywhere is defensive programming.

Relying on direct testing

Suppose you have a facade class that depends on a utility class. Testing the facade class can cover the utility class. This is an example of indirect testing. The following Facade class depends on a StringService class for formatting; when we test the Facade class with a String value, then the StringService class is also tested:

```
public class Facade {
  private final StringService stringService;
  public Facade(StringService utility) {
    this.stringService= utility;
  }

  public Object doSomething(Object o) {
    if (o instanceof String) {
```

```
      return stringService.format((String) o);
   }

   if (o instanceof Integer) {
     return Integer.MIN_VALUE;
   }

   return null;
   }
}
```

We should test `StringService` directly, even though its methods are also invoked by the tests of the `Facade` class. We should have two test classes: `FacadeTest` and `StringServiceTest`.

It's not a good idea to rely on indirect testing because if we change the implementation of the `Facade` class, then the dependent class may be uncovered. Suppose we change the implementation of the `Facade` class, so that it no longer depends on `StringService`. The tests in `StringServiceTest` will no longer invoke the methods of `StringService`, so we will lose code coverage.

Staying away from debugging

A common practice when we find a bug is to start debugging an application—stop doing this. Rather, add more tests to break the code; this will enrich your test suite and improve the system documentation. Similarly, don't put a catch block to print stacktrace. Rather, assert the exception message using the `ExpectedException` rule (explained in the *Handling exceptions* section). Sometimes, it's not possible to avoid debugging entirely. So anyway, before starting to debug, create a (integration) test that reproduces the issue and then debug it. This will narrow down the problem, create a unit test for the lowest possible unit, and keep both the tests for future reference.

Avoiding generic matchers

We tend to use wildcard matchers to stub mock object methods; in the same way, verify the method invocations with generic matchers. This is a bad practice; you should go for an exact parameter match when possible. The following example demonstrates the wildcard argument matching.

The `StringDecorator` class decorates the input with an exclamation symbol:

```
public class StringDecorator {
  public String decorate(String object) {
    return object+"!";
  }
}
```

The `PrinterService` interface connects to a LAN printer and prints the input text as follows:

```
public interface PrinterService {
  void print(String text);
}
```

The `Facade` class accepts an input, decorates the input, and sends it to `PrinterService` for printing. To unit test this behavior, we need to mock out `PrinterService` with a mock object using the following code:

```
public class Facade {
  private final Decorator decorator;
  private final PrinterService printerService;

  public Facade(Decorator decorator, PrinterService
    printerService) {
    this.decorator = decorator;
    this.printerService = printerService;
  }

  public void process(String object) {
    printerService.print(decorator.decorate(object));
  }

}
```

Generally, `PrintService` is stubbed with an `anyString()` generic matcher, and the `PrintService` call is verified using `verify(mockService).print(anyString());`, as follows:

```
@RunWith(MockitoJUnitRunner.class)
public class FacadeTest {

  @Mock PrinterService mockService;
  Facade facade;

  @Before
```

```
    public void setUp() throws Exception {
      facade = new Facade(new StringDecorator(), mockService);
    }

    @Test
    public void test() {
      String input = "hello";
      doNothing().when(mockService).print(anyString());
      facade.process(input);
      verify(mockService).print(anyString());
    }

  }
```

We can use `eq("hello!")` instead of `anyString()`, as we know the `StringDecorator` method appends an exclamation to the `String` input; the test will fail if the `StringDecorator` method doesn't append the exclamation symbol. So, the side effects of `StringDecorator` can be identified immediately.

Keeping away from @ignore

Do not skip unit tests using the `@ignore` or `@exclude` annotations. As we know dead code removal is a refactoring technique, dead codes are never used. However, they create confusion. Similarly, when we ignore tests using the `@ignore` annotations, the tests are skipped, but the code remains in the file as dead code and creates confusion. Unit tests that are skipped provide no benefit. Instead of skipping unit tests, remove them from source control. If you need the test, you can get it from the source control history. Sometimes people create tests to easily understand some sort of APIs, but they don't want the tests to be executed when the test suite runs, or it may not be possible to run some tests on all platforms. With Maven (and Gradle), you can have different profiles with different test suites. For utility tests, it's always helpful to create a specific module for this.

Eluding debug messages

In early days, we used print (`System.out` or `System.err`) messages to console for debugging or unit testing code. Unit tests are system documentation, and a print statement does not fit in there. If you need to print something, just write a test and assert the expected value. Also, you can add a logging utility such as Log4J and log the debug messages. If a problem occurs in production, you just turn on these logs and see what's going on there to be able to reproduce the issue with tests better. So, tests and logs should rather complement each other.

Automating JUnit tests

Chapter 2, *Automating JUnit Tests*, covered the importance of test automation, CI, and test automation with Gradle, Maven, and Ant. This section reiterates the benefits of test automation.

The following are the benefits of test automation:

- Assumptions are continually verified. We refactor the code (change the internal structure of the code without affecting the output of the system) to improve code quality such as maintainability, readability, or extensibility. We can refactor the code with confidence if automated unit tests are running and providing feedback.

- Side effects are detected immediately. This is useful for fragile, tightly coupled systems when a change in one module breaks another module.

- Test automation saves time and there is no need of immediate regression testing. Suppose you are adding a scientific computation behavior to an existing calculator program and modifying the code. After every piece of change, you perform regression testing to verify the integrity of the system. Regression testing is tedious and time consuming, but if you have an automated unit test suite, then you can delay the regression testing until the functionality is done. This is because the automated suite will inform you at every stage if you disrupt an existing feature.

Always integrate your JUnits with build script and configure CI.

Configuring tests

This section deals with the test configuration. Unit tests are not testing the system. In TDD, unit tests are written to obtain the following benefits:

- They drive your design. You write a test, add code to fix the test, refactor code with confidence, and apply the design. This results in a simple, clean, maintainable, loosely coupled, and cohesive design. You write code to satisfy a failing test, so it limits the code you write to only what is needed.

- The tests provide fast, automated regression for refactoring and enhancing the code.

You should configure your tests to follow the following principles:

- Unit tests should be executed extremely fast so that they can provide quick feedback. Would you withdraw money from an ATM that takes 10 minutes to dispense money?
- Tests should be reliable. Tests should fail if the production code is broken. Your tests will be considered unreliable in situations where you break the production logic but the tests pass, or you don't touch the production code but still your tests fail.

The following section covers the test configuration.

Running in-memory tests

Do not write unit tests that make HTTP requests, look up JNDI resources, access a database, call SOAP-based web services, or read from the filesystem. These actions are slow and unreliable, so they should not be considered as unit tests; rather, they are integration tests. You can mock out such external dependencies using Mockito. *Chapter 4, Progressive Mockito*, explains the mocking external dependencies.

Staying away from Thread.sleep

Thread.sleep is used in the production code to halt the current execution for some time so that the current execution can sync up with the system, such that the current thread waits for a resource used by another thread. Why do we need Thread.sleep in a unit test? Unit tests are meant to get executed faster.

Thread.sleep can be used to wait for a long running process (this is usually used to test concurrency), but what if the process takes time in a slow machine? The test will fail though the code is not broken, and this defeats the test reliability principle. Avoid using Thread.sleep in unit tests; rather, simulate the long running process using a mock object.

Keeping unit tests away from the production code

Don't deliver unit tests to customers; they are not going to execute the tests. The test code should be separated from the production code. Keep them in their respective source directory tree with the same package naming structure. This will keep them separate during a build.

The following Eclipse screenshot shows the separate source folder structure. Source files are located under the `src` folder, and the tests are placed under the `test` source folder. Note that the `Adder.java` and `AdderTest.java` files are placed in the same package named `com.packt.bestpractices.invalidinput`:

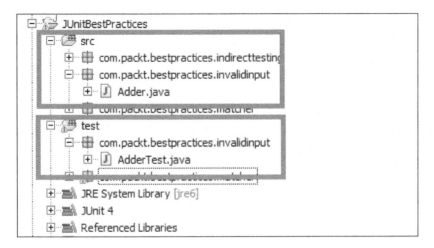

Avoiding static variables

Static variables hold state. When you use a static variable in your test, it signifies that you want to save the state of something. So, you are creating inter-test dependency. If the execution order changes, the test will fail though the code is not broken, and this defeats the test reliability principle. Do not use static variables in unit tests to store global state.

Don't initialize the class to be tested as static and use the `setUp` method (annotated with `@Before`) to initialize objects. These will protect you from accidental modification problems. The following example demonstrates the accidental modification side effects.

The `Employee` class stores employee names:

```java
public class Employee {
  private String lastName;
  private String name;

  public Employee(String lastName , String name) {
    this.lastName = lastName;
    this.name = name;
  }
```

```
      public String getLastName() {
        return lastName;
      }


      public String getName() {
        return name;
      }

    }
```

The `HRService` class has a `generateUniqueIdFor(Employee emp)` method. It returns a unique employee ID based on the surname. Two employees with the surname Smith will have the IDs `smith01` and `smith02`, respectively. Consider the following code:

```
    public class HRService {

      private Hashtable<String, Integer> employeeCountMap =
        new Hashtable<String, Integer>();

      public String generateUniqueIdFor(Employee emp) {
        Integer count = employeeCountMap.get(emp.getLastName());
        if (count == null) {
          count = 1;
        } else {
          count++;
        }
        employeeCountMap.put(emp.getLastName(), count);
        return emp.getLastName()+(count < 9 ? "0"+count:
          ""+count);
      }
    }
```

The unit test class initializes the service as static. The service stores the input of the first test and fails the second test, as follows:

```
    public class HRServiceTest {
      String familyName = "Smith";
      static HRService service = new HRService();

      @Test
      public void when_one_employee_RETURNS_familyName01()
        throws Exception {
        Employee johnSmith = new Employee(familyName, "John");
        String id = service.generateUniqueIdFor(johnSmith);
```

```
      assertEquals(familyName + "01", id);
  }

  //This test will fail, to fix this problem remove the static
    modifier
  @Test
  public void when_many_employees_RETURNS_familyName_and_count() {
    Employee johnSmith = new Employee(familyName, "John");
    Employee bobSmith = new Employee(familyName, "Bob");

    String id = service.generateUniqueIdFor(johnSmith);
    id = service.generateUniqueIdFor(bobSmith);
    assertEquals(familyName + "02", id);
  }

}
```

The following JUnit output shows the error details:

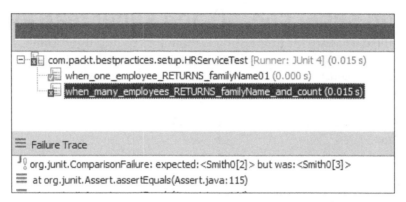

Assuming the test execution order

JUnit was designed to execute the tests in random order. It depends on the Java reflection API to execute the tests. So, the execution of one test should not depend on another. Suppose you are testing the database integration of `EmployeeService`, where the `createEmployee()` test creates a new `Employee`, `updateEmployee()` method and updates the new employee created in `createEmployee()`, and `deleteEmployee()` deletes the employee. So, we are dependent on the test execution order; if `deleteEmployee()` or `updateEmployee()` is executed before `createEmployee()`, the test will fail as the employee is not created yet.

To fix this problem, just merge the tests into a single test named
`verifyEmployeePersistence()`.

So, don't believe in the test execution order; if you have to change one test case,
then you need to make changes in multiple test cases unnecessarily.

Loading data from files

The JUnit `Theory` framework offers an `abstract` class `ParameterSupplier` for
supplying test data for test cases. The `ParameterSupplier` implementation can read
from a filesystem, such as a CSV or an Excel file. However, it is not recommended
that you read from the filesystem. This is because reading a file is an I/O (input/
output) process, and it is unpredictable and slow. We don't want our tests to create
a delay. Also, reading from a hardcoded file path may fail in different machines.
Instead of reading from a file, create a test data supplier class and return the
hardcoded data.

Invoking super.setUp() and super.tearDown()

Sometimes the data setup for unit testing is monotonous and ugly. Often, we create a
base test class, set up the data, and create subclasses to use the data. From subclasses,
always invoke the setup of the super classes and teardown methods. The following
example shows the fault of not invoking the super class.

We have `EmployeeService` and `EmployeeServiceImpl` to perform some
business logic:

```
public interface EmployeeService {
   public void doSomething(Employee emp);
}
```

The `BaseEmployeeTest` class is an `abstract` class, and it sets up the data for
subclasses, as follows:

```
public abstract class BaseEmployeeTest {

   protected HashMap<String, Employee> employee ;

   @Before
   public void setUp() {
     employee = new HashMap<String, Employee>();
     employee.put("1", new Employee("English", "Will"));
     employee.put("2", new Employee("Cushing", "Robert"));
   }
}
```

The `EmployeeServiceTest` class extends the `BaseEmployeeTest` class and uses the `employee` map, as follows:

```
public class EmployeeServiceTest extends BaseEmployeeTest {

  EmployeeService service;
  @Before
  public void setUp() {
    service = new EmployeeServiceImpl();
  }
  @Test
  public void someTest() throws Exception {
    for(Employee emp:employee.values()) {
      service.doSomething(emp);
    }
  }
}
```

The test execution fails with a `NullPointerException`. The following is the JUnit output:

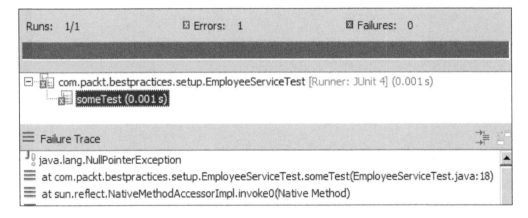

To fix this, call `super.setUp()` from the `setUp()` method. The following is the modified `setUp()` method in `EmployeeServiceTest`:

```
@Before
public void setUp() {
  super.setUp();
  service = new EmployeeServiceImpl();
}
```

Staying away from side effects

Do not write test cases that affect the data of other test cases, for example, you are examining the JDBC API call using an in-memory `HashMap` and a test case clears the map, or you are testing the database integration and a test case deletes the data from the database. It may affect the other test cases or external systems. When a test case removes data from a database, any application using the data can fail. It's important to roll back the changes in the final block and not just at the end of the test.

Working with locales

Be aware of internationalization while working with `NumberFormat`, `DateFormat`, `DecimalFormat`, and `TimeZones`. Unit tests can fail if they are run on a machine with a different locale.

The following example demonstrates the internationalization context.

Suppose you have a class that formats money. When you pass 100.99, it rounds up the amount to 101.00. The following formatter class uses `NumberFormat` to add a currency symbol and format the amount:

```
class CurrencyFormatter{

  public static String format(double amount) {
    NumberFormat format =
      NumberFormat.getCurrencyInstance();
    return format.format(amount);
  }
}
```

The following JUnit test verifies the formatting:

```
public class LocaleTest {

  @Test
  public void currencyRoundsOff() throws Exception {
    assertEquals("$101.00",
      CurrencyFormatter.format(100.999));
  }
}
```

If you run this test in a different locale, the test will fail. We can simulate this by changing the locale and restoring back to the default locale, as follows:

```
public class LocaleTest {
  private Locale defaultLocale;
```

```
@Before
public void setUp() {
    defaultLocale = Locale.getDefault();
    Locale.setDefault(Locale.GERMANY);
}
@After
public void restore() {
    Locale.setDefault(defaultLocale);
}
@Test
public void currencyRoundsOff() throws Exception {
    assertEquals("$101.00",
        CurrencyFormatter.format(100.999));
}
}
```

Before test execution, the default locale value is stored to `defaultLocale`, the default locale is changed to GERMANY, and after test execution, the default locale is restored. The following is the JUnit execution failure output. In GERMANY, the currency will be formatted to **101,00 €** but our test expects **$101.00**:

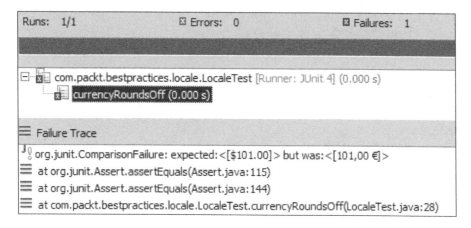

You can change your code to always return the USD format, or you can change your test to run in the US locale by changing the default locale to US, and after test execution, restore it back to the default one. Similarly, be careful while working with date and decimal formatters.

Working with dates

If not used carefully, dates may act bizarrely in tests. Be careful when using hardcoded dates in unit tests. You are working with dates and checking business logic with a future date. On January 1, 2014, you set a future date as April 10, 2014. The test works fine till April 9 and starts failing thereafter.

Do not use hardcoded dates. Instead use `Calendar` to get the current date and time and add MONTH, DATE, YEAR, HOUR, MINUTE, or SECOND to it to get a future date time. The following self explanatory code snippet demonstrates how to create a dynamic future date:

```
Calendar cal = Calendar.getInstance ();
Date now = cal.getTime();

//Next month
cal.add(Calendar.MONTH,1);
Date futureMonth = cal.getTime();


//Adding two days
cal.add(Calendar.DATE,2);
Date futureDate = cal.getTime();

//Adding a year
cal.add(Calendar.YEAR,1);
Date futureYear = cal.getTime();

//Adding 6 hours
cal.add(Calendar.HOUR,6);
Date futureHour = cal.getTime();

//Adding 10 minutes
cal.add(Calendar.MINUTE,10);
Date futureMinutes = cal.getTime();

//Adding 19 minutes
cal.add(Calendar.SECOND,19);
Date futureSec = cal.getTime();
```

The following are the future dates when the program was run on April 16, 2014:

```
Current date    = Wed Apr 16 11:18:17 IST 2014
Adding a month  = Fri May 16 11:18:17 IST 2014
Adding 2 days   = Sun May 18 11:18:17 IST 2014
Adding a year   = Mon May 18 11:18:17 IST 2015
Adding 6 hours  = Mon May 18 17:18:17 IST 2015
Adding 10 mins  = Mon May 18 17:28:17 IST 2015
Adding 19 secs  = Mon May 18 17:28:36 IST 2015
```

Working with assertions

An assertion is a predicate used to verify a programmer assumption (expectation) with an actual outcome of a program implementation. For example, a programmer can expect that the addition of two positive numbers will result in a positive number. So, the programmer can write a program to add two numbers and assert the expected result with the actual result.

The `org.junit.Assert` package provides static overloaded methods for asserting expected and actual values for all primitive types, objects, and arrays.

This section covers the proper usage of the `Assertion` APIs. The following are the best practices.

Using the correct assertion

Use the correct assertion method. JUnit supports many assertion options, such as `assertEquals`, `assertTrue`, `assertFalse`, `assertNull`, `assertNotNull`, `assertSame`, and `assertThat`. Use the most appropriate one. The following are the examples:

- Use `assertTrue(yourClass.someMethod())` instead of using `assertEquals(true, yourClass.someMethod())`
- Use `assertFalse(yourClass.someMethod())` instead of calling `assertTrue(!yourClass.someMethod())`
- Use `assertNull(yourClass.someMethod())` rather than `assertEquals(null, yourClass.someMethod())`
- Use `assertEquals(expected, yourClass.someMethod())` instead of using `assertTrue(expected.equals(yourClass.someMethod()))`
- The `assertThat(age, is(30))` method is more readable than `assertEquals(30, age)`
- Similarly, `assertThat(age, is(not(33)))` is more readable than `assertTrue(age != 33)`

Maintaining the assertEquals parameter order

The `assertEquals` method is a very useful method to verify the expectation.
The `assertEquals` method has the `assertEquals(Object expected, Object actual)` signature.

Maintain the parameter order: first the expected value and then the actual result.
The following JUnit snippet reverses the order, passes the actual value first, and
then the expected result:

```
@Test
public void currencyRoundsOff() throws Exception {
    assertEquals(CurrencyFormatter.format(100.999),
      "$101.00");
}
```

When the test fails, the error message says that the expected value is **101,00 €** but
actually the expected value is **$101.00**.

So, `assertEquals` shows misleading error messages when the parameter
order changes.

The following screenshot shows the error message. It says the test expects euros (€)
but receives dollars ($):

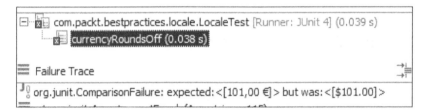

Optionally, you can pass a meaningful message to `assertEquals` to describe the
cause. The `assertEquals(String message, Object expected, Object actual)`
signature takes a `String` message to display a meaningful error message when the
actual value doesn't match the expected value.

The following JUnit snippet passes a meaningful error message:

```
@Test
public void currencyRoundsOff() throws Exception {
    assertEquals("Currency formatting failed",
      $101.00", CurrencyFormatter.format(100.999));
}
```

The following is the `Assertion` failure output with an informative message:

Striving for one assertion per test

Strive for one assertion per test method. When you check one assertion per test and a unit test fails, it is much easier to determine what went wrong. When a unit test has more than one assertion, and one assertion fails, extra effort is required to determine which one failed; for one assertion per test, no extra effort is required.

When a unit test performs more than one assertion, and a runtime exception is thrown, the assertions after the exception do not get verified; the JUnit framework marks the unit test as erroneous and proceeds to the next test method.

The following JUnit test asserts three conditions—the formatted amount is not null, the formatted amount contains a $ symbol, and the exact formatting:

```
@Test
public void currencyRoundsOff() throws Exception {
  assertNotNull(CurrencyFormatter.format(100.999));
  assertTrue(CurrencyFormatter.format(100.999).
    contains("$"));
  assertEquals("$101.00",
    CurrencyFormatter.format(100.999));
}
```

When any assertion fails, the output doesn't tell you what is wrong (you get the line number in the source code file, though, it is not very convenient to work with). The following is the JUnit output:

Instead of using three assertions, you can create three tests, or you can pass meaningful error messages to the assertion methods. The following JUnit test is modified to pass error messages:

```
@Test
public void currencyRoundsOff() throws Exception {
  assertNotNull("Currency is NULL",
    CurrencyFormatter.format(100.999));
  assertTrue("Currency is not USD($)",
    CurrencyFormatter.format(100.999).contains("$"));
  assertEquals("Wrong formatting",
    "$101.00", CurrencyFormatter.format(100.999));
}
```

Now, the failing test gives you additional information about the failure. The following is the test output. It reads **Currency is not USD($)**, which means the second assertion failed:

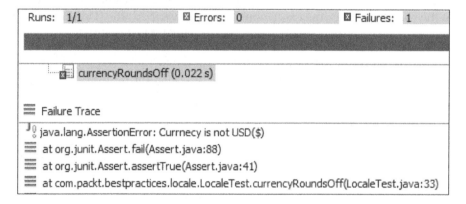

Handling exceptions

Exception handling is an important part of Java coding. The Java community follows a set of best practices about exception handling. The following are the exception handling best practices for unit testing:

- Do not write catch blocks to pass a unit test. Consider the following example where a `Calculator` program has a `divide` method. It takes two integers, divides, and returns a result. When `divide` encounters a divide by zero, the program should throw an exception. The following is the code:

```
public class Calculator {

  public int divide(int op1, int op2)  {
```

```
    return op1/op2;
  }
}
```

The following is the test:

```
@Test
public void divideByZero_throws_exception() throws
  Exception {
  try {
    calc.divide(1, 0);
    fail("Should not reach here");
  } catch (ArithmeticException e) {

  }
}
```

Instead of catching `ArithmeticException`, we can apply the JUnit 4 pattern as follows:

```
@Test(expected = ArithmeticException.class)
public void divideByZero_throws_exception() throws
  Exception {
  calc.divide(1, 0);
}
```

A more elegant way is to check the `ExpectedException` rule. The following is the modified test with `ExpectedException`:

```
public class CalculatorTest {

  @Rule
  public ExpectedException expectedException=
    ExpectedException.none();

  Calculator calc = new Calculator();

  @Test
  public void divideByZero_throws_exception(){
    expectedException.expect(ArithmeticException.class);
    expectedException.expectMessage("/ by zero");
    calc.divide(1, 0);
  }
}
```

`ExpectedException` expects an exception and an error message. If the exception is not thrown, or the message doesn't match, the test fails.

- Do not write catch blocks to fail a test; the JUnit framework takes care of runtime exceptions. The following is an example of an unnecessary catch block:

```
@Test
public void fails_when_an_exception_is_thrown()  {
  try {
    calc.divide(1, 0);
  }catch(Exception ex) {
    fail("Should not throw an exception");
  }
}
```

Instead, just write the following lines. The test will fail automatically if any exception is thrown:

```
@Test
public void fails_when_an_exception_is_thrown()  {
  calc.divide(1, 0);
}
```

- Do not catch an exception and assert the failure to pass a test. The following test code catches ArithmeticException and sets a Boolean flag, and finally asserts the flag. If no exception is thrown, the flag remains false and the test fails:

```
@Test
public void fails_when_an_exception_is_thrown()  {
  boolean isFailed = false;
  try {
    calc.divide(1, 0);
  }catch(Exception ex) {
    isFailed = true;
  }

  assertTrue(isFailed);
}
```

Use the JUnit 4 patterns explained in the preceding example.

- Do not add catch blocks to test a method that throws **checked** exceptions. The following example explains the problem. The sum(int... arg) method throws a NumberOverflowException checked exception when the integer overflows:

```
public int sum(int... args) throws NumberOverflowException{
  int sum = 0;
  for(int val:args) {
```

```
if(Integer.MAX_VALUE - sum < val) {
  throw new NumberOverflowException("Number overflow");
}
sum+=val;
}

return sum;

}
```

A catch block is used to catch a checked exception and compile the test, as follows:

```
@Test
public void fails_when_an_exception_is_thrown()  {
  try {
    int sum = calc.sum(1,2,3);
    assertEquals(6, sum);
  } catch (NumberOverflowException e) {

  }
}
```

Do not follow this pattern; instead, use throws Exception. The following JUnit test uses the throws Exception clause:

```
@Test
public void fails_when_an_exception_is_thrown() throws
  Exception {
  int sum = calc.sum(1,2,3);
  assertEquals(6, sum);
}
```

- Do not throw specific Exceptions from your tests. Instead, use the generic throws Exception.

  The following example throws a specific NumberOverflowException exception:

```
public void fails_when_an_exception_is_thrown() throws
  NumberOverflowException{

}
```

  Suppose the code is changed such that it could throw either NumberOverflowException or a ParseException. In that case, we have to change the test method to throw both the exceptions to compile the test. If we use the generic throws Exception clause, then this problem won't arise.

Working with test smells

Code smell is a technical debt or symptom that indicates a deeper problem. Smells are not bugs, or they don't fail tests. Instead, they indicate a problem in design or code such that a rigid code cannot be enhanced or can create a maintenance issue. This section covers the test smells that should be refactored for maintenance and readability. The following topics are covered:

- Test code duplication
- Conditions in test code
- Test logic in the production code
- Over engineering

Refactoring duplicates

Code duplication is the simplest code smell. It creates maintainability problems. The same code is written in many places; if any bug is found, then you need to modify all other places. This subsection elaborates on the duplicate code in test cases.

Suppose you are designing a hospital management system and writing a test for checking a patient in. The following objects are needed for the patient check-in process: a person, a guarantor, reason for hospitalization, the attending physician, and the check-in date. A person should have an address. A guarantor can be a person or an organization, such as a jail authority, a government authority, or a corporate sponsor. A guarantor should have an address.

The following test snippet creates two `Person` objects for check in, a patient `johnPeterson`, and his guarantor `johnsDad`:

```
Person johnsDad = new Person();
    Address newYorkBayArea = new Address();
    newYorkBayArea.setAddressType(AddressType.Residential);
    newYorkBayArea.setCountry("US");
    newYorkBayArea.setState("NY");
    newYorkBayArea.setZip("49355");
    newYorkBayArea.setStreet("12/e xyz Avenue");
    johnsDad.addAddress(newYorkBayArea);
    johnsDad.setEmail("dontDisturb@my.org");
    johnsDad.setFirstName("Freddy");
    johnsDad.setLastName("Peterson");
    daddy.setPerson(johnsDad);

    Person johnPeterson = new Person();
```

```
Address mavernPhilly = new Address();
mavernPhilly.setAddressType(AddressType.Residential);
mavernPhilly.setCountry("US");
mavernPhilly.setState("PA");
mavernPhilly.setZip("19355");
mavernPhilly.setStreet("123 Frazer");
johnPeterson.addAddress(mavernPhilly);
johnPeterson.setEmail("johnYou12345@gmail.com");
johnPeterson.setFirstName("John");
johnPeterson.setLastName("Peterson");
```

Two `Person` objects and two `Address` objects are created and initialized. They are logically duplicate statements. Many other tests can write similar duplicate statements. Extract the method to refactor the duplicate smell. Extract the builder methods for the `Person` and `Address` objects as follows:

```
protected Person newPerson(Address newYorkBayArea, String
    lastName, String email, String firstName) {
  Person person = new Person();
  person.addAddress(newYorkBayArea);
  person.setEmail(email);
  person.setFirstName(firstName);
  person.setLastName(lastName);
  return person;
}

protected Address newAddress(String street, String country,
    String state, String zip, AddressType residential) {
  Address address = new Address();
  address.setAddressType(residential);
  address.setCountry(country);
  address.setState(state);
  address.setZip(zip);
  address.setStreet(street);
  return address;
}
```

From the test code, just pass the required values and call the build methods as follows:

```
Address newYorkBayArea = newAddress("12/e xyz Avenue", "US",
    "NY","49355", AddressType.Residential);

Person johnsDad = newPerson(newYorkBayArea, "Peterson",
    "dontDisturb@my.org", "Freddy");
```

```
Address mavernPhilly = newAddress("123 Frazer", "US", "PA",
    "19355", AddressType.Residential);

Person johnPeterson = newPerson(mavernPhilly, "Peterson",
    "johnYou12345@gmail.com", "John");
```

We can refactor the duplicate code in many test classes by moving the common code to a base test class or a helper class.

Refactoring the test control logic

Unit test code verifies the behavior of the code under test, and usually, no conditional logic is written to verify the code. However, when a test contains code that is executed based on some condition, it gets complicated for the reader. The test executes fine but creates a maintainability problem.

When we post JMS messages to a destination (such as the TIBCO Enterprise Messaging Service), internally, the JMS provider posts administrative messages such as message received, message sent, and message acknowledged. However, each message contains the same JMS message ID. If we create a message logger program to listen to the JMS events (including administrative events), and log all events to a database for an audit trail, then the logger will save many messages with the same JMS message ID.

The following is an example of the test control logic. The message is defined as follows:

```
public class Message {
    private String jmsMessageID;
    private String header;
    private Object payload;
    private int eventType;
}
```

The eventType variable indicates the administrative message type (received is 1, sent is 2, and acknowledged is 3).

The MessagingService interface is defined as follows:

```
public interface MessagingService {
    String publish(Object message);
    List<Message> retrieveByMessageId(String jmsMessageId);
}
```

We'll verify the logging capability as follows:

```
@RunWith(MockitoJUnitRunner.class)
public class MessagingServiceTest {
  MessagingService service = new MessagingServiceImpl();

  @Test
  public void logs_messages() throws Exception {
    String msgId = service.publish(new String("hello world"));
    for(Message msg:service.retrieveByMessageId(msgId)) {
      if(msg.getEventType() == 2) {
        assertEquals("hello world", msg.getPayload());
        break;
      }
    }
  }
}
```

The `Test` method loops through the messages, finds a message, and then verifies the payload. The test contains logic. Do we need another test for this test? This is confusing.

To refactor our test, you can move the logic to the code under test. The API should have a method to return a specific type of message. That way, we can check the message object directly instead of looping and checking.

Removing the test logic from the production code

Writing code for testability is a quality. Often, we put testing logic into the production code for unit testing, such as a new constructor or new method. To make the code testable, the tests require extra logic in production code to gain access to the code's internal state for testing configuration or result verification. Testing logic in production code is a smell, though it doesn't break the code under test but increases the complexity of the code, and this can create severe maintainability problems or system failure if anything gets misconfigured.

The testing logic is inserted into the production code under the following conditions:

* Adding conditional logic to return a hardcoded value during testing. The code under test acts as a dynamic stub as shown in the following example:
  ```
  public final class EncounterManager {
    public boolean isHack = false;

    public boolean save(Map data) {
  ```

```
    if(isHack) {
      return true;
    }
    Encounter enc = new EncounterServiceImpl().
      checkIn(buildCheckinRqst(data));
    return enc != null;
  }
}
```

EncounterManager cannot be overridden as the class is declared as `final`; so, you cannot create a mock or fake object of this class. If your code under test needs to stub the `save()` behavior, then somehow you need to bypass the database call made in the `EncounterServiceImpl` method to persist the check-in data into a database. So, the `save()` method has an `isHack` conditional logic. This Boolean variable is added for testing purposes. From test, the Boolean variable `isHack` is set to `true`. If accidentally this variable is set to `true`, then encounters will not be created in production.

- Additional code is written only for test execution, or private variables are exposed as public. The following is an example:

```
public final class EncounterManager {
  private List<Encounter> retrieveEncounters() {
    if (encounters == null) {
      Patient patient = new Patient();
      patient.setPatientId(patientId);
      new EncounterServiceImpl().
        retreiveBy(patient);
    }
    return encounters;
  }

  public List<Encounter> encounters;
  public void setEncounters(List<Encounter> encounters) {
    this.encounters = encounters;
  }
}
```

The `retrieveEncounters()` method is a private method used for lazy instantiation of `encounters` `List`. However, for testing purposes, `encounters` `List` is exposed as `public` and a `public` setter method is used. From test, either the setter method is called with a hardcoded `List` or directly the `encounters` `List` is set. If `encounters` `List` is accidentally set in production, users will see the wrong data in the UI.

- Mockito doesn't allow stubbing the `equals()` and `hashcode()` methods, as they should not be overridden unless the logic is comprehensible. Yet, often for testing, we override the `equals()` and `hashcode()` methods and perform testing logic or return the hardcoded value. This is very dangerous. In production, if we need to put the objects in a collection or need to perform an equality check, then the system behaves in a bizarre fashion. The following code snippet overrides the `hashcode()` and `equals()` methods:

```
@Override
public int hashCode() {
  return isHack ? HACKED_NUMBER : 0;
}

@Override
public boolean equals(Object obj) {
  if (obj instanceof EncounterManager) {
    return isHack && ((EncounterManager) obj).isHack;
  }
  return false;
}
```

The `equals()` method returns `false` in the production code and `hashcode()` returns `0`. The `EncounterManager` class cannot be used in conjunction with the Java collection framework.

To refactor the production code, remove the final keyword, override the class in the test context, and return the hardcoded values. However, never ever touch the `equals()` and `hashcode()` methods for testing.

Refactoring over engineered tests

Tests are system documentation. They should tell the reader what is being executed. Often, we put too much documentation and make it more complex for the reader to understand the intention. Sometimes, we refactor the test and extract clean, meaningful methods, pass variables to the extracted methods, and from test just invoke the methods. Now the reader fails to understand the utility of the test case, and everything is carried out elsewhere.

The following test example demonstrates `Test` with less or no information:

```
@Test
public void checks_in_patient() throws Exception {
  createCheckInRequestForAPatientWithAGuarantor();
  checkInaPatient();
  assertResult();
}
```

The unit test calls three methods:
createCheckInRequestForAPatientWithAGuarantor, checkInaPatient, and
assertResult. From the test body, it is not possible to understand what is being
tested, what data is created, and what is asserted. A test should configure data,
call the actual method, and assert results.

The following is an example of a test with overly verbose documentation:

```
public void checks_in_patient() throws Exception {
   CheckInRequest request = new CheckInRequest();
   request.setCheckInDate(new Date());
   request.setDisease("Vomiting");
   request.setDoctor("Dr. Mike Hussey");

   String country = "US";
   String johnsStreetAddress = "123 Frazer";
   String johnsState = "PA";
   String johnsZipCode = "19355";
   Address johnsAddressMavernPhilly =
      buildAddress(johnsStreetAddress, country, johnsState,
      johnsZipCode,  AddressType.Residential);

   String johnsEmailId = "johnYou12345@gmail.com";
   String johnsFirstName = "John";
   String familyName = "Peterson";

   Person johnPeterson =
      buildPerson(johnsAddressMavernPhilly, familyName,
      johnsEmailId, johnsFirstName);

   request.setPerson(johnPeterson);

   Guarantor daddy = new Guarantor();
   daddy.setGuarantorType(GuarantorType.Person);
   String dadsStreetAddress = "12/e xyz Avenue";
   String dadsState = "NY";
   String dadsZipCode = "49355";
   Address dadsAddressNYBayArea =
      buildAddress(dadsStreetAddress, country, dadsState,
      dadsZipCode, AddressType.Residential);
   String dadsEmail = "dontDisturb@my.org";
   String dadsFirstName = "Freddy";
   Person johnsDad = buildPerson(dadsAddressNYBayArea,
      familyName,  dadsEmail, dadsFirstName);
   daddy.setPerson(johnsDad);
   request.setGuarantor(daddy);
}
```

The test builds two `Person` objects and two `Address` objects. Two builder methods are extracted for code reuse. For better documentation, variables are created and the hardcoded values are set and passed to the builder methods. These hardcoded variables make it tough to understand what is going on.

Instead of creating a custom builder method in test class, you can modify the main data class to follow the builder pattern and build the object in multiple steps. That way, we don't have to create hardcoded variables such as `johnsStreetAddress`, we can directly call the methods we need.

The `Person` class is modified; the setter methods return an instance of `this` as follows:

```
public Person setFirstName(String firstName) {
  this.firstName = firstName;
  return this;
}

public Person setLastName(String lastName) {
  this.lastName = lastName;
  return this;
}
```

From test, we can build the object easily. The following test example needs only an e-mail ID, first name, and phone number for testing, so it should not populate other values.

We can build the object in three steps, and we no longer need the hardcoded strings to document the behavior:

```
Person mark = new Person().setEmail("mark@gmail.com").
  setFirstName("Mark").setPhoneNumber1("444-999-0090");
```

Summary

This chapter covered the JUnit best practices and explained the underlying principles. The best practices are writing meaningful tests, automating unit tests, test configuration, working with assertions, exception handling in test cases, identifying test smells, and refactoring test smells.

Now you will be able to write clean and maintainable test cases.

Index

atLeast(int minNumberOfInvocations)
    method 115
atLeastOnce() method 115
atMost(int maxNumberOfInvocations)
    method 115
automated tests 216
automated tools, static code analysis
  Checkstyle 157
  FindBugs 158
  PMD 158

B

bad practice examples,
        FindBugs-supported error
  Cloneable idiom 162
  examples 162
  Hash code and equals problems 162
  Misuse of finalize 163
  serializable problems 163
BDD 135
BDD style
  JUnit test, implementing in 136
  tests, writing 136
BDD syntax
  tests, writing in 137
Behavior-driven development. See BDD
benefits, CI 58
best practices, assertion
  assertEquals parameter order,
        maintaining 272
  correct assertion, using 271
  one assertion per test, striving for 273
best practices, exception handling 274-277
best practices, test writing
  @ignore annotation, avoiding 260
  application debugging 258
  debug messages, eluding 260
  direct testing 257, 258
  generic matchers, avoiding 258-260
  input combinations, trying 255
  invalid parameters, verifying 255-257
  readability, improving 254
  trivial test cases, ignoring 255
BI 193
blue chip share 119
BookingErrorController class 219

book() method 218
brownfield project 215
builder pattern 26
building blocks
  data store 194
  process 194
  what 194
  who 194
build life cycle, Maven
  clean 80
  default 80
  project, compiling 80
  project, testing 81
  site 80
built-in matchers
  exploring 30
Business Intelligence. See BI

C

CALLS_REAL_METHODS setting 132
checked exceptions 276
Checkstyle plugin
  configuring 158-160
  downloading, URL 158
  rules, verifying 158
Checkstyle tool
  URL 157
CI
  about 57
  Ant 82
  benefits 58
  Gradle 59
  Maven project management 75
  tools 58
class test 9
clean life cycle, Maven 81
Clover plugin
  executing 143, 144
  installing 143, 144
Clover tool 142
Cobertura Ant task
  configuring 152, 153
Cobertura tool 142
code
  analyzing, SonarQube runner used 168-172
  unit testing, impediments 216, 217

unit testing 182-185
jaCoCo plugin **149**
JaCoCo tool **143**
Java code coverage tools
Clover 142
Cobertura 142
EMMA 142
JaCoCo 143
Java Development Kit (JDK) 75
Java Development Tools (JDT) 65
Java plugin
about 65-74
used, for creating Gradle build script 65-72
Java Virtual Machine (JVM) 59
JBehave
URL 137
JBehave framework 135
JDBC code
testing 208, 209
JDBC JAR
URL 204
Jenkins
about 23, 85
Ant project, building 93, 94
configuring, for Maven build job
execution 92, 93
Gradle plugin, installing in 87-91
installation, URL 85, 87
wiki, URL 94
jMock framework
URL 137
JUnit 10
JUnit 4
@AfterClass annotation 13
@Before annotation 13
@RunWith annotation 20
@Test annotation 12
advantages 11
Eclipse, setting up 11, 12
exception handling, working with 19
JUnit 4++
assumption, using 23, 24
test, executing in order 21, 22
test, ignoring 20, 21
test suite, exploring 25
JUnit (4.11)
URL 10

JUnit categories
exploring 55
JUnit rules
about 47
ErrorCollector rule 49, 50
ExpectedException rule 48, 49
external resources, handling 53-55
TemporaryFolder rule 49
TestName rule 53
TestWatcher rule 51, 52
timeout rule 47, 48
Verifier rule 50
JUnit test automation
benefits 261
JUnit theory
@DataPoint annotation 40
@DataPoints annotation 41
@ParametersSuppliedBy annotation 41
@Theory annotation 40
about 40
data externalization, @Parameters
SuppliedBy used 44-47
exploring 41, 42
ParameterSupplier annotation 41
Theories annotation 41
Juno 11

K

KEPLER (4.3) 11

L

legacy code (legacy)
working with 216
loadDriver() method 197
Luna 11

M

matchers
equalTo method 27
not attribute 27
Matchers.argThat(Matcher) method 117
Maven
about 75
build life cycle 80
clean life cycle 81

PMD plugin
   URL 165
   working with 165
PMD tool 158
POM file 78
PotentialAssignment class 44
PowerMock 110
PowerMockito 110
private methods
   working with 230-232
process, building blocks 194
Project Object Model. *See* POM file

Q

quality
   improving, with Sonar Eclipse
      plugin 172-174
   monitoring, with Ant and SonarQube 178
   monitoring, with Gradle and
      SonarQube 174-177
   monitoring, with SonarQube and Ant 178
Quality Assurance (QA) 251

R

reset method 133
retrieveEncounters() method 282
RETURNS_DEFAULTS setting 132
RETURNS_MOCKS setting 132
RETURNS_SMART_NULLS setting 132
runtime dependencies 69

S

sanity check 9
selling point (USP) 59
SingletonDependency class 235
site life cycle, Maven 81
SONAR 23
Sonar Eclipse plugin
   download, URL 172
   used, for quality improvement 172-174
SonarQube
   about 166
   and Ant, used for quality monitoring 178
   configuring, steps 167
   features 166

quality, monitoring with Ant 177-179
quality, monitoring with Gradle 174-176
quality, monitoring with Maven 176, 177
URL 167
SonarQube runner
   used, for code analyzing 168-172
sonar:sonar command 177
Spring
   used, for integration test writing 209-212
Spring JDBC
   implementing, steps 205-207
Spring MVC
   about 186-188
   request handling mechanism 186
   Spring web application, building 186-191
spy 101, 102
spy object 124
StaticBlockOwner class 240
static code analysis
   about 156
   automated tools 157
   metrics 156, 157
static methods 234
string matchers
   containsString matcher 30
   endsWith matcher 30
   startsWith matcher 30
stub 99
subtask
   ordering, doFirst closure used 61, 62
   ordering, doLast closure used 61, 62
   super.setUp() method 266, 267
   super.tearDown() method 266, 267
SurveyResultCompiler class 243

T

target folder
   cobertura 152
   generated-classes 152
   site 152
   surefire-reports 152
task
   --daemon option 63, 64
   about 60
   creating 61
   daemon process 63

U

unit testing
about 9, 10, 253
code-driven unit frameworks, for Java 10
code, impediments 216-224
unit test, principles
effortless execution 105
Formula 1 execution 105
Order independent and isolated 104
trouble-free setup and run 105
unit tests 217

V

Verifier rule
working with 50
verify() method 114
verifyNoMoreInteractions(Object... mocks)
method 116

verifyZeroInteractions(Object... mocks)
method 116
void methods
stubbing 126-128

W

what, building blocks 194
when_ten_percent_gain_then_the_stock_is_
sold method 113
who, building blocks 194
wildcard matchers 118
willAnswer method 137
willCallRealMethod() method 137
will method 137
willReturn method 137
willThrow method 137

X

XML namespaces 178

Thank you for buying
Mastering Unit Testing Using Mockito and JUnit

About Packt Publishing

Packt, pronounced 'packed', published its first book "*Mastering phpMyAdmin for Effective MySQL Management*" in April 2004 and subsequently continued to specialize in publishing highly focused books on specific technologies and solutions.

Our books and publications share the experiences of your fellow IT professionals in adapting and customizing today's systems, applications, and frameworks. Our solution based books give you the knowledge and power to customize the software and technologies you're using to get the job done. Packt books are more specific and less general than the IT books you have seen in the past. Our unique business model allows us to bring you more focused information, giving you more of what you need to know, and less of what you don't.

Packt is a modern, yet unique publishing company, which focuses on producing quality, cutting-edge books for communities of developers, administrators, and newbies alike. For more information, please visit our website: www.packtpub.com.

About Packt Open Source

In 2010, Packt launched two new brands, Packt Open Source and Packt Enterprise, in order to continue its focus on specialization. This book is part of the Packt Open Source brand, home to books published on software built around Open Source licenses, and offering information to anybody from advanced developers to budding web designers. The Open Source brand also runs Packt's Open Source Royalty Scheme, by which Packt gives a royalty to each Open Source project about whose software a book is sold.

Writing for Packt

We welcome all inquiries from people who are interested in authoring. Book proposals should be sent to author@packtpub.com. If your book idea is still at an early stage and you would like to discuss it first before writing a formal book proposal, contact us; one of our commissioning editors will get in touch with you.

We're not just looking for published authors; if you have strong technical skills but no writing experience, our experienced editors can help you develop a writing career, or simply get some additional reward for your expertise.

Test-Driven Development with Mockito

ISBN: 978-1-78328-329-3   Paperback: 172 pages

Learn how to apply Test-Driven Development and the Mockito framework in real life projects, using realistic, hands-on examples

1. Start writing clean, high quality code to apply Design Patterns and principles.

2. Add new features to your project by applying Test-first development—JUnit 4.0 and Mockito framework.

3. Make legacy code testable and clean up technical debts.

Instant Eclipse Application Testing How-to

ISBN: 978-1-78216-324-4   Paperback: 62 pages

An easy-to-use guide on how to test Java applications of any scope using Eclipse IDE

1. Learn something new in an Instant! A short, fast, focused guide delivering immediate results.

2. Learn how to install Eclipse and Java for any platform.

3. Get to grips with how to efficiently navigate in the Eclipse environment using shortcuts.

Please check **www.PacktPub.com** for information on our titles

Instant Mockito

ISBN: 978-1-78216-797-6   Paperback: 66 pages

Learn how to create stubs, mocks, and spies and verify their behavior using Mockito

1. Learn something new in an Instant!
    A short, fast, focused guide delivering immediate results.

2. Stub methods with callbacks.

3. Verify the behavior of test mocks.

Instant Mock Testing with PowerMock

ISBN: 978-1-78328-995-0   Paperback: 82 pages

Discover unit testing using PowerMock

1. Learn something new in an Instant!
    A short, fast, focused guide delivering immediate results.

2. Understand how to test unit code using PowerMock, through hands-on-examples.

3. Learn how to avoid unwanted behavior of code using PowerMock for testing.

Please check **www.PacktPub.com** for information on our titles

Made in the USA
Middletown, DE
13 December 2018